LOUISIANA GOVERNORS

Louisiana Governors

Rulers, Rascals, and Reformers

Walter Greaves Cowan
and Jack B. McGuire

UNIVERSITY PRESS OF MISSISSIPPI
Jackson

www.upress.state.ms.us

The University Press of Mississippi is a member of the Association of American University Presses.

Manufactured in the United States of America

First paperback printing 2010
Paperback ISBN 978-1-60473-501-7

∞

Library of Congress Cataloging-in-Publication Data

Cowan, Walter G.
Louisiana governors : rulers, rascals, and reformers / Walter Greaves Cowan and Jack B. McGuire.
p. cm.
Includes bibliographical references and index.
ISBN 978-1-934110-90-4 (cloth : alk. paper) 1. Governors—Louisiana—Biography. 2. Louisiana—Biography. 3. Governors—Louisiana—History. 4. Louisiana—Politics and government. I. McGuire, Jack B. II. Title.
F368.C69 2008
976.3009′9—dc22
[B]

2008006390

British Library Cataloging-in-Publication Data available

To Margaret Martinez Cowan
For her enduring encouragement and help through life.
W.G.C.

For Sue, with whom I would do all things all over again, and for Shannon, Barrett, David, and Holland, four of those things.
J.B.McG.

Contents

Acknowledgments

Special thanks for manuscript research to:

Dr. Wilbur F. Meneray, Assistant Librarian and Head of Special Collections at the Tulane University Library, and Ken Owen and Leon Miller of the staff.

Nancy Burris, Librarian for the *Times-Picayune*, and her staff.

Colin Hamer, retired head of the Louisiana Department of the New Orleans Public Library, and the library's general staff.

And for their continuing encouragement to see the book produced: Dr. Edward D. Frohlich, Dorothy Marchal, Walter Greaves Cowan Jr., and William Douglas Cowan, along with their wives, Nancy and Carol.

Computerized by Marie Dufour Goodwin, who assisted in the editing.

Special thanks to Barrett C. McGuire for his invaluable assistance with computerization of the manuscript, and to Sharon Pepperman for her skill in formatting it.

Preface

France ruled Louisiana through eleven governors and Spain followed with nine, leading up to the Louisiana Purchase of 1803. The history of the state was set in motion with discovery of the great Mississippi River in 1682, when René Robert Cavalier, Sieur de La Salle, claimed for France all the territory drained by the river.

The lives of the governors—who they were and what they did—are what this book is about, through the colonial periods and the American era. Their experiences in battles with native Indians and competing English forces trying to gain a foothold in the Louisiana province are fascinating. French and Spanish governors, appointed by their respective crowns, quarreled among themselves and answered to leaders of their respective countries, while Americans had to answer to the constituted authority of the newly founded United States. Corruption crept into the governance early, and physical skirmishes highlighted the period.

Following the Purchase, politics moved front stage and has held the spotlight since. The Whigs prevailed first but disintegrated into the Know Nothings, who held sway during a period before the Civil War. Creoles and Cajuns entered the public fray for dominance as time elapsed, and in the mid-nineteenth century the Republican Party was born to oppose slavery both nationally and in Louisiana. The Democratic Party was well established at that time.

Massacres by Indians protesting the loss of their land and uprisings by Negroes brought from Africa to till the soil on Southern plantations became dominant problems. Thus, Louisiana's governors had to deal with social issues as well as the mechanics of government. In all, the period evolved into the era of slavery, secession, suffrage, and segregation. Consequences of these times have dogged the state through the eighteenth, nineteenth, and twentieth centuries and affect life in the twenty-first century as well, especially in the public sector.

After the fall of New Orleans to Union forces on April 25, 1862, Louisiana felt the hardships of war. Occupation of seventeen parishes (of the forty-three total at the time) resulted in great upheaval: as Confederate governors sought to escape the authority of the Union army, the state capital was moved from New Orleans to Baton Rouge, to Opelousas, to Shreveport, and back to New Orleans before being located in Baton Rouge after the war.

Meanwhile, continuing racial problems brought on by the occupation plagued the state's lawmakers. Twice in the state's tumultuous history, two opposing governors and legislatures were seated simultaneously. Adding to its woes, the state had to deal with a lottery that corrupted public officials.

Reconstruction existed in Louisiana for twelve years, 1865 to 1877. This was the last state from which Union troops were withdrawn, following a deal in which Rutherford B. Hayes was awarded the presidency of the United States as Louisiana bargained to seat its Democratic governor and terminate Reconstruction.

The state was dominated by Bourbon rule in the post-Reconstruction period, in which planters joined with the New Orleans political machine to elect governors, in essence turning governance back to the kind of rule that existed before the war. Blacks were largely disenfranchised through the poll tax, grandfather clause, and other restrictions. The Democratic party became supreme in the last quarter of the nineteenth century. Politics took a dramatic turn with the election of Huey P. Long to the governorship in 1928. Through manipulation of the legislature, Long molded the electorate into a virtual dictatorship. His ability to mobilize support led to vast, socialistic changes in state government, and his vituperative actions brought on his demise.

In the wake of Huey Long's onslaught on state government, Louisiana developed a virtual two-party system (pro- and anti-Long) within the Democratic Party that lasted until the 1960s. Widespread scandals in the late 1930s caused the Longites to be swept out of office, but reform administrations were interrupted by Earl K. Long's return to power in 1948 and 1956. In the 1959 session of the legislature, the state was rocked by Earl's collapse and commitment to two mental hospitals while governor.

The succeeding years saw the rise of Edwin W. Edwards, who won four terms and became the second governor to go to federal prison. Racial tensions returned briefly during the Edwards years as David Duke espoused the cause of the Ku Klux Klan, but his prominence was short-lived. In the mid-1990s a new lottery was authorized, along with legalization of other forms of gambling—casino gambling, riverboat gambling, and video poker—to help fund state budgets.

The most spectacular development in the final quarter of the twentieth century was the rise of the Republican Party, due principally to enactment of the state's unique open primary election system. But 2004 witnessed another landmark achievement, the election of the first woman governor in state history.

— The Authors

LOUISIANA GOVERNORS

Pierre Le Moyne, Sieur d'Iberville et d'Ardillieres

1699–1702

Finding the mouth of the Mississippi River turned into a dramatic search headed by the now-famous Iberville, who eventually was credited with being the founder of the fledgling French colony of Louisiana. Some historians say he was unquestionably the greatest Canadian of his generation.

Historian Edwin Adams Davis noted that Iberville succeeded where René-Robert Cavalier de La Salle had failed in planting a firmly rooted colony that survived and generally prospered, following many disappointments. While Iberville was never given the title of governor, he was everything else, which included leading the voyage from France to colonize Louisiana, selecting sites for fortifications, and developing plans to head off attempts by Spain and England to gain a greater foothold in America.

La Salle discovered the great river in 1682, but France failed to capitalize on his claim, and La Salle had only descended the river from Canada. In 1684 he did try to find the river's mouth, but his voyage ended in tragedy because of faulty compass readings. La Salle and his expedi-

Pierre Le Moyne, Sieur d'Iberville et d'Ardillieres. Courtesy of Special Collections, Tulane Libraries.

tion sailed past the Mississippi's mouth and ended up in Matagorda Bay, Texas, from where they undertook to locate the river by walking northward. La Salle's men mutinied and killed him.

It was imperative that France learn how to navigate the river from the Gulf of Mexico, into which it flowed. France's minister of marine, Louis Phelypeaux, the Count de Pontchartrain (for whom the lake at New Orleans is named), taking note of Iberville's naval exploits against the British on Hudson Bay, proposed to King Louis XIV that he select Iberville to undertake the search.

Pierre Le Moyne, the third of fourteen children of Charles Le Moyne and Catherine Primot of Montreal, Canada, was baptized on July 20, 1661, (his date of birth is unknown). His father, a Dieppe, France, innkeeper, had been ennobled by the king and bestowed seignories upon his twelve sons. Historian Jack D. L. Holmes notes that, though Iberville entrusted most of the administration of Louisiana to his younger brother, Bienville, the elder brother must be included in any list of early Louisiana governors.

Responding to King Louis XIV's order, Iberville assembled a flotilla of two oceangoing ships, the *Badine* and the *Marin*, with small boats aboard to navigate shoreline waters. The *Badine* carried thirty guns and a crew of 150, commanded by Iberville. The *Marin* had thirty guns and a crew of 130. Aboard the *Marin* was Father Anastasius Douay, companion of La Salle and eyewitness to his murder.

By the time Iberville sailed from Brest on October 24, 1698, the Gulf of Mexico had become the goal of Spain, France, and England, making it important that France develop its Louisiana discoveries.

Arriving in the Gulf of Mexico in 1699, Iberville scouted the coast for a harbor with water deep enough to accommodate his ships. The ships stopped at Pensacola and Mobile en route, then ended up at Ship Island, some twelve miles off the coast of Biloxi, Mississippi. The island lies about 85 miles from the Mississippi River.

What happened next was graphically described by Nellis M. Crouse in his volume *LeMoyne d'Iberville: Soldier of France*. Using two *traversiers*, small boats brought along for such a venture, the search was launched. Beginning on February 27 Iberville and his brother Bienville and twenty other men, with supplies for twenty days and two cannons, threaded their way through a maze of impediments, encountering high winds, torrential rains, thunder and lightning. Progress was slow and difficult.

On March 2, 1699, the little vessels buffeted their way near the shoreline, scudding before a northerly gale, the water kept back by tarpaulins stretched above the railings. Iberville dared not get too close to the shore, lest the river be passed, though a heavy sea made the going dangerous in deep water.

Suddenly, his careful navigating paid off. What looked like a rocky palisade projecting into the gulf on close inspection turned out to be masses of petrified logs and driftwood blackened by age and cemented together by fluvial sediment. The river's current was felt for three-quarters of a league into the sea (a league is approximately three miles), and the water tasted fresh, unlike the salty water of the gulf. Iberville took a compass reading and it showed a latitude of 28 degrees 50 minutes, some twenty-eight leagues from Ship Island. On the following day, Iberville and his party moved upriver and found that the river separated into three passes, now known as North, South, and Southwest. Iberville had entered via the North Pass.

Over centuries the swift river currents had cut deep channels in the outlets to the sea. As logs from fallen trees and driftwood stacked up, troughs were created. Growth alongside or atop the fallen trees and driftwood created the effect of palisades, something the Indians and Spanish sailors had alluded to through the years.

Victory at finding the river's mouth now assured, Iberville headed north, and the party camped for the night at a spot they named Mardi Gras Point. The day was Shrove Tuesday, which is Mardi Gras, and the name became the first place name on the mainland of Louisiana.

After breaking camp, Iberville and his group began to search for Indians. He found the village of the Bayougoulas and Mougoulachas, and later the Quinipissas, also known as the Colapissas.

There were no Indians in sight until March 7, when the Iberville group ran into six canoes of them paddling furiously to get out of sight. One Indian, however, was curious and waited for Iberville to come ashore. His fellow Indians, after they had fled into the reeds, saw that Iberville meant no harm and returned to greet him. Iberville then gave them knives, axes, and beads, and the savages reciprocated with gifts of smoked beef and bear steak.

Iberville was now interested in finding a location suitable for erection of a fort where his group could headquarter. He went back to Biloxi, which his men previously eliminated as a suitable harbor because the channels were too shallow for the small boats. But Iberville located a channel on the Ocean Springs side of Biloxi Bay that was seven feet deep, enough to permit passage of his *traversiers*. Iberville ordered construction of a fort in this area. The fort, built in April of 1699, was named for the Count de Maurepas. Preceding that, a smaller fort—de la Boulaye—had been built on the Mississippi River near the Indian settlement of Phoenix. It was the first French settlement on the banks of the river and was only a troop-gathering facility.

In 1702, following an outbreak of fever at Fort Maurepas, Fort Saint Louis de la Mobile was built on the Mobile River, and Mobile became the capital of Louisiana until 1720, when it was moved to Biloxi, and then, in 1723, to New Orleans.

Iberville made three trips to Louisiana and had scheduled a fourth, but fate cut his service short. He had developed a special bond with the Indians, employing the practice of giving usable gifts to keep them happy. For instance, when Henri de Tonti, who had descended the Mississippi long before Iberville and his group set out to find the Mississippi's mouth, appeared on a visit on March 25, 1702, he had with him a number of chiefs of the Chickasaw and Choctaw tribes. Iberville lavished presents upon them and lectured them, telling them they should not deal with the English because all the English wanted was to make them slaves and occupy their lands and villages. He is said to have won the allegiance of the Chickasaws and Choctaws. With the fort at Mobile completed and the Indians placated, he prepared to return to France.

Iberville left Louisiana for the last time on April 27, 1702. He had hoped to plant several strong, permanent settlements along the Gulf Coast to counter any move by the English and Spanish to encroach on French territory.

Shortly before his arrival in France, war broke out between France and England. Iberville was sent with a fleet of eleven vessels to the West Indies, where he occupied the islands of St. Christopher and Nevis, but found Martinique and the Barbados islands too strong to conquer. Iberville then sailed to Havana to join Spanish forces there.

He was seized with yellow fever, of which he died on July 9, 1706. Iberville was within two weeks of his forty-fifth year. He died on board his flagship, the *Pelican*, and was buried in the Church of San Cristobal in Havana.

Historian Davis observed that Iberville had given his colonists sound advice in urging the extension of agriculture, and had encouraged the coming of families and of young women to make homes for unmarried settlers. No French colonizer had a better record of heroism, work, and self-sacrifice than this inspiring leader, who finally gave his life for the empire of France. "He well deserves to be called the 'Founder of Louisiana,'" Davis concluded.

—W.G.C.

Crouse, Nellis M. *LeMoyne d'Iberville: Soldier of New France*. 1954. Baton Rouge: Louisiana State University Press, 2001.

Davis, Edwin Adams. *Louisiana: A Narrative History*. Baton Rouge: Claitor's Publishing Division, 1971.

Dufour, Charles L. *Ten Flags in the Wind: The Story of Louisiana*. New York: Harper & Row, 1967.

Giraud, Marcel. *A History of French Louisiana*. Vol I. Translated by Brian Pierce. Baton Rouge: Louisiana State University Press, 1990.

Holmes, Jack D. L. "Pierre Le Moyne, Sieur d'Iberville et d'Ardillieres, Colonial Explorer, 1699–1702." *The Louisiana Governors: From Iberville to Edwards*. Joseph G. Dawson III, ed. Baton Rouge: Louisiana State University Press, 1990.

Wall, Bennett H., ed. *Louisiana: A History*. Wheeling, IL: Harlan Davidson, 1997.

Sieur de Sauvole

1699–1700

The most important thing about the Sieur de Sauvole, Louisiana's second governor, is not who he was, but who he was not.

Sauvole became the colony's acting governor in 1699, when Iberville sailed for France to seek additional troops and resources. His tenure was brief, as he died of fever on August 22, 1700.

There is no image of Sauvole to study, and his name is spelled in various ways, given by the Louisiana secretary of state's office as Sauvole but with an additional *l* (Sauvolle) by historian Charles L. Dufour. The confusion about the spelling of his name is minor, however, in comparison with the misinformation about his lineage.

In his standard history of Louisiana, Dr. Edwin Adams Davis wrote that Ensign Sauvole was one of the Le Moyne brothers, although, "even in recent years," some historians "have confused Sauvole with another of Iberville's brothers, Francois Marie le Moyne."

Dufour wrote that "no man has caused as much confusion among Louisiana historians. He was not a Le Moyne and was not the brother of Iberville and Bienville as many historians have repeated for the better part of a hundred and fifty years." Francois Xavier Martin, Charles Gayarré, and Alcee Fortier all perpetuated this error, with Gayarré describing a pathetic scene in which a tearful Bienville mourned his "brother's" passing at Sauvole's grave.

A naval officer who appears to have had some training in engineering and surveying, Sauvole was a member of Iberville's first expedition. Frequent mention of him in Iberville's logs indicates that he was a trusted lieutenant: when Iberville departed for France he placed Sauvole in command at Fort Maurepas, with Bienville as second in command.

Sauvole left a journal which describes his activities. He received emissaries from the local tribes and established friendly relations with them, dispatched expeditions to explore the coast and the interior, and strengthened the defenses of the crude fort. The little garrison, not even a colony as yet, was beset by problems, including chronic food shortages and the ravages of the fever that claimed him, but it was no mean accomplishment on Sauvole's part that he maintained and enhanced the foothold the French had established on the Gulf Coast.

—J.B.McG.

Davis, Edwin Adams. *Louisiana: A Narrative History*. Baton Rouge: Claitor's Publishing Division, 1971.
Dawson, Joseph G. III, ed. *The Louisiana Governors: From Iberville to Edwards*. Baton Rouge: Louisiana State University Press, 1990.
Dufour, Charles L. *Ten Flags in the Wind: The Story of Louisiana*. New York: Harper & Row, 1967.
Gayarré, Charles, *History of Louisiana. Vol. 1: The French Domination*. Gretna, LA: Pelican, 1965.
Wall, Bennett H., ed. *Louisiana: A History*. Wheeling, IL: Harlan Davidson, 1997.

Jean Baptiste Le Moyne, Sieur de Bienville

1701–1713; 1716–1717; 1718–1725; 1733–1743

On a calm day in 1699, Jean Baptiste Le Moyne, Sieur de Bienville, was descending the Mississippi River with five men in two canoes when he encountered an English warship anchored in a bend, waiting for favorable winds to carry it upstream. Its captain advised Bienville that he had been sent by the Carolina proprietors to explore the river and determine whether the French, who claimed all lands drained by it, had established a settlement. Bienville bluffed the Englishman, telling him there was a French fort a short distance upriver, with cannon and soldiers prepared to defend Louis XIV's claim to the vast territory called Louisiana. The English raised anchor and left. The bend where Bienville encountered them was thereafter called *le detour des anglais*, or English Turn.

Bienville thus exhibited his resourcefulness, daring, and cheekiness at an early stage of his long career in the Louisiana colony.

The story of Louisiana, historian Charles L. "Pie" Dufour wrote, is "colorful, stormy, and dramatic," and the Le Moyne brothers fit that description in all particulars.

Jean Baptiste Le Moyne, Sieur de Bienville. Courtesy of Special Collections, Tulane Libraries.

11

René-Robert Cavalier, Sieur de La Salle, discovered the mouth of the Mississippi River and claimed an enormous slice of the North American continent for France on April 9, 1682. With tensions between the European powers during a succession of wars, the French crown belatedly determined to secure La Salle's claim by establishing a post. Pierre Le Moyne, Sieur d'Iberville, a distinguished naval officer, was entrusted with this mission, on which he took his younger brother, Bienville. They rediscovered the river's mouth on March 2, 1699, Mardi Gras day.

The twelfth of fourteen children, Bienville was baptized in Montreal on February 23, 1680, which is given as his birthday since the exact date is unknown. His father, Charles Le Moyne, had left France to seek his fortune in Canada as a trapper and trader. He became wealthy, and the king gave him the title of Canadian nobility, "Sieur," as in Sieur de Longueuil or Sieur de Chateaugay. The elder Le Moyne named his twelve sons, born in New France, after estates in his homeland.

Bienville grew up in Montreal and was commissioned a naval cadet at twelve. He was nineteen when he explored the Mississippi with his older brother and showed a remarkable skill in learning the language of the Indians and dealing with them on friendly terms. He remained in Louisiana when Iberville sailed for France in 1702 to report on the nascent colony and recruit settlers for it. Iberville did not return to Louisiana. He went on active service against England in the War of the Spanish Succession and commanded a French squadron in the West Indies, but died of yellow fever in Havana in 1706.

Bienville was placed in command of the colony in 1701, when he was twenty-one, as successor to Sieur de Sauvole, who had died. He held the post until 1713 and, while he was technically the commandant general, he functioned as governor.

With France suffering defeats in its European wars, the infant colony was left to its own devices. The first French settlement was Fort Maurepas on Biloxi Bay, from which the post was moved to Mobile in 1711. The first French post on the Mississippi River was Fort de la Boulaye, a small garrison fifty miles above its mouth. It was abandoned in 1707 because Bienville did not have enough troops to garrison it. Beset by a shortage of food and other supplies, with a handful of colonists living in miserable conditions, Bienville urged upon the court the importance of locating a permanent settlement on the Mississippi to cement France's claims. The ongoing rivalries with other European powers, the establishment of a Spanish colony at Pensacola, and the desire of English traders in the Carolinas to expand westward were reasons enough for Bienville to want to develop the Louisiana colony; but he also believed that over time, and with the proper resources, great riches could be gained.

From the beginning, Bienville was dogged by rumors and accusations that made the French court suspicious of him and his intentions. Iberville and Bienville were both accused of profiting from their official positions, and although these charges were never substantiated they followed Bienville for years. He was also accused of being dictatorial, difficult to work with, and insubordinate when placed in a junior position.

The commandant general, or governor, was in charge of military and naval affairs and the civil government, while the commissary, an officer of equal rank, was the storekeeper, treasurer, and auditor. The division of powers between these two officials inevitably led to conflicts. Bienville bickered and quarreled with the commissary, Nicolas de La Salle, as well as with the pastor during his first years as governor, and they responded by vilifying him in reports to the authorities in France. La Salle charged that Iberville, Bienville, and a third Le Moyne brother, Chateaugay, had stolen the king's goods, embezzled funds, and engaged in illegal trade from which they reaped enormous profits. In a lengthy paper to Pontchartrain, the Minister of the Marine, who oversaw France's colonial empire, La Salle undermined the Le Moynes and planted seeds of distrust that never died.

Louis XIV removed both Bienville and La Salle and ordered an investigation of the charges. The new commissary, Martin d'Artaguiette, was instructed to send Bienville under arrest to France if his inquiry established guilt. After viewing the evidence and interviewing several people, d'Artaguiette absolved Bienville.

The Louisiana colony, despite its importance in staking France's claim to a vast mid-American territory and blocking expansion westward by the English, was never provided the attention, resources, and manpower it so desperately needed. There were chronic shortages of food and other resources, and the poor settlers barely existed. They lived under miserable conditions, as soldiers deserted and mosquitoes, fever, and other illnesses plagued them.

Bienville may have benefited from his official position, but he also spent his own resources to keep the colony afloat. In 1708, he had to take provisions from the settlers to feed the troops. He also dispensed provisions from the crown warehouses to the needy and gave food to sailors without deducting its cost from their meager wages. French law prohibited trade with anyone other than the mother country, a policy Bienville violated by trading with the English and Spanish when he found such smuggling necessary to obtain needed provisions for his impoverished colony. While he doubtless smuggled for his own account as well, that was a common practice for colonial officials of all stripes.

Bienville's greatest frustrations involved the lack of support from France.

The Sun King had depleted the treasury to finance European wars and maintain a lavish court, and the Louisiana colony was not a high priority for the crown but rather was viewed as a costly burden. In 1712, Louis XIV gave a wealthy merchant, Antoine Crozat, a royal charter that granted him the exclusive right to trade in Louisiana for a fifteen-year term, making him the virtual proprietor of the colony.

Crozat was expected to develop the colony but, like the crown, he never committed sufficient resources to it.

Bienville remained as the king's lieutenant and military commandant, but was disappointed that he was not appointed governor. Antoine de la Mothe Cadillac had been named governor in 1710, before the transfer to Crozat, but he did not arrive in Louisiana to assume his duties until 1713. Cadillac was the first colonial administrator to hold the title of governor; Bienville remained as the troop commander, a Superior Council was created to advise the governor, and the stage was set for friction.

Cadillac and Bienville bickered and fell out, with Bienville claiming that his refusal to marry the governor's daughter was the basis of Cadillac's enmity. Bienville said that his own popularity with the colonists and the respect that the Indians had for him made Cadillac jealous. The French historian, Marcel Giraud, wrote that "the presence of a governor provoked the resentment of Bienville, who had once again failed to get the office that he wanted so badly."

Philomena Hauck, in her biography of Bienville, wrote that while he would have resented anyone placed over him, "Cadillac was an easy man to resent" as there was a "wealth of evidence to suggest that he never let honesty or truthfulness get in the way of his progress." Cadillac, however, was the founder of Detroit and had powerful patrons, including Pontchartrain, at the court, and Frontenac, the governor of New France.

Bienville's resentment and frustration were vented in a letter he sent to Pontchartrain in reaction to Cadillac's appointment. "I have been here for thirteen years," he wrote. "I have spent my youth here. I have worn out my health here, and I have not, my lord, certainly made any profit here." Bienville wrote that he had spent his own funds to pay expenses that should have been borne by the crown, had not amassed any property, and was still but a lowly naval guard, with no advancement in rank having been given despite his years of service. "I have been here, one day on Indian corn, another on wheat, and often without either," he complained. "It has been seven years since I received one sou of my salary, which is very moderate, and which would not even be enough to receive the Indians who drop in to see me every day."

Pontchartrain showed no sympathy for Bienville, instead ordering him to observe "strict subordination" to Cadillac, but Crozat tired of the in-fighting and recalled Cadillac in 1716. A new governor, the Sieur d'Epinay, had no better relations with Bienville, while Crozat, disappointed at the failure to discover mines of silver and gold and rivers rich with pearls, decided to cut his losses and return the colony to the crown.

Bienville served as acting governor again during part of 1716 and 1717 and built alliances with the Natchez and Choctaw Indians. When the Natchez killed several Canadian fur traders in 1716, in a show of force he established Fort Rosalie near their principal village, and punished the offenders. His artful diplomacy caused the Natchez to both respect and fear him, and they resisted overtures from the English traders, whose gifts to them were more plentiful and valuable than those Bienville had available to dispense.

With the death of Louis XIV in 1715 after a reign of seventy-two years, his younger brother, the Duc d'Orleans, became regent, acting for the youthful Louis XV, the late king's four-year-old great-grandson. The court saw no reason to take on the burden of the Louisiana colony again, and in 1717 the Company of the West, chartered by John Law, was given control of Louisiana. A wealthy Scotsman who had settled in France, Law thought that Louisiana would be profitable if the colony was developed properly. He was given a monopoly on Louisiana's trade for twenty-five years in return for agreeing to send out six thousand settlers and three thousand slaves within ten years.

Responsibility for colonial affairs was transferred from the Minister of the Marine, Pontchartrain, to the Council of the Navy. Bienville was appointed the company's director general, making him governor in all but title, and the Regent awarded him the Cross of St. Louis, a decoration he had coveted.

The Company of the West, desiring to establish a commercial center for the colony, directed Bienville to establish a town on the Mississippi River, to be named for the Regent. Bienville founded New Orleans in 1718, on what he described as "one of the most beautiful crescents of the river." In a dispatch in June 1718, he reported that "we are working on New Orleans with such diligence as the dearth of workmen will allow. I myself went to the spot to choose the best site." New Orleans became the capital in 1723 and grew to a population of a thousand by 1728.

John Law had enjoyed immense success with his financial schemes. He started a bank that replaced coinage made from precious metals with paper money, and the Regent, impressed with Law's financial wizardry, made his private bank the Royal Bank of France.

Law's propaganda machine distributed tracts in Europe that promised untold riches in the Louisiana colony. These brochures described mines of gold and silver, and investors rushed to buy shares in Law's new Company of the Indies, in which the Company of the West, the East India Company, and the Company of China were merged.

Law attracted many investors but few colonists. He had planned on awarding large land concessions to investors who would agree to send out two hundred settlers, and the colony was promoted as a land of wealth and opportunity in propaganda distributed in France, Germany, Switzerland, and Holland.

When it became apparent that voluntary immigration would not be sufficient to populate the colony, the Company recruited criminals and street riff-raff to fill the ranks of settlers, and the population went from 400 in 1717 to 8,000 in 1721. Philomena Hauck wrote that "prisons and workhouses were combed for able-bodied men and women, and groups of armed thugs, nicknamed the 'bandoliers of Louisiana,' were hired to round up vagabonds, tramps, and domestic servants out of work for more than four days." She said that in many cases, these press gangs seized innocent people and held them under lock and key for shipment to Louisiana.

When Bienville complained about the low types Law's agents were sending to Louisiana, the Regent forbade additional deportations, and the Company recruited a number of Germans. Hauck said that "although the number of undesirables who actually reached the colony was never as high as has been made out, they were enough to cause endless frustrations" to Bienville. "The damage was done. Louisiana had acquired the reputation of a penal colony, a reputation it took a long time to live down."

Bienville had to deal with the colonists who were rounded up by Law's agents and dumped in Louisiana with no resources, and he had to contend with the Indians, encroachments by the English traders from the Carolinas, and a multitude of other problems. The first hurricane on record struck New Orleans on September 11, 1722, demolishing over half the structures.

The Superior Council, established to advise the governor and assist in administering the colony, addressed price controls and the suppression of gambling, a notorious vice among settlers and soldiers. In 1724 the Code Noir, or Black Code, promulgated by the monarchy, was implemented in Louisiana by the Superior Council. It required that slaves receive religious instruction and observe Sundays and Holy Days as holidays from their labor. Masters were required to provide their slaves housing, food, and proper clothing. Penalties for infractions by slaves, such as striking a master or a member of his family, were severe. The code granted to freed slaves all of the rights enjoyed by freeborn colonists.

The introduction of slavery had allowed agriculture to expand, and the colony became more self-sufficient, but conditions were still poor. Bienville's greatest asset in sustaining the colony was his ability to deal with the Indians and achieve good relations with them. When they visited his home, he treated their chiefs as equals, and his Indian diplomacy was critical to the survival of the colony.

Unfortunately for Bienville, he was never as adept in dealing with his colleagues and superiors as he was with the natives. The story of his governorships is a chronicle of one quarrel after another with just about every official with whom he dealt. Dufour said that "One may well ask whether Bienville was not a difficult man to get along with, so recurrent were his quarrels. But his obvious resentment and antagonism to newcomers to Louisiana, to whom he became subordinate, is understandable. Humiliation piled upon frustration spread over eighteen years could hardly spawn any other feelings."

The sad state of the colony, impoverished and miserable, probably accounted for much of the bickering among its officials. While the Louisiana colony barely hung on, Law's financial empire collapsed. The speculation in the stock of the Company of the Indies, known as the "Mississippi Bubble," brought down Law's financial empire, and he fled France in the wake of the financial panic that ensued.

Bienville was named interim commandant by the crown, but was still suspected of corruption. Sieur Jacques de La Chaise was sent to Louisiana in 1723 as commissary, with instructions to investigate complaints about Bienville's conduct. While La Chaise initially found no fault with Bienville's treatment of him, he reported that "everybody [spoke] in general complaints of him, even those who appear to be his best friends."

Despite their initial cordiality, La Chaise was soon embroiled in a feud with Bienville and now characterized him as a troublemaker. La Chaise recommended that both Bienville and his younger brother Chateaugay, who had commanded at Mobile, be recalled, and his view was supported by the royal engineer, Le Blond de La Tour, who accused Bienville of despotism.

The Regent ordered Bienville's recall to France in 1724, to answer charges of malfeasance and corruption lodged by his enemies, and he and Chateaugay returned there together in 1725. He submitted a paper to the crown in which he took credit for establishing the colony, recounted his long years of service, and defended his conduct.

While the colony was still impoverished and weak, Bienville had made the most of the resources that he had. His governorship from 1718 to 1725 was his most effective period of service. He had kept the English traders who sought alliances with the Indians at bay, New Orleans had been established, and during a war between France and Spain, he had defended Mobile against a Spanish expedition and captured Pensacola, thereby pushing the boundary of Louisiana to the Perdido River in the peace that followed.

In evaluating Bienville's conduct, the crown made no determination of guilt, but he was formally removed from his position in Louisiana and forbidden to return. Given a small pension, he retired to an apartment in Paris. While serving as governor under the authority of the Company of the West and awarding tracts of land to Law's investors and other settlers, Bienville designated large concessions on both sides of the Mississippi River in New Orleans for himself. He derived an income from rentals on these and other properties and from investments in France.

While Bienville sought to recover from bad health, his successor, Etienne de Perier, named governor in 1727, failed to follow Bienville's Indian diplomacy. A naval officer with a record for courage and leadership, Perier took firm control of the colony and was generally well received. Although he had no prior dealings with Indians, he was confident that he could handle the natives without treating them as equals in Bienville's fashion.

Perier declined to recognize the Indians' ownership of their tribal lands, a cornerstone of Bienville's Indian policy. The Natchez tribe felt deceived when the commandant at Fort Rosalie, adjacent to the Grand Village of the Natchez, told their principal chief, the Great Sun, that they would have to turn over their town and its cultivated fields to the French.

The Natchez visited within the fort on the pretext of trading game for trinkets, but instead attacked the garrison, killing 200 soldiers and settlers and taking captive women, children, and slaves. Perier responded swiftly, sending troops and Choctaw allies to capture and disarm the Natchez village. The tribe was destroyed; many Natchez were sent to the Caribbean to work sugar plantations as slaves. A handful of survivors took refuge with the Chickasaws.

The Company of the Indies returned the colony to the monarchy in 1730, and Perier was recalled in 1732. Relations with the Indians were at a low point and the colony was fighting for survival when Bienville was brought out of retirement to serve as governor for a final time. This was the first instance in which he was actually given the title of royal governor, although he had filled the office in practice during three prior appointments.

Bienville returned to New Orleans in 1733, at age fifty-two, having spent the better part of his life in Louisiana. The residents were pleased at his reinstatement, as the colony was in a sad state of affairs, with the most basic necessities in short supply or lacking entirely. He sought to correct problems that had long plagued the colony; among his improvements were a central warehouse for goods and a proper barracks for soldiers. He had to contend with years of political and religious difficulties, with the Jesuits and the Capuchins vying for supremacy in the French colonial empire.

The English in the Carolinas and Georgia sought to expand into French territory and succeeded in gaining the allegiance of several Indian tribes, including the Alibamons and the Chickasaws, who were particularly troublesome to the French. Bienville had to command the loyalty of the Chickasaws through gifts, threats, and diplomacy; failing that, he would have to force their submission. He was determined to punish them for giving shelter to the remaining Natchez, because he feared French prestige would suffer if he did nothing.

When the Chickasaws refused to turn the Natchez over to him, Bienville led a large force of soldiers and Choctaws against them at their villages near present-day Memphis. He planned a coordinated attack with a French force, commanded by Pierre d'Artaguette, that marched south from the Illinois country to join him for a concerted assault. Bienville was delayed in his march, however, and the Illinois army made a fatal mistake in attacking without him. They compelled the Chickasaws to abandon one fort, but in their attack on a second stronghold the French were abandoned by their Indian allies. They were routed by the Chickasaws, who killed many French and captured others, including d'Artaguette, whom they burned at the stake.

Bienville's troops and Choctaws finally reached the scene and attacked the Chickasaw forts. Two assaults failed, and the French withdrew in defeat. Bienville took responsibility for the debacle, although he remained convinced that if the Illinois army had waited for him, they would have gained a decisive victory.

Bienville, accused of mismanaging the military campaign, defended his actions in dispatches. He received reinforcements from France, with munitions and supplies, and in 1739 he marched against the Chickasaws with 1,200 soldiers and 2,000 Indians. He built a fort near the Chickasaws and attacked them. While he did not gain a decisive victory, he killed a number, and the Chickasaws sued for peace, turning the few Natchez in their care over to him. Bienville called the expedition a victory, but he had not destroyed their villages or bound them to him. The Chickasaws remained a threat to the French colony.

While Bienville had a "marked capacity for creating enemies" during his prior service, in his last ten years as governor his relations were good. He was aware of continued dissatisfaction with him at the court, however. Rumors of corruption and self-dealing were never extinguished, and the cost of the military campaign against the Chickasaws had been enormous. However, his last years in Louisiana saw marked improvement in the colony, including the establishment of a charity hospital made possible by a trader's bequest. But Bienville felt he had failed in most respects and that his accomplishments over a lifetime of service had never been fairly appreciated or recognized.

Disappointed by what he considered the crown's lack of attention to and support of the colony, and frustrated by the inroads the English had made with the Indians, in 1743, at age sixty-two, Bienville asked to be relieved. He remained in Louisiana until a successor, the Marquis de Vaudreuil, arrived. When Bienville boarded ship for France on August 17, 1743, never to see his birthplace in Canada or Louisiana again, he had devoted forty of his sixty-two years to the colony. In his petition for relief he said that, despite being dogged by "ill fortune," he felt he could "flatter myself that I am leaving everything in better order than it has ever been."

Bienville had labored under many burdens, not least of which was the crown's failure to devote adequate resources to the colony. At various times, he found himself out of favor with colleagues, some colonists, the companies of Crozat and Law, and the crown, and spent much time in disputes and recriminations. His successes included the founding of New Orleans, which was made the capital of French Louisiana, the establishment of Charity Hospital, and bringing the Ursuline nuns to the colony to oversee the hospital and open a school for girls.

His most remarkable talent, evidenced from the very outset, lay in his manner of dealing with the Indians. While he could not lavish gifts on them to the extent the English did, they liked and trusted him, and to the very end asked about him. He was fair but firm when depredations against colonists and traders required retribution. Giraud noted his "cunning" in dealing with the Indians and wrote "the fact that he could retain his own Indian allies against the higher bid of the British is significant testimony to his ability." Through a combination of artful diplomacy and guile, he maintained the loyalty of the Choctaws and kept the Chickasaws from destroying the colony. He held Louisiana together during the battles between the French and English for supremacy on the North American continent and saved the colony from economic and military collapse.

Bienville lived in comfort for another twenty-three years with his government pension, income from investments, and rents from his Louisiana properties, still regarded as ill-gotten gains by his adversaries. He saw France turn Canada over to the English and his beloved Louisiana to Spain. He died in Paris on March 7, 1767, the last of the Le Moyne brothers who left indelible marks on the pages of Louisiana history.

If Iberville was the Discoverer of Louisiana, then surely Bienville was the Father of Louisiana and the Founder of New Orleans.

—J.B.McG.

Davis, Edwin Adams. *Louisiana: A Narrative History*. Baton Rouge: Claitor's Publishing Division, 1971.

Dawson, Joseph G. III, ed. *The Louisiana Governors: From Iberville to Edwards*. Baton Rouge: Louisiana State University Press, 1990.

Dufour, Charles L. *Ten Flags in the Wind: The Story of Louisiana*. New York: Harper & Row, 1967.

Giraud, Marcel. *A History of French Louisiana: The Reign of Louis XIV, 1698–1715*. Baton Rouge: Louisiana State University Press, 1974.

Hauck, Philomena. *Bienville: Father of Louisiana*. Lafayette: Center for Louisiana Studies, University of Southwestern Louisiana, 1998.

Wall, Bennett H., ed. *Louisiana: A History*. Wheeling, IL: Harlan Davidson, 1997.

Antoine de Lamothe, Sieur de Cadillac

1713–1716

Antoine de Lamothe, Sieur de Cadillac, Louisiana's fourth governor, found himself in a swirl of controversy from the time he was named to the post in 1713. Actually, a report on what he had done in the founding of Detroit just prior to his appointment in Louisiana was so critical that it should have ended his career, some historians claim.

But Cadillac had great persuasive qualities and talked his way into positions of authority. This was especially true in his role in Louisiana, for he persuaded Antoine Crozat, the wealthy French financier, to take over the territory and its troubles in 1713, when France decided the colony had become a burden. Cadillac, however, was deluded by his own rhetorical powers, finding upon arrival in Louisiana that he had oversold the value of the territory as it existed at the time.

It did not take long for factional division to spring up between Cadillac and Bienville, who had opposed Cadillac's appointment and refused to help him. DuBois DuClos, the commissary who was in charge of finances and commerce, and Bienville became allies and worked against Cadillac. While the governor controlled the military and shared authority with the commissary in police power, DuClos closed his eyes to illegal trade with Spain and even took part in it.

The bickering between Cadillac and Bienville led Crozat to become disillusioned with the colony. He petitioned for an end to his monopoly, which was granted in August 1717. Cadillac's administration was largely a failure, and it was Crozat who requested that he be recalled.

However, there were some positive gains in Cadillac's term: He encouraged farming, and the population increased. Natchez and Natchitoches, as well as several outposts beyond Mobile, were established to expand Indian trade and thwart Spanish and English competition to France in the east. He also made an effort to develop mines and to trade with Mexico, in order to satisfy Crozat, but failed in these attempts.

A proper man, Cadillac was offended by the moral tone of Louisiana, describing the inhabitants as "scum, refuse, ruffians who cheat the gibbet—vagabonds steeped in vice." He commented, "If I send away all the loose females, there will be no women at all."

Born in Gascony, France, on March 5, 1658, Cadillac was the son of a minor provincial judge. He appeared in America in 1683 and settled at Port Royal, Nova Scotia, after marrying Marie Therese Guion, niece of Francois Guion, a privateer. After being recalled to France in 1716, Cadillac ran afoul of the French government in promoting Louisiana to John Law and the Company of the West, Crozat's successor.

This time Cadillac told the truth about Louisiana. For giving a realistic view of the colony, he was imprisoned in the Bastille for four months. Later, however, he was restored to dignity and granted the Cross of St. Louis. He ultimately bought the governorship of Castelsarrasin, France, where he died on October 16, 1730.

—W.G.C.

Fortier, Alcee. *A History of Louisiana*, vol. I. 2nd ed. Jo Ann Carrigen, ed. Baton Rouge: Claitor's Book Store, 1966.

Gayarré, Charles. *History of Louisiana: The French Domination*. Gretna, LA: Pelican, 1965.

Jean Michel De l'Epinay

1717–1718

Antoine Crozat, the wealthy Frenchman granted a twenty-five-year commercial monopoly of Louisiana in 1712, did not approve of Cadillac's administration and saw to it that he was removed from office in 1717. Bienville was to be in command until the arrival of Cadillac's successor, Jean Michel De l'Epinay.

De l'Epinay arrived on March 9, 1717, accompanied by Marc-Antoine Hubert, who had been appointed intendant. Bienville, disappointed that he was not chosen governor again, gave De l'Epinay a cold shoulder, and he and his friends organized a party of opposition to the new authorities. Bienville had been awarded the Cross of St. Louis for his work in the colony and reasoned that he should be returned to the office of governor.

Louisiana at that time contained only 700 persons "of all ages, sexes, and colors." Major settlements were located at Mobile Bay, along the coast westward from Biloxi, two small groups on the Red River near Natchitoches, and at Alexandria. Several small forts had been built, including Fort Rosalie at Natchez. Fort Louis, established at Mobile on the river, had to be moved to what became the city of Mobile, where it was renamed Fort Conde.

In August 1717 Crozat surrendered his charter, and the French regent chose the Mississippi or Western Company, headed by the Scotsman John Law to administer the colony, again for twenty-five years.

The Mississippi or Western Company, as it was described, evolved into the Company of the Indies when Law's company fizzled, ruining him financially and leading to his administration being referred to as the "Mississippi Bubble."

De l'Epinay found himself in controversy, especially when he decreed that liquor could not be sold to Indians at a time when it was the most profitable item of commerce. He was removed from the governorship, and Bienville was chosen again. Bienville served his second term until January 1724, when he was recalled to France to answer charges of malfeasance.

—W.G.C.

Fortier, Alcee. *A History of Louisiana*, vol. I. 2nd ed. Jo Ann Carrigen, ed. Baton Rouge: Claitor's Book Store, 1966.

Pierre Sidrac Dugué, Sieur de Boisbriant

1725–1727

One of the French founding fathers of Colonial Louisiana, Pierre Sidrac Dugué, Sieur de Boisbriant (or Boisbriand), was ordered to replace Bienville when the latter was recalled to France. Dugué served as acting governor from February 1725 until March 1727.

Little is known of Dugué's accomplishments in Louisiana, except that he became involved in a controversy concerning use of the company stores. His connection with Bienville led him into repeated conflicts with Jacques de La Chaise, chief financial officer of the colony. But Dugué had a lot going for him because of his ability to court favor with the Indian tribes of the region. He inherited from his father, Michel Sidrac Dugué, a love of the frontier.

Iberville recruited Dugué for the second expedition from France to Louisiana, and the two led numerous reconnaissance missions in the Gulf Coast area. Dugué aided in the construction of Fort Louis de Louisiane in Mobile in 1700. He remained in Mobile for twelve years and did a lot to solidify French control among the Indian tribes. He served as commandant of the Mobile and Illinois districts. During his Illinois tenure, he led one hundred men into the area seeking silver mines, but found only a lead mine that yielded little silver.

Dugué, who was born in Montreal February 21, 1675, entered military service with Iberville and, in 1697, accompanied him in the conquest of Fort Bourbon on Hudson Bay. Dugué's career began as a half-pay ensign in 1691. Promoted to major, he became commandant of Mobile and the Dauphine district in 1717. The controversy with de La Chaise caused him to be stripped of his command, and he returned to France in 1729, where he died on June 7, 1736.

—W.G.C.

Coutts, Brian E. "Jean-Michel, Seigneur de Lepinay et de Longueville, Governor, 1717–1718; Pierre Sidrac Dugue de Boisbriand, Governor, 1724–1726; and Etienne de Perier, Governor, 1727–1733." *The Louisiana Governors: From Iberville to Edwards.* Joseph C. Dawson III, ed. Baton Rouge: Louisiana State University Press, 1990.

Reeves, Miriam G. *The Governors of Louisiana.* Gretna, LA: Pelican, 1976.

Etienne de Perier

1727–1733

Etienne de Perier had never seen an Indian until he came to Louisiana as its governor, and the mistakes he made in believing that he could handle the native inhabitants led to the massacre of the soldiers and settlers at Fort Rosalie by the Natchez tribe.

Born in LeHavre in 1690, he rendered commendable service in the closing engagements of the War of the Spanish Succession. He commanded ships for the Company of the West and won praise for his abilities, with the command in Louisiana given by its directors as a reward for his accomplishments.

Perier's lack of any experience in colonial administration was an unforeseen drawback, but historian Marcel Giraud noted that he "performed his duties with a zeal and a sense of equity that gave the population a little more stability, for a short time at least."

As commandant-general for the Company of the West, or governor in practice, Perier was responsible for military matters and Indian relations, while the commissary, Jacques de La Chaise, oversaw the justice system, police, financial matters, and trade.

The company, feeling that Bienville's family members and supporters had "revolted" against its authority, removed them from any roles in the colony. With Bienville gone, there was less discord and dissention, but the colony remained divided into pro- and anti-Bienville camps. Perier was soon undermined by his subordinates, including de La Chaise, whom he accused of intriguing against him.

Perier was very active in the administration of the colony, although his efforts were hampered by a chronic shortage of funds. He tried unsuccessfully to promote development of a citrus industry, and he visited all of the outposts. In an essay about Perier, Brian E. Coutts wrote that his "greatest accomplishments came in the area of public and charitable works." He built levees to protect New Orleans from flooding and deepened the mouth of the Mississippi's main channel so that larger vessels could ascend the river. Construction of a prison was completed, and Perier provided funds to care for orphans from the meager resources at his disposal. Soon after he took over, the first Ursuline nuns arrived in New Orleans to care for patients at the hospital and establish a school for girls. They were followed by the Casket Girls, named for the small trunks in which they carried their possessions. These were single young women sent out as wives for colonists.

Perier did not treat the Indians as did Bienville, who welcomed them into his quarters and dealt with them as equals. Perier refused to recognize the Indians' ownership of their tribal lands, which was a cornerstone of Bienville's Indian policy, and the Natchez felt deceived.

The French had enjoyed friendly relations with the Natchez, and several hundred settlers had established themselves on farms, or "habitations," at Fort Rosalie, near the Grand Village of the Natchez. While there is dispute among historians about all of the circumstances of the Natchez revolt, it appears that Governor Perier wanted to establish a plantation for himself at Fort Rosalie. He appointed a new commandant there, a Captain Chepart (or Detcheparre in some accounts), whose handling of affairs angered the settlers. Chepart was called before the Superior Council in New Orleans, which dismissed him. Perier then overruled that body and reinstated Chepart.

One historian has suggested that Perier promised to give Chepart an interest in the plantation, and that greed motivated Chepart's desire to take the most fertile lands for it. Rather than mark out a section of vacant land, Chepart foolishly determined to seize the land and cultivated fields on which the White Apple Village of the Natchez was located. He ordered the Indians to abandon it once their harvest was completed.

Chepart paid no heed to the protests of the principal chief of the Natchez, the Great Sun, and discounted rumors that the Indians were going to rise up against the French.

On November 28, 1729, a large number of Natchez entered the fort, carrying guns, to trade with the settlers. Welcomed by the garrison and colonists, they suddenly turned on the French, killing many of them in their first volley. Captain Chepart, found hiding in a garden, was clubbed to death, while 145 men, 35 women, and 56 children were killed. The captives included 80 women and 150 black slaves. The Indians pillaged the fort's storehouses, torching the habitations of the settlers.

When news of the massacre reached New Orleans, panic ensued. With the blow that one tribe had struck, the inhabitants recognized that if the Indian tribes had acted in concert in a general uprising, the colony would have been wiped out. Perier had only a handful of soldiers, and the city's defenses were weak, but he calmed the populace and acted decisively.

Perier sent a punitive expedition of 200 soldiers and volunteers and 300 Indian allies from tribes near New Orleans against the Natchez. They planned on meeting up with 800 Choctaws to attack While Apple Village. The Choctaws, finding the unsuspecting Natchez outside of their forts in the area, attacked them without waiting for the French expedition. They killed over 70 Natchez warriors and rescued 50 women and children and 100 black slaves.

When the French arrived, they brought up cannon to lay siege to the Natchez forts. They beat back a counterattack and prepared to mount their own assault, but were persuaded by the Choctaws to allow them to negotiate with the Natchez. The Natchez released their remaining captives, the French left a small force near the remains of Fort Rosalie, and the rest of the expedition returned to New Orleans.

Perier was not satisfied with the success of this expedition. He now believed that the only thing the Natchez understood was force and determined to exterminate the tribe.

By the end of 1730, when reinforcements arrived from France, Perier struck. The remaining Natchez had harassed the French, attacked and burned several settlers' habitations, and established a new Indian fort on the Black River, in present-day Concordia Parish.

With 150 fresh troops, soldiers from the garrisons at New Orleans, Natchitoches, and Natchez, volunteers from among the settlers, and a large number of Indian allies, Perier left New Orleans on December 9, 1730. He laid siege to the Natchez fort, promising to spare the remaining tribesmen if they released their captives and surrendered. Most of the women and children came out, but a number of warriors escaped.

Perier took 450 prisoners and pronounced his campaign a great success. His enemies reported otherwise, claiming that he had missed an opportunity to annihilate the tribe. The Natchez who surrendered were sent to St. Domingue, with many dying on the voyage there, to work the sugar plantations as slaves. Perier was accused of duplicity in deporting the Indians, to whom he had promised no harm if they surrendered. Both the French king and the minister felt that he had been too harsh. The few Natchez who were left in Louisiana took refuge with the Chickasaw tribe.

The directors of the Company of the West, disheartened by the Natchez massacre and disappointed at their failure to find riches in Louisiana, petitioned the king to reclaim the colony, which Louis XV did upon payment to the crown of an indemnity to settle the company's accounts in Louisiana. With relations with the Indians a primary concern, the king ordered Perier home and brought Bienville from retirement to serve as governor once again.

Perier returned to France in 1733. His service to the crown was recognized with the Cross of St. Louis and a pension. He died at Brest in 1755.

—J.B.McG.

Coutts, Brian E. "Jean-Michel, Seigneur de Lepinay et de Longueville, Governor, 1717–1718; Pierre Sidrac Dugue de Boisbriand, Governor, 1724–1726; and Etienne de Perier, Governor, 1727–1733." *The Louisiana Governors: From Iberville to Edwards*. Joseph G. Dawson, III, ed. Baton Rouge: Louisiana State University, Press 1990.

Davis, Edwin Adams. *Louisiana: A Narrative History*. Baton Rouge: Claitor's Publishing Division, 1971.

Dufour, Charles L. *Ten Flags in the Wind: The Story of Louisiana*. New York: Harper & Row, 1967.

Giraud, Marcel. *A History of French Louisiana: The Company of the Indies, 1723–1731*. Baton Rouge: Louisiana State University Press, 1991.

Wall, Bennett H., ed. *Louisiana: A History*. Wheeling, IL: Harlan Davidson, 1997.

Pierre de Rigaud de Cavagnial, Marquis de Vaudreuil

1743–1753

The closest that Louisiana came to having its own royalty, at least until the advent of the Cajun Prince, Edwin Edwards, was the reign as governor of Pierre de Rigaud de Cavagnial, Marquis de Vaudreuil.

Descended from a noble family of Languedoc, Vaudreuil was born in Canada in 1698. He was commissioned an ensign in the colonial regulars at age ten, and served in the army and held administrative posts in New France, including as Governor of Montreal. He was an experienced colonial officer when he was named governor of Louisiana. His ambition was to follow his own father as Governor General of New France, now Canada.

Vaudreuil arrived in New Orleans on May 10, 1743. Historian Dufour notes that, from the outset, the Marquis and his wife impressed the citizens with their "elegant manners, good taste, and elaborate entertainments." His decade-long administration was "a sort of golden age for the long-suffering colony," marked by prosperity and harmony. He was quick to respond when the Chickasaws attacked several plantations. French troops razed several of the Indian villages; the Chickasaws eventually capitulated and pledged their loyalty in a treaty dictated by Vaudreuil.

Vaudreuil, called by the people the "Grand Marquis," was immensely popular. His wife, fifteen years older, was less so; she was disliked for her imperious ways and her demands that merchants honor her high station by giving her discounts on purchases. The unfavorable view of his consort was not carried over to the governor, however; he presided at glittering social occasions in the city and at surrounding plantations. One historian said that the king may have had his court at Versailles, but on the French frontier in Louisiana, Vaudreuil "maintained an impressive formal court at New Orleans. His sponsorship of a regular series of balls, dinners, and formal social engagements increased his popularity with French officials and members of the upper class in New Orleans, all of whom were hungry for pomp and splendor."

Among the notable events of Vaudreuil's governorship was the start of the sugar cane industry, which became so important to the economy of Louisiana in later years. It began on a small basis under the Grand Marquis when Jesuits in Santo Domingo sent samples of cane to their brethren in New Orleans to see if the plants would thrive in the Louisiana climate. He also promoted the successful production of indigo.

The crown rewarded Vaudreuil's success in Louisiana with appointment as Governor General of Canada. His administration there was marred by disagreements over military affairs with the Marquis de Montcalm and accusations of corruption in civil matters. Montcalm was promoted to lieutenant general, a military rank senior to a colonial governor, and while Vaudreuil was responsible for the security of New France, Montcalm commanded its armed forces. A Canadian biographical dictionary said " The lines of command were now hopelessly confused between two men who could not abide each other." After Montcalm's defeat and death in the battle for Quebec, Vaudreuil surrendered Montreal to the British rather than sacrifice his troops. Vaudreuil returned to France, where he was blamed for the loss of New France, imprisoned in the Bastille, and put on trial for financial misconduct. He was exonerated, however, and the king awarded him the Grand Cross of the Order of St. Louis for his years of service. Granted a pension, he lived quietly in retirement until his death in Paris in 1788.

Vaudreuil made a lasting impression in Louisiana and was fondly remembered there. The *Dictionary of Canadian Biography* said Vaudreuil "won the acclaim of the Louisiana colonists. He left the colony in a far more secure and prosperous condition than he had found it." Dufour said that when his successor, Kerlerec, arrived, Vaudreuil, "the Grand Marquis to the end," gave an elaborate reception for him, with fountains of wine flowing in the Place d'Armes, "so that the soldiers and inhabitants of New Orleans could join in the celebration."

—J.B.McG.

Davis, Edwin Adams. *Louisiana: A Narrative History*. Baton Rouge: Claitor's Publishing Division, 1971.

Dawson, Joseph G. III, ed. *The Louisiana Governors: From Iberville to Edwards*. Baton Rouge: Louisiana State University Press, 1990.

Dufour, Charles L. *Ten Flags in the Wind: The Story of Louisiana*. New York: Harper & Row, 1967.

Eccles, W. J. *Dictionary of Canadian Biography*, online edition.

Wall, Bennett H., ed. *Louisiana: A History*. Wheeling, IL: Harlan Davidson, 1997.

Louis Billouart, Chevalier de Kerlerec

1753–1763

Dissension, even war, confronted Governor Louis Billouart, Chevalier de Kerlerec, when he assumed control of Louisiana February 3, 1753. This was some three years before the outbreak of the Seven Years' War in Europe, but hostilities between France and England had already begun in America.

The English posed a continual threat because they sought the allegiance of the powerful Indian tribes who vacillated between the French and English. Friendship with the Indians had to be bought over and over again with presents, but Kerlerec maintained this procedure was preferable to war. The Choctaws had fifty-two villages and four thousand warriors, the Alibamons three thousand warriors and an untold number of villages.

In spite of repeated threats by the English, the French government reduced the number of its troops in Louisiana. Louis XV paid little attention to the colony, and great discord developed within its borders. The Jesuit and Capuchin religious orders quarreled, and the commissary, Rochemore, grew hostile to Kerlerec. When Rochemore charged Kerlerec with violations of the king's orders, an investigation was ordered. Rochemore contended Kerlerec let interloper ships from Jamaica engage in illegal traffic with Louisiana. Also, Rochemore was charged with irregularities in his office. A report exonerated Rochemore, but not Kerlerec, who was ordered to return to France, where he was thrown in the Bastille for "some time." Kerlerec died after his release, but records do not stipulate the date.

As a result of the fight between the Jesuit and Capuchin orders, the Jesuits were expelled from Louisiana in 1763. They returned in 1835 and established a number of schools and a university, which still exist.

Kerlerec's administration, which lasted ten years and five months, also was marked by lesser events that were troublesome. In 1737, Kerlerec appointed Sieur Duroux commandant of Cat Island, which lies off the Mississippi Gulf Coast, next to Ship Island, where Iberville and his fleet found anchorage in 1699. A Swiss regiment and a detachment of marines were assigned to guard it.

A French officer named Bossu, stationed in Louisiana, said Duroux compelled the soldiers to work his garden and do other chores, and severely punished those who refused. The soldiers complained to Kerlerec, who would do nothing. So they killed Duroux and tossed his body into the Gulf of Mexico. They liberated a planter named Beaudreaux, who had been put in irons for refusing to share goods from a wrecked ship, then pillaged the stores and escaped.

Beaudreaux and a soldier were arrested in 1758 and taken to New Orleans to face trial. Found guilty, they were condemned to death, their bodies broken on the wheel and thrown into the river. The Swiss soldier was placed in a coffin and sawn through alive, according to the custom of the Swiss regiment.

—W.G.C.

Fortier, Alcee. *A History of Louisiana*. 2nd ed. Jo Ann Carrigen, ed. Baton Rouge: Claitor's Book Store, 1966.

Gayarré, Charles. *History of Louisiana. Vol. I: The French Domination*. Gretna, LA: Pelican, 1965.

Jean Jacques Blaise d'Abbadie

1763–1765

With Kerlerec's recall, Louis XV named three officials to govern matters in Louisiana. Jean Jacques Blaise d'Abbadie was commissioned director general, with Nicolas Chauvin de la Freniere as attorney general and Nicolas Foucault as intendant. D'Abbadie, who was the comptroller general and chief administrator of the colony, was the senior official, and was regarded as the governor.

D'Abbadie had served as a naval officer, both at sea and in administrative posts, and was an experienced colonial administrator. He arrived in New Orleans in June 1763 and made a good impression from the beginning. He restored the colony's finances and strengthened its defenses. Economic conditions improved because d'Abbadie allowed British merchant ships to come up the Mississippi to reach English posts at Manchac, Baton Rouge, St. Francisville, and Natchez. The French sold their goods and produce to the British in this profitable, though illegal, trade.

D'Abbadie found himself in the unique position of serving as the French governor of a Spanish possession when he received dispatches di-

Jean Jacques Blaise d'Abbadie. Courtesy of Special Collections, Tulane Libraries.

recting him to deliver the colony to representatives of the Spanish king when they arrived. By the Treaty of Paris, Louis XV had transferred the territory of French Louisiana that was east of the Mississippi River to Great Britain. The secret Treaty of Fontainebleau in 1762 gave Charles III of Spain all of Louisiana west of the river and the "Isle of Orleans," New Orleans. It was over a year and a half before the monarchs published the articles of cession, and official notification did not reach d'Abbadie until October 1764.

D'Abbadie had been under much stress in dealing with the problems of the colony, and the king's decree doubtless aggravated his condition. He issued a proclamation announcing the cession and stating that French rule would end as soon as Spanish officials arrived. The news caused an uproar in New Orleans; la Freniere and other leading citizens organized a mass meeting, which resolved to send an emissary to Louis XV to beg him to rescind the transfer of the colony to Spain. Jean Milhet, the richest man in Louisiana, took the citizens' petition to France, but was rebuffed by the minister, who declined to give him an audience with the king.

Bedridden with a nervous disorder, d'Abbadie did not live to transfer Louisiana to Spain. He died of a stroke on February 4, 1765, before the Spanish arrived. "He had been a patriotic and just Governor, and now the people began to appreciate his work and his true character," Dr. Edwin Adams Davis wrote. "They held a mass meeting and paid tribute to his memory."

—J.B.McG.

Davis, Edwin Adams. *Louisiana: A Narrative History*. Baton Rouge: Claitor's Publishing Division, 1971.

Dawson, Joseph G. III, ed. *The Louisiana Governors: From Iberville to Edwards*. Baton Rouge: Louisiana State University Press, 1990.

Dufour, Charles L. *Ten Flags in the Wind: The Story of Louisiana*. New York: Harper & Row, 1967.

Wall, Bennett H., ed. *Louisiana: A History*. Wheeling, IL: Harlan Davidson, 1997.

Charles Philippe Aubry

1765–1766

History does not accord a kind role to Charles Philippe Aubry, the last French governor, who served at a time of great unrest in Louisiana as the colony sought to avoid the yoke of Spanish domination.

Aubry was commandant and governor when General Alexandro O'Reilly took command following the expulsion of Spain's first governor, Antonio de Ulloa, when colonists vowed they would not submit to any power other than French. It was Aubry, named governor in 1765 but who served during the period of the investigation of the Revolt of 1768 and beyond, upon whose shoulders fell the task of greeting General O'Reilly, who had come to punish the colony for its brazen efforts in trying to avoid Spanish rule.

Imagine the scene: twenty-three ships, plus the general's, bearing some three thousand soldiers, anchored in a quay of the Mississippi River in front of the Place d'Armes, where General O'Reilly stepped off the frigate in a public ceremony filled with colorful but tragic moments. Aubry stepped up to the head of the troops as they marched off the ships and lined the square. Then Aubry addressed the crowd, reading the orders of Spanish King Carlos III and handing over the keys to the gates of New Orleans to O'Reilly. Salutes boomed from the vessels, and the Spanish flag was raised, with the people chorusing, "Vive le Roil."

Although the revolt had taken place during three days of October 1768, O'Reilly did not arrive until August 17, 1769. After O'Reilly took command, said Fortier in his history, "It was not necessary that he [Aubry] should give any information to O'Reilly, because at that moment Aubry ceased to be governor."

However, Aubry felt obliged to inform O'Reilly of details of the rebellion and name the conspirators. "Posterity must certainly judge Aubry very severely for his conduct," observed Fortier, from the point of view of a descendant of the French settlers. A later generation might not be so harsh on a soldier following orders that were neither illegal nor immoral.

While the place and date of Aubry's birth have been lost, records show that he died near Bordeaux, France, on February 17, 1770. He entered the military service in France as a second lieutenant in 1742, served the French crown with distinction in the War of the Austrian Succession in

1742–48, and in 1750 was commissioned a captain of colonial troops and assigned to Louisiana.

He fought the British during the Seven Years' War at Fort Duquesne, after being assigned to the Illinois district of Louisiana. In July 1759, in a skirmish with superior enemy forces, his Indian allies deserted him. Aubry was captured and sent to New York for permanent detention, but his actual imprisonment was short-lived. In 1760, after the capitulation of the French resistance in Canada, the French prisoners of war were sent to France. In March 1763, Aubry was placed in charge of Louisiana's garrison. When Governor D'Abbadie died suddenly on February 4, 1765, Aubry was compelled to take charge of the government.

—W.G.C.

Fortier, Alcee. *A History of Louisiana*, vol. I. 2nd ed. Jo Ann Carrigen, ed. Baton Rouge: Claitor's Book Store, 1966.

Gayarré, Charles. *History of Louisiana. Vol. I: The French Domination*. Gretna, LA: Pelican, 1965.

Martin, Francois Xavier. *A History of Louisiana from the Earliest Period Until 1815*. Gretna, LA: Pelican, 1975.

Antonio de Ulloa de la Torre-Guiral

1765–1768

Alejandro O'Reilly

1769

The first Spanish governor of Louisiana, Antonio de Ulloa, got off to a bad start. As he took over administration of the colony, he refused to present his credentials to the Superior Council, the governing body under French rule. He further snubbed that body by governing through the French military governor, Captain Charles Philippe Aubry. Ulloa's orders were dispatched from the Balize, a military station at the mouth of the Mississippi River, where he remained for months after his arrival.

Alejandro O'Reilly. Courtesy of Special Collections, Tulane Libraries.

His contempt of the council, as well as authoritative orders restricting all shipping to certain Spanish ports, angered the general populace and cost him dearly, resulting in his expulsion in an insurrection hailed by some historians as the opening chapter in the movement for American independence seven years later. In the French colonists' view, they had reason to refuse to submit to Spanish rule. After all, Louisiana had been transferred from French to Spanish ownership in a secret deal reached on November 3, 1762, by the Treaty of Fontainebleau, though nobody had bothered to tell the people of Louisiana. Moreover, the terms of the treaty were not known in Paris for nearly two years. Six months after the revelation of these terms in Paris, the news finally hit New Orleans and caused an uproar. The colony sent a delegation to Paris, trying to get King Louis XV to reverse his edict, but their efforts failed.

Who was Ulloa anyway? His full name was Antonio de Ulloa de la Torre-Guiral, born in Seville on January 12, 1716, to an aristocratic family connected to Portuguese royalty. Fifty years old when he arrived in Louisiana, he was a naval officer, scientist, author, and colonial administrator. His first experience as a colonial administrator was in 1758 as governor of a colony in Peru, but he had had little success. He had also failed as superintendent of a mining operation in Peru.

How then could he have been chosen to administer Louisiana? Historian Charles Gayarré noted that although Ulloa was an introvert, he had unusual drive and energy, the marks of a good politician. He had also been elected to the Royal Society in London, in recognition of his outstanding knowledge of astronomy, chemistry, and mathematics. He was also a member of the Royal Academies of Stockholm and Berlin and a scholar honored by the Royal Academy of Science in Paris.

After arriving at the Balize, Ulloa was married by proxy to a prominent young woman of Santiago, Chile, who was related to the old families of Seville. Although they were later married in a formal ceremony in New Orleans, the proxy ceremony was considered offensive to Creole custom, giving the couple an aversion to the social life of the port city.

Ulloa found the political atmosphere hostile when he later settled in New Orleans. Named governor in May 1765, he did not arrive in Louisiana until March 5, 1766, and did not take full control of the colony until August 1767. He brought only ninety soldiers and three civil officers, hoping to enlist the aid of French troops already serving in the area. The French refused to help. To make matters worse, the colony faced austere economic times, forcing Ulloa to reduce both Spanish and French troops to half-rations.

Furthermore, by delaying his move to New Orleans and not raising the Spanish flag in the Place d'Armes, he caused his credibility to suffer.

When in March 1766 he declared that the colony would only do business with nine Spanish ports, ending the trade with French ports, the people became angrier. Among other things, the order deprived the colony of their French wines! His order proved to be a disaster, severing Louisiana from its traditional markets.

During the time Ulloa directed affairs from the Balize, hostility brewed in the city. Two prominent colonists, Nicolas Chauvin de La Freniere, the attorney general, and Nicolas Foucault, the commissary, spearheaded a campaign against Ulloa's rule. Planters and merchants joined the protest, which culminated in twenty-one formal charges of misadministration filed against Ulloa. When, on October 28, 1769, members of the Superior Council debated the charges, hundreds of Creoles, Acadians, and Germans gathered in the main square, brandishing muskets and other firearms. The colonists proclaimed that they would never submit to any governor other than one from France.

Suddenly, a dramatic scene unfolded as the council put Ulloa on notice to leave. He, his wife, and their baby daughter boarded the *El Volante*, the ship that had brought him to New Orleans. They hoped to leave on October 31, but this was deemed unsafe, so Ulloa chartered the French frigate *Cesar*. The next morning, bearing Ulloa and his family, several monks and close advisors, the vessel set sail for Havana. (During the American Revolution, Ulloa was commander of a Spanish navy force in the Caribbean and was promoted to lieutenant general and admiral of the fleet. He died in Cadiz in 1795.)

With Ulloa's departure, however, the drama had only begun. Ulloa sent a full report of the insurrection to King Charles, III, who appointed one of his favorites, General Alejandro O'Reilly, governor and captain-general of Louisiana and directed him to suppress the rebellion that had ousted Ulloa.

O'Reilly, born in Ireland, entered the Spanish army and rose to the rank of field marshal. Prior to going to Louisiana, he commanded in Puerto Rico, where he organized a regiment of native troops.

With an expedition of warships and 2,600 troops, O'Reilly arrived in New Orleans in August 1769. He was met at the Balize and escorted to the city by Aubry.

O'Reilly assured the nervous population of 3,200, who feared reprisals, that his interest was in establishing order and punishing the ringleaders of the rebellion. He ordered the arrest of six men and imprisoned or expelled several others from the colony, but issued a general pardon to all other participants on condition they take an oath of allegiance to Spain.

The six ringleaders were put on trial without jury for treason and sedition. Their defense claimed that since Spanish law had not yet been instituted when their alleged crimes occurred, they could not be convicted for violating it. O'Reilly, however, following the recommendations of the Spanish judge advocate, found them guilty and imposed the death sentence on five of the men.

They were executed at 3 p.m. on October 25, 1769, in the yard of the barracks adjoining the Ursuline Convent, as the nuns and members of the doomed men's families prayed. "It was a terrible moment for those gathered," said Fortier in his history. "The report of firearms caused the windows of the chapel to shake."

The five executed by a firing squad were Pierre Caresse; Jean-Baptiste Noyan, a nephew of Bienville; Pierre Marquis, who had commanded the militia that paraded through the streets; Joseph Milhet; and de La Freniere. Five other men charged as accomplices were imprisoned in Havana, but their sentences were soon commuted.

Joseph Villere, another instigator of the revolt, was on his plantation on the German Coast at the time of the roundup. He was thinking of fleeing to British protection when he received a letter from Aubry, reassuring him that he had nothing to fear from O'Reilly, that he could come to New Orleans in perfect safety. As he arrived in New Orleans, he was arrested. Indignant, Villere struck an officer, and a struggle ensued. Guards joined the fight, and Villere was bayoneted. He was taken aboard a frigate, where he died a few days later. Aubry had double-crossed him!

The executed men, and Villere, were soon labeled the "Martyrs of Louisiana." Fortier said of them: "Posterity, the judge of men in power, will doom this act to public execration. No necessity demanded, no policy justified it. Ulloa's conduct had provoked the measures to which the inhabitants had resorted. Charles III would have pardoned men whose only crime was to have loved liberty and France . . . there is surely no nobler page in any history than that which is presented to us by The Martyrs of Louisiana."

Furthermore, the Marquis de Grimaldi, a minister of Charles III, in a letter to Count de Fuentes, Spanish ambassador to France, said that O'Reilly had gone beyond his instructions in executing the men. O'Reilly's authority was only to expel the guilty colonists.

Known throughout Louisiana history as "Bloody" O'Reilly, with that reputation firmly established by the French historians of Louisiana Gayarré and Fortier, he sought to conciliate the people after the executions. During the five months of his governorship, he abolished the French Superior Council and established the Cabildo, a Spanish-style government.

O'Reilly sent most of his troops to Havana and retained the French commandants at most posts. He instituted the Code O'Reilly as the basis of Spanish law, proclaimed it a crime to hold captive Indians as slaves, and ordered a census.

O'Reilly appointed Luis Unzaga y Amerzaga governor on December 1, 1769, but remained in New Orleans as captain-general until his departure on October 29, 1770. He later served as governor of Cadiz, dying in 1794.

Under O'Reilly's firm hand, Spain stabilized its rule and sought to improve the colony's economy for the next thirty-four years, until the brief retrocession to France and the Louisiana Purchase.

—W.G.C.

Fortier, Alcee. *A History of Louisiana*, vol. III. 2nd ed. Jo Ann Carrigen, ed. Baton Rouge: Claitor's Book Store, 1966.

Gayarré, Charles. *A History of Louisiana. Vol. IV: The American Domination.* Gretna, LA: Pelican, 1965.

Moore, J. Preston. "Antonio de Ulloa, Colonial Governor, 1766–1768." *The Louisiana Governors: From Iberville to Edwards.* Joseph G. Dawson III, ed. Baton Rouge: Louisiana State University Press, 1990.

www.enlou.com. The Spanish Governors of Louisiana: Antonio de Ulloa; Alejandro O'Reilly.

Luis Unzaga y Amerzaga

1769–1777

Luis Unzaga y Amerzaga accompanied O'Reilly to Louisiana; O'Reilly held the titles of captain-general and governor, and Unzaga was deputized as his successor. O'Reilly seated Unzaga as acting governor after the revolt was dealt with, and Unzaga presided over the Cabildo, the Spanish superior council for the colony, at its first meeting. As captain-general O'Reilly outranked him, but he continued as governor after O'Reilly returned to Havana, serving in that position from December 1, 1769, until August 1772. His commission was made permanent then, and he held the office until January 1, 1777.

Born in Málaga in 1721, Unzaga spent over thirty years in the military. He was colonel of the regiment of Havana when he was posted to Louisiana. As governor, he improved conditions in the colony during a peaceful era. Dr. Edwin Adams Davis said that Unzaga was "placid, mild, even-tempered, conciliatory, and possessed the ability to make friends and inspire confidence."

He eased the difficult transition to Spanish rule, after the executions of the leaders of the Revolt of 1768, by naming French citizens to government posts, and he "endeared himself to the colonists when he married the daughter of the wealthy and powerful New Orleans merchant, Gilbert Antoine St. Maxent." Perhaps what they liked him best for, however, was his willingness to tolerate the illegal trade with the neighboring British colonies. The British had been granted rights to navigation of the Mississippi by the Peace of 1763, but Unzaga allowed their ships to anchor near its banks as "floating warehouses" to sell their goods.

Unzaga's health failed during his governorship, and his eyesight diminished. He asked the crown to relieve him and allow him to retire to Spain, but his services were so valued that he was promoted to brigadier-general and appointed captain general of Caracas, one of the most important Spanish colonial offices. He later was named governor and captain general of Venezuela and interim governor and captain general of Cuba, and at the end of his long career was promoted to lieutenant general. He died in Málaga on July 21, 1793.

Charles Gayarré said that during Unzaga's tenure in Louisiana, "he had won the esteem and affection of the population," while Dr. Davis concluded that he had left the colony "prosperous beyond all experience."

One of the most interesting stories about Unzaga is that while governor of Louisiana, during the start of the American Revolution, he allowed the Congress's agent in New Orleans, the merchant Oliver Pollock, to purchase needed supplies, including gunpowder, for the American colonists. A few years later, while captain-general of Cuba, when his government wanted to curb the activities of American merchants and traders in Havana, he had Pollock, then living there, arrested and briefly imprisoned. It was an example of Unzaga's devotion to duty as he saw it.

—J.B.McG.

Cummins, Light Townsend. "Luis de Unzaga y Amerzaga, Colonial Governor, 1770–1777." *The Louisiana Governors: From Iberville to Edwards.* Joseph G. Dawson III, ed. Baton Rouge: Louisiana State University Press, 1990.

Davis, Edwin Adams. *Louisiana: A Narrative History.* Baton Rouge: Claitor's Publishing Division, 1971.

Fortier, Alcee. *A History of Louisiana*, vol. III. 2nd ed. Jo Ann Carrigen, ed. Baton Rouge: Claitor's Book Store, 1966.

Gayarré, Charles. *A History of Louisiana. Vol. IV: The American Domination.* Gretna, LA: Pelican, 1965.

Wall, Bennett H., ed. *Louisiana: A History.* Wheeling, IL: Harlan Davidson, 1997.

Wilson, James Grant, et al. *Appleton's Cyclopedia of American Biography.* New York: D. Appleton, 1889.

Bernardo de Galvez

1777–1782

Bernardo de Galvez, who succeeded Luis Unzaga as governor of Louisiana on January 1, 1777, proved himself a hero in fighting the British and a diplomat in arranging treaties with the peaceful Indians.

Charles III of Spain heaped praise on Galvez, especially for his exploits in capturing Baton Rouge and Mobile, and was so pleased with Galvez's performance at Pensacola that he promoted him from lieutenant general to viscount of Galveztown (the name of his ship). The king also named Galvez captain general of Louisiana and the Floridas. Galvez's victories at Baton Rouge and Mobile were hailed with enthusiasm in Spain and the United States. George Washington wrote him congratulations.

Spain declared war against the British in 1779, with the goal of pushing them out of the Gulf South. In early October 1780, Galvez led an expedition of fifteen ships, including some fifty transports carrying 4,000 men, from Havana en route to Pensacola, but the fleet met disaster in a storm. Galvez was determined to reach his goal, so he rounded up another fleet and reached Pensacola on March 9, 1781, where he was joined by a small number of ships from Louisiana.

The Spanish admiral in charge, Jose Calbo de Irazabal, held up the at-

Bernardo de Galvez. Courtesy of Special Collections, Tulane Libraries.

tack, saying the water was too shallow to cross at the bar of Pensacola. Galvez, under cover of night, had his men check the depth and decided his ships could cross the bar safely. Irazabal again refused permission, but Galvez defied the admiral. He raised the Spanish flag and ordered his ships to sail. The guns of Fort Barrancas Coloradas opened fire as the Spanish came within range, but Galvez's fleet crossed the bar unscathed. Irazabal, seeing what Galvez had done, followed, and in short order the Spanish forces claimed victory. Pensacola and the colony of West Florida surrendered on May 10, 1781. Thus Spain closed forever the door of the Floridas to the British.

Prior to hostilities against the British, Galvez had worked closely with Oliver Pollock in supplying money and materials to American forces during the War of Independence. He also brought refugees from the Canary Islands, known as the Isleños, to Louisiana.

Galvez's marriage to twenty-one-year-old Felicite St. Mazent gained him favor among the French Creole families of Louisiana. He was born on July 23, 1746, in Macharaviage, Spain, and was a military cadet at 16. Following his service in Louisiana he was appointed captain-general of Cuba, Louisiana, and the Floridas, and when his father died, succeeded him as viceroy of Mexico, where he died on November 30, 1786.

—W.G.C.

Davis, Edwin Adams. *Louisiana: A Narrative History*. 3r ed. Baton Rouge: Claitor's Publishing Division, 1971.

Fortier, Alcee. *A History of Louisiana*, vol. III. 2nd ed. Jo Ann Carrigen, ed. Baton Rouge: Claitor's Book Store, 1966.

Holmes, Jack D. L. "Bernardo de Galvez: Spain's Man of the Hour during the American Revolution." *Cardinales de los independencias*. Beatris Gaytan, ed. Mexico City: Noreste de Mexico—Sureste de los Estados Unidos, 1978.

Esteban Rodriguez Miro

1782–1791

Esteban Rodriguez Miro, who served approximately ten years as governor of Louisiana, presided during a period of relative prosperity, according to historians. His tenure, however, was marred by a great fire, which destroyed 856 of the 1,100 buildings in New Orleans in 1788, and by efforts of Mississippi River pirates to seize Spanish lands in the Natchez area. Miro is credited with rebuilding much of New Orleans' French Quarter, the main sector of the city at the time of the fire, and in successfully halting the river pirates' actions. He also negotiated treaties with Indian tribes who opposed encroachment on their lands and prohibited importation of slaves from the Caribbean.

When the colony faced hard economic times, Miro arranged for the Spanish crown to purchase tobacco crops, the main source of farmers' revenues prior to the introduction of cotton.

Miro was born in Reus, Catalonia, Spain, in 1742 and died in the Pyrenees mountains in June 1795. As a cadet he took part in a campaign against Portugal in 1762, and later served in Mexico and Algiers. He came to Louisiana as colonel of the Regiment of Louisiana and was second in command to Galvez in the conquest of West Florida. After a tour as pro-

Esteban Rodriguez Miro. Courtesy of Special Collections, Tulane Libraries.

visional governor of St. Domingo, he was appointed acting civil and military governor of Louisiana on March 1, 1782. At that time he was a brigadier general, the highest-ranking officer in Louisiana after Galvez. He served concurrently as intendant of the New Orleans port for three years. He was confirmed as permanent governor in 1785.

Miro won the favor of the populace by marrying Marie Celeste Elenore de Macarty of New Orleans.

—W.G.C.

Fortier, Alcee. *A History of Louisiana*, vol. III. 2nd ed. Jo Ann Carrigen, ed. Baton Rouge: Claitor's Book Store, 1966.

www.enlou.com. The Spanish Governors of Louisiana: Esteban Miro.

Francois-Louis Hector, Baron de Carondelet et Noyelles

1791–1797

Francois-Louis Hector, Baron de Carondelet et Noyelles (Carondelet in the history books) is best remembered for the now nonexistent canal named for him and the street in New Orleans which bears his name.

The Carondelet Canal, which linked the Mississippi River with Lake Pontchartrain through Bayou St. John, was important for marine transportation between the two bodies of water until the early 1920s. Built between 1794 and 1796, the canal permitted shallow draft vessels to transport commodities to ships anchored in the river. It was a vital link, since tons of goods could be quickly moved through New Orleans.

Carondelet, who succeeded Miro, was governor of Louisiana for approximately six years, from 1791 to 1797. His biggest problem during his administration was a slave insurrection in Pointe Coupee Parish, the result of a confused policy in governing slaves. He also had to deal with re-

Francois-Louis Hector, Baron de Carondelet et Noyelles. Courtesy of Special Collections, Tulane Libraries.

building of government and other buildings after the second great fire of 1794, which destroyed 200 structures, and a yellow fever outbreak in 1796.

Born in Cambray, France, on July 29, 1747, Carondelet was the scion of a distinguished family of Burgundy. He became a Spanish army officer and served under General O'Reilly in 1775 in an invasion of Algiers, where he was seriously wounded. He also served under Galvez in the siege of Pensacola, Florida, in 1781, after which he was promoted to lieutenant colonel. His initial leadership role was as governor and intendant of San Salvador, then a province of Guatemala. He took over the Louisiana governorship on December 30, 1791, and resigned the post in 1797 to accept the presidency of the Royal Audiencia of Quito, Ecuador, where he died on August 10, 1807.

—W.G.C.

Dawson, Joseph G. III, ed. *The Louisiana Governors: From Iberville to Edwards.* Baton Rouge: Louisiana State University Press, 1990.

Fortier, Alcee. *A History of Louisiana*, vol. III. 2nd ed. Jo Ann Carrigen, ed. Baton Rouge: Claitor's Book Store, 1966.

www.enlou.com. The Spanish Governors of Louisiana: Baron de Carondelet.

Manuel Gayoso de Lemos

1797–1799

Manuel Gayoso de Lemos became governor of Louisiana at a key point in the colony's young history. Discontent had spread because of boundary disputes with England, the bordering Indian nations, and farmers seeking to ship their goods through the port of New Orleans.

Gayoso was governor for approximately two years. Educated in England, Gayoso went to Spain in 1771 to join Alexandro O'Reilly's forces as an aide-de-camp in the siege of Gibraltar. An infantry soldier, he showed from the outset an ability for diplomacy. When Spain won the Natchez district in 1779, an English-speaking military officer was needed to deal with the restless American frontiersmen and the Choctaw, Cherokee, Chickasaw, and Creek Indians. Gayoso was tapped for the job and was appointed governor of the Natchez District, under the governor of Louisiana.

Under terms of the 1795 Treaty of San Lorenzo, Spain relinquished exclusive control over the Mississippi River and recognized the 31st parallel as the northern boundary of Spanish East and West Florida, which then bordered Louisiana. Spain also promised to provide places of deposit for transshipment of goods through New Orleans. Thus, Gayoso was a busy man from the day he became governor.

He renewed the slave trade in New Orleans, brought about several municipal changes in the city, and strengthened the colony's military defenses. He also began the first garbage collection in the city.

Gayoso was born in Oporto, Portugal, on May 30, 1747. He died during a yellow fever epidemic in New Orleans, on July 18, 1799, and was buried in St. Louis Cathedral.

Following Gayoso's death, the affairs of the colony were directed by interim administrators until arrival of Juan Manuel de Salcedo, who was appointed governor on October 24, 1799, but did not come to Louisiana until 1801, and took office on July 15th.

Nicholas Vidal, appointed lieutenant governor under Carondelet in 1795, became the acting civil governor after Gayoso died on July 18, 1799, and held that position until de Salcedo took office on July 15, 1801.

Francisco Bouligny, who had served as acting governor during May and June 1784 while Miro was treating with Indians at Mobile and Pensacola, became the acting military governor in the vacuum following Gayoso's death.

Bouligny was born in Alicante, Spain, in 1736 to a noble family from Italy. He changed his name from Bolognini to Bouligny. He came to Louisiana as an aide to O'Reilly. Fluent in French, he arranged for O'Reilly's arrival from the Balize with Aubry. Bouligny remained in Louisiana as an aide to Carondelet and Gayoso and was acting military governor from July 17 to September 17, 1799. He married the French colonial Louise de Senechal d'Auberville. When he died in 1800 he was commander of the Louisiana Fixed Regiment.

—W.G.C.

Holmes, Jack D. L. "Manuel Gayoso de Lemos, Colonial Governor, 1797-1799." *The Louisiana Governors: From Iberville to Edwards*. Joseph G. Dawson III, ed. Baton Rouge: Louisiana State University Press, 1990.

Martin, Fontaine. *A History of the Bouligny Family and Allied Families*. Lafayette: Center for Louisiana Studies, University of Southwestern Louisiana, 1990.

Martin, Francois-Xavier. *A History of Louisiana from the Earliest Period*. Gretna, LA: Pelican, 1975.

www.enlou.com. The Spanish Governors of Louisiana: Manuel Gayoso de Lemos.

Sebastian Calvo de la Puerta Y O'Fariel, Marquis de Casa Calvo

1799–1801

As the 1800s neared, Americans were pushing across the boundaries of Spanish Louisiana and the fledgling United States at will, to settle and trade. That was the scene as Casa Calvo was sent to New Orleans to become interim governor on September 18, 1799, following the death of Manuel Gayoso de Lemos.

Little information has survived from the period when Casa Calvo ruled. It was apparent that his administration could not restrain the settlers. He served until July, 1801, when Juan Manuel de Salcedo came.

Casa Calvo also had to deal with the burgeoning number of Americans over the issue of free navigation of the Mississippi River, a battle Spain eventually lost.

Casa Calvo accompanied General O'Reilly to New Orleans in 1769. Born in Havana on August 11, 1751, he served in the Spanish army against the British at Mobile and Pensacola, and later in Santo Domingo. When Gayoso died, Casa Calvo was a judge advocate in Havana. The captain-general of Cuba and Louisiana appointed him interim military governor of Louisiana, where Nicholas Vidal was the acting civil governor. With Gayoso's death, Salcedo was appointed governor on October 24, 1799, but, in ill health, he did not come to New Orleans until 1801, which left affairs in the hands of Casa Calvo until then.

In 1803 he was appointed a joint commissioner with Salcedo for the transfer of Louisiana to France. Once the French colonial prefect, Laussat, transferred Louisiana to the United States, Casa Calvo remained in Louisiana, ostensibly as a Spanish commissioner to determine the western boundary of the territory, for which he retained a company of soldiers. The territorial governor, W. C. C. Claiborne, did not trust him, and in 1806 ordered that he leave Louisiana. He died in 1825.

—W.G.C.

Fortier, Alcee. *A History of Louisiana*, vol. III. 2nd ed. Jo Ann Carrigen, ed. Baton Rouge: Claitor's Book Store, 1966.
Gayarré, Charles. *History of Louisiana*. Gretna, LA: Pelican, 1965.
www.enlou.com. The Spanish Governors of Louisiana: Casa Calvo.

Juan Manuel de Salcedo

1801–1803

The last of the Spanish governors, Juan Manuel de Salcedo, faded away to the Canary Islands after serving from July 14, 1801, until the transfer of Louisiana back to France on November 30, 1803. He was appointed governor, to succeed Gayoso, on October 24, 1799, but he suffered ill health, and did not take office until July 15, 1801.

Salcedo, who served under Charles IV, did not fit the assignment very well, it seems, although little has been written about his administration. What was written was unfavorable. He boycotted meetings of the Cabildo and humiliated its members, it was said. Contemporaries who visited New Orleans during his term declared him unfit for office, and when the Spanish government decided to suspend the right of deposit on the Mississippi River to upriver tradesmen, it did not bother to let Salcedo know.

In addition, the captain general of Cuba did not believe Salcedo fit to surrender Louisiana to France in 1803; he sent Casa Calvo back to assist him. On May 18, 1803, Salcedo and Casa Calvo jointly issued a proclamation informing the inhabitants of the retrocession. On November 30, 1803, they transferred Louisiana to France, and on December 20, 1803, the French colonial prefect, Laussat, transferred the colony to the United States.

Salcedo was later the governor of Texas.

—W.G.C.

Gayarré, Charles. *History of Louisiana*. Gretna, LA: Pelican, 1965.
www.enlou.com. The Spanish Governors of Louisiana: Juan Manuel de Salcedo.

Transfer

Flags unfurled and cannons roared as a breeze swept over the Place d'Armes, New Orleans' public square, but the people in attendance appeared to be unmoved by the ceremonies in which Louisiana went from thirty-four years of Spanish rule back to French domination, and then in an instant the colony was delivered into the hands of the United States of America.

This was Louisiana's turning point in history: December 20, 1803, a day in which the size of the continental United States was doubled. The U.S. took possession of the Louisiana Territory in a deal engineered by President Thomas Jefferson and his diplomats, who arranged to buy Louisiana from France for a paltry $15 million, or about four cents an acre.

Pierre Clement Laussat, Napoleon's colonial prefect, who was clothed with authority to consummate the transaction, had come from France, and Don Juan Manuel de Salcedo, a former Louisiana military governor, had come from Havana to assist. William C. C. Claiborne and General James Wilkinson, United States commissioners, were on hand to accept the prize. While some historians have treated Laussat as a governor, he did not hold that title or commission by French authority.

And a prize it was, in the view of President Jefferson, who had said that the nation that controlled New Orleans, a burgeoning world port, would control the destiny of what had become the United States. Still, the transaction's importance apparently had not sunk in with the inhabitants of New Orleans.

Surprisingly, no emotion was shown by a crowd of onlookers as Laussat, Claiborne, and Wilkinson exchanged warm congratulations. As historian Francois Xavier Martin put it, "The colonists did not appear conscious they were reaching the '*Latium sedes ubi fata quietas ostendunt.*'" Broadly translated, this Latin tag confirms the general reaction that the peaceful transfer of authority from France to the United States was simply an act of destiny.

From the powerful regal authority of France and Spain, then back to French Napoleonic authority, the Louisiana Territory would be carved into individual states, each governed under a republican form of government by elected governors. It is from that vantage point this book is written, as a history itself of the founding of the United States and telling the story of one state's governors.

—W.G.C.

Dufour, Charles L. *Ten Flags in the Wind: The Story of Louisiana*. New York: Harper & Row, 1967.

Fortier, Alcee. *A History of Louisiana*, vol. III. 2nd ed. Jo Ann Carrigen, ed. Baton Rouge: Claitor's Book Store, 1966.

Martin, Francois-Xavier. *A History of Louisiana from the Earliest Period*. Gretna, LA: Pelican, 1975.

William Charles Cole Claiborne

Territorial Governor 1803–1812
Governor 1812–1816

William Charles Cole Claiborne served as territorial governor and as the first elected governor of Louisiana. While he had many notable accomplishments in a short-lived but distinguished career, none was more important than the success he enjoyed in securing acceptance of the U.S. regime by the largely foreign population of Louisiana, for whom the customs, religion, language, and government of the Americans were strange.

Claiborne was born near Richmond, Virginia, in 1775, son of a Revolutionary officer. He attended the Richmond Academy and the College of William and Mary, and was evidently a quick learner. At age fifteen, he went to New York for employment as a clerk for a congressman, and while there he met Thomas Jefferson and John Sevier, who urged him to become an attorney and relocate to Tennessee. Claiborne returned to Richmond, read law for several months, and was admitted to the bar. He moved to Sullivan County, Tennessee, where he opened his practice, and

William Charles Cole Claiborne. Courtesy of Special Collections, Tulane Libraries.

at age 21 was a delegate to the convention that adopted the first state constitution. Sevier was elected the state's first governor, and he appointed Claiborne a justice of the supreme court. When Andrew Jackson resigned his seat in Congress in 1797, the twenty-two-year-old Claiborne won a special election and was reelected to a full term in 1798.

In the national election of 1800, Jefferson and Aaron Burr ran as a ticket for president and vice-president. The recipient of the greatest number of electoral votes would become president and the runner-up vice-president. A crisis resulted when Burr received as many electoral votes as Jefferson, and with neither holding a majority, the election of a president fell on the House of Representatives, with each state holding one vote. Burr schemed to obtain the presidency but failed. Claiborne was a staunch ally of Jefferson and helped hold the vote of Tennessee for him. His reward was appointment as governor of the Mississippi Territory by the new president.

In 1803, Jefferson named Claiborne and General James Wilkinson, commanding general of the U.S. army, as the United States commissioners to take possession of Louisiana, which they did in a December 20, 1803, transfer ceremony. Claiborne functioned as governor from the outset, but he was not appointed until 1804, when Jefferson named him governor of the Territory of Orleans. The newly acquired Louisiana Territory was split into upper and lower areas, and Claiborne's responsibility included all of modern Louisiana except the "Florida Parishes," which were brought in after the West Florida Rebellion in 1810.

Claiborne was faced with the daunting task of establishing a government and working to instill principles of representative democracy in a jurisdiction that had no familiarity with them. He had a legislative council of thirteen members to advise him, although his decisions were final. Its members were appointed by the president, but Jefferson had sufficient confidence in his proconsul in New Orleans to give him blank commissions of office, allowing Claiborne to fill in the names. In 1805, Congress provided for an organized territorial government, with a popularly elected lower house of twenty-five representatives and an upper house consisting of a governor's council of five members appointed by the president.

Jackson had sought appointment as governor, and Jefferson offered the post to James Madison and the Marquis de Lafayette, both of whom declined. Jefferson had been intrigued with the idea of appointing Lafayette, whom he thought an ideal choice who would have the confidence of both the French and Americans. When Jefferson appointed Claiborne, he indicated that he had hoped for Lafayette's acceptance, which must have bruised Claiborne's feelings. They would have been assuaged by the fact that he was appointed and reappointed six times by Presidents Jefferson and Madison. Jefferson had indicated that Claiborne was to serve on an interim basis only, but was so impressed by the reports he received from the governor and others that he told a cabinet member that Claiborne's "conduct has on the whole been so prudent and conciliatory that no secondary character could have a better right" to the office.

The territory was thrown into an uproar by the Burr Conspiracy in 1806, when the discredited former vice-president, who had killed Alexander Hamilton in a duel, arrived in New Orleans with a small force to confer with General Wilkinson. Burr's actual motives may never be known, as it is unclear whether his objective was to seize the territory, take control of Texas, or march against the Spanish in Mexico and establish his own empire there. His accomplices apparently included a wealthy New Orleans merchant, Daniel Clark, and General Wilkinson, who was in the pay of Spain as its agent. Wilkinson, fearing discovery of his role in the Burr plot, betrayed him and rushed to New Orleans with troops to defend the city. Claiborne was convinced that Wilkinson was a patriot and praised the general's decisive action to foil the plot. He raised no objection when Wilkinson established martial law in New Orleans until the emergency passed.

Claiborne devoted much attention to the defense of the territory, fearing internal threats from its polyglot population, which continued to grow. It was swelled by the arrival of "Kaintucks" from Kentucky and Tennessee and other Anglos from Virginia, the Carolinas, and Georgia, whose rough ways offended the Frenchmen. Refugees from St. Domingue poured in after the bloody slave revolt that established the country of Haiti there. While the foreign slave trade had been prohibited by Congress, an exception was made for the slaves the refugees brought with them, and 3,000 slaves and as many free men of color came into the territory.

Claiborne's fears of a slave revolt came true in 1811, when 500 slaves working sugar plantations in St. Charles and St. John the Baptist Parishes rose in rebellion. Their plans to march on New Orleans were forestalled by lack of arms, and with only farm tools as weapons, they were crushed in an encounter that saw over sixty of them killed. Those identified as leaders, twenty-one in number, were executed.

Jefferson and Claiborne had agreed that the people had to be trained in principles of democracy before statehood could be entertained. The Americans in the territory continued to press for early statehood, and as the Frenchmen became familiar with the benefits of representative government, they supported that goal. Claiborne, in one of his first reports to Jefferson, said that the people he found in Louisiana were "uninformed, indolent, luxurious—in a word illy fit to be useful citizens of a Republic." He wrote that while he wished that Louisiana could become a state immediately, he felt that admission to the union would be "impolitic" until the people were brought along in their understanding of democratic government.

Daniel Clark, arguing for statehood at the earliest date, became Claiborne's leading political opponent and inflicted a severe wound on the governor in a duel. The Northwest Ordinance had set 60,000 as the minimum population for a territory to gain statehood, so Jefferson and Claiborne delayed matters until the Census of 1810 could establish the population. When it tallied 76,000 inhabitants, Congress, in 1811, authorized a constitutional convention. The delegates simply copied Kentucky's recent constitution, Congress approved it, and Louisiana, including part of West Florida to the Pearl River, became the eighteenth state on April 30, 1812.

The new constitution provided an unusual process for election of the governor. Candidates would run in a popular election, but the legislature would select between the two top candidates, with no requirement that it favor the one with the greatest number of votes. The candidates were Claiborne, Jacques Villere, and Jean Noel Destrehan. Creoles comprised a majority of the voters, but Claiborne outpolled his rivals, with 2,700 votes to fewer than 1,000 for Villere and 200 for Destrehan. The election must have been a pleasant surprise for Claiborne, made doubly so when the legislature, dominated by Creoles, elected him governor over Villere by a vote of 33 to 6, in a vote of confidence in his administration and appreciation of his service.

After the slave revolt, Claiborne continued to reorganize and strengthen the militia, and as governor he was very active in urging measures for the defense of Louisiana during the War 1812, fearing a British attack on the Gulf Coast. He was unsure of the loyalty of some of the population, who doubted the ability of the United States to defend the state, and he determined to suppress the Baratarians at Grand Terre, who he feared would throw in with the British. This enclave of smugglers, led by brothers Jean and Pierre Lafitte, preyed on Spanish ships under privateers' commissions issued by the paper republic of Cartagena, but they were generally regarded as freebooters. Claiborne denounced them as "banditti" committing "depredations and piracies."

The Baratarians were very popular with the merchants of the city and the planters, since they provided smuggled goods of every description, including slaves. When the legislature failed to suppress them, Claiborne turned to the navy, which transported U.S. regulars to the Lafittes' stronghold on Barataria Bay. The Baratarians withdrew rather than resist, and their warehouses were burned and several ships seized.

Claiborne had provided Jean Lafitte ample reason to cooperate with a British invasion. He was offered a commission in the Royal Navy and a large sum in gold to guide the British through the approaches to New Orleans, but he refused and sent word of an imminent attack to Claiborne. Anticipating a British strike on the Gulf Coast, but unsure whether it would fall at Pensacola, Mobile, or New Orleans, General Andrew Jackson guessed that New Orleans would be the target. His surmise was confirmed by the British attempt to deal with Lafitte. Jackson had denounced the Baratarians as "hellish banditti," but he brought them into his ranks to defend the city.

Any fears that Claiborne and Jackson may have entertained about the loyalty of the diverse population or its willingness to fight were dispelled in the campaign and battle of New Orleans. Jackson's ragtag army of U.S. regulars, Tennessee, Kentucky, and Mississippi volunteers, Louisiana militia, free men of color, Choctaw Indians, and the Baratarians slaughtered the British in the decisive battle of January 8, 1815. The euphoria over the victory was clouded by Jackson's refusal to withdraw martial law while the British fleet remained in the gulf. His actions so annoyed the governor and legislature that the state's proclamation commending those responsible for the successful defense of the state failed even to mention General Andrew Jackson.

With all that he had accomplished, Claiborne had reasons to be proud as his term in office drew to a close. The 1812 constitution had limited a governor to a single term, so he could not seek reelection. Jacques Villere, the frontrunner in the 1816 popular vote, then was elected governor by the legislature, which also elected Claiborne a U.S. senator. With his distinguished résumé, it is interesting to speculate how far he might have gone in a political career at the national level had he taken his seat in the Senate, but he died in New Orleans of a liver illness in 1817 at only forty-two.

Surprisingly, for so public a man, little is known of Claiborne's private life. His first wife, Eliza Lewis, whom he married in Nashville before taking up the governorship of the Mississippi Territory, died in 1804. In 1806, he married Clarissa Duralde in New Orleans, in a union that received the approbation of the Creole families. She and a daughter both died of yellow fever, and in 1812 he married Suzette Bosque, with whom he had a son and a daughter. Claiborne initially disdained the *joie de vivre* of the Creoles, believing that they spent too much time on frivolities, but he came to enjoy the frequent balls in the city and evidently was a participant in its social life. The fact that he won acceptance from them, and was elected the state's first governor at their hands, is testimony to the regard in which he came to be held.

In an early dispatch to Secretary of State Madison, Claiborne wrote that he had "great cause to fear that through want of judgment, I shall commit many errors, but . . . I shall do nothing but with honest intentions, and a sincere desire to promote the interests of my country."

Claiborne's greatest contribution to the history of Louisiana was his success in bringing together a disparate population in a foreign, French-speaking, Catholic colony and making it meld together into an American state. In an evaluation, Dr. Joe Gray Taylor wrote, "He took over an indifferent, if not hostile, province, and in less than a decade brought it into the Union as one of eighteen equal states. He did not accomplish this through any brilliant stratagem or bold policy. Rather he met each crisis as it came, and simply did the best he could. In retrospect, his best seems to have been very good indeed. It is difficult to see how any other man could have accomplished so much so permanently in so short a time."

—J.B.McG.

Davis, Edwin Adams. *Louisiana: A Narrative History*. Baton Rouge: Claitor's Publishing Division, 1971.

Dawson, Joseph G. III, ed. *The Louisiana Governors: From Iberville to Edwards*. Baton Rouge: Louisiana State University Press, 1990.

Dufour, Charles L. *Ten Flags in the Wind: The Story of Louisiana*. New York: Harper & Row, 1967.

Wall, Bennett H., ed. *Louisiana: A History*. Wheeling, IL: Harlan Davidson, 1997.

Winters, John D. "William C. C. Claiborne: Profile of a Democrat." *Louisiana History* 10 (Summer 1969).

Jacques Philippe Villere

1816–1820

Jacques Philippe Villere, son of the Villere who lost his life in the Rebellion of 1769 trying to prevent the Spanish takeover of Louisiana, became the first native-born governor of the state in 1816. He had run for the office in 1812, but Governor Claiborne held the post until 1816.

Jacques Philippe Villere was but eight years old when his father, Joseph Roy de Villere, was marked for execution but died after defying General O'Reilly's troops when they occupied New Orleans. Young Villere, born on April 28, 1761, was sent to France to be educated and following that was commissioned a lieutenant of artillery and assigned to St. Domingue Island. Permitted to return to Louisiana in 1782, he became a sugar planter and took interest in state affairs, being appointed a colonel of the Louisiana Militia and later advancing to major general. He served as a member of the first state constitutional convention in 1811 and ran for governor the following year, but lost to Claiborne. Four years later, he won.

Louisiana's government had settled down to peaceful pursuits under Claiborne, but by the time Villere took office factionalism had been born, and it has been with the state ever since. In that campaign 1816, the "Old

Jacques Philippe Villere. Courtesy of Special Collections, Tulane Libraries.

Inhabitants" squared off against the "American" party, the principal issue being which could best serve the state.

Villere faced Judge Joshua Lewis, a Virginia native who had been named to the Superior Council by President Thomas Jefferson. Villere polled 2,314 votes to Lewis's 2,146. Twenty-six parishes took part in the election. But the fact that Villere had won a majority did not mean he was elected, because the new constitution put the final say in the hands of the state legislators. There was much speculation that the legislature might select Lewis, as newspapers took sides promoting the candidates. The big questions posed in the state's fledgling *Louisiana Gazette* were, "Is the man fit for office?" and "Did he vote on our side?"

While Villere sought to bring about a balance between the new Americans and the Creoles in his appointments, animosity between the two forces continued. The *Gazette*, which backed Lewis, editorialized that Villere "begins pretty early to show his contempt for the swinish multitude, his own and his General Assembly's legitimate masters."

Elected by the legislature, Villere took office as Louisiana experienced a period of prosperity, with sugar and cotton crops propelling it forward, and this did much to quiet factionalism, historians observed. Dueling, the way men settled matters of honor, had increased greatly. Villere shepherded an act through the General Assembly in 1818 that provided death for the winner of a duel if it was found that he provoked it.

Turning his attention to education, in 1819 Villere pushed to adoption a measure providing annual appropriations for each parish to establish public schools. He credited President Jefferson with stimulating his interest.

Mostly, Villere was known as a law-and-order governor. He ordered the militia to quell disturbances when trouble occurred, and he bolstered the criminal code of the state.

The Villere family of Louisiana was descended from Rouer de Villeray (the name being changed over the years). Jacques Rouer de Villeray emigrated to Canada from Italy about 1650, and the family came later to Louisiana.

The state constitution made it impossible for a governor to succeed himself, though he could run again after sitting out a term. Villere did run again in 1824 but had to face two candidates, one of them a fellow Creole, Bernard de Marigny. Henry Johnson, a newly arrived American, swept to victory because the two Creoles divided that vote. Villere spent the rest of his life devoted to his family. He died March 7, 1830, and is buried in St. Louis Cemetery No. 2.

—W.G.C.

Fortier, Alcee. *A History of Louisiana*, vol. I. 2nd ed. Jo Ann Carrigen, ed. Baton Rouge: Claitor's Book Store, 1966.
Martin, Francois-Xavier. *A History of Louisiana from the Earliest Period*. Gretna, LA: Pelican, 1975.
Wall, Bennett H., ed. *Louisiana: A History*. Wheeling, IL: Harlan Davidson, 1997.

Thomas Bolling Robertson

1820–1824

Thomas Bolling Robertson, elected Louisiana's governor in 1820, exploited his Virginia roots at a time when the embryonic state felt the push of Virginia transplants. His election brought to the political surface a simmering feeling of competitiveness between the established Gallic French forces and the incoming new Americans, a divisiveness that would express itself many times in elections as Louisiana became part of the federal union.

Named by President Jefferson in 1807 as one of three land commissioners in the Territory of Orleans, Robertson was elected to Congress in 1812 following a short stint as attorney general. Louisiana's only representative in Congress in the early years, Robertson attracted support by championing sugar tariffs in protecting the state's only crop. He and Governor Claiborne frequently quarreled over public matters, and in 1818 Robertson quit Congress to seek the governorship. Governor Villere soothed relations between the Creoles and the newly arrived Americans, with the hope a rotation could be established in the governorship between the French and American forces. Robertson lost no time in exploiting this situation and swept to victory, defeating Abner L. Duncan and Pierre Derbigny. It was indeed the Americans' turn to occupy the statehouse.

But Robertson soon found the going tough. He was rebuffed in an attempt to move the state capital from New Orleans to Baton Rouge, and stirred up opposition when he vetoed a usury bill, under the guise of protecting free enterprise. This brought attacks claiming he was defending usurers, most of whom, the Gallic press charged, were members of the Anglo-American financial community.

Another source of disruption to his rule was the refusal of Americans in the state militia to obey the orders of unnaturalized officers. As a result, riots broke out in the period 1823–25, and Robertson did nothing to quell them. It remained for his successor, Henry S. Johnson, to bring them under control.

While Robertson was generally regarded as an inept governor, he did accomplish a number of things, among them the opening to commerce of the Red and Pearl Rivers and building Louisiana's portion of the national road from Madisonville to Nashville. Also, he helped create the Bank of

Louisiana and the College of Orleans and increased funding of Charity Hospital.

Confronted with budgetary problems and general unrest, Robertson resigned the governorship in November 1824 to become a federal district judge, but was passed over for appointment to a federal circuit judgeship in 1826.

Robertson was born in Prince George County, Virginia, in 1773, the son of Petersburg merchant William Robertson and Elizabeth Bolling, who claimed descent from Pocahontas. He graduated from the College of William and Mary and married Lelia Skipwith of Baton Rouge. He died on October 5, 1828, at White Sulphur Springs, Virginia.

—W.G.C.

Fortier, Alcee. *A History of Louisiana*. 2nd ed. Jo Ann Carrigen, ed. Baton Rouge: Claitor's Book Store, 1966.

Tregle, Joseph G., Jr. "Thomas Bolling Robertson, Governor, 1820–1824." *The Louisiana Governors: From Iberville to Edwards*. Joseph G. Dawson III, ed. Baton Rouge: Louisiana State University Press, 1990.

Five Governors

1824–1831

Louisiana had five governors between 1824 and early 1831, a period of less than seven years. They included Henry S. Thibodaux, who as president of the Senate served the final month of Robertson's term; Henry S. Johnson; Pierre Auguste Bourguignon Derbigny; Armand Julie Beauvais; and Jacques Dupre.

Johnson served a full four-year term, from 1824 to 1828; Derbigny from December 15, 1828, until October 7, 1829; Beauvais from then until January 14, 1830, when he resigned to run for governor; and Dupre served for a year, completing Derbigny's term. Both Beauvais and Dupre had served for short periods as president of the Senate and succeeded to the governorship during the turnover period created by Derbigny's death.

Johnson, a native Virginian, became a congressman and senator after serving as governor. A highlight of Johnson's term was the visit of the famous French hero, the Marquis de Lafayette, who had been made an American major general when he volunteered his services in America's War of Independence. On April 10, 1825, General Lafayette stood with Governor Johnson at Andrew Jackson's lines of defense in the Battle of

Armand Julie Beauvais. Courtesy of Special Collections, Tulane Libraries.

New Orleans at Chalmette. His visit was cause for a great celebration in New Orleans.

Derbigny, the sixth elected American-era governor, was fatally injured in October 1829 when he was thrown from his horse-drawn carriage. In the ten months he was the state's chief executive, he promoted education and warned of excessive spending. A native of Laon, France, the exact date of his birth in 1778 is not known. Prior to his election as governor, he served on the Louisiana Supreme Court, resigning to run for governor.

In the approximately three months Beauvais served as governor, the General Assembly authorized incorporation of the Pontchartrain Railroad, one of the earliest rail lines in the United States. At the time the legislative body met at Donaldsonville, but the capital was moved to New Orleans on January 8, 1830.

Dupre succeeded Beauvais and served for approximately one year, actually relinquishing the office to Andre Bienvenu Roman before the Derbigny term expired. Dupre spoke out against further importation of slaves, saying, "The annual supply is gradually pouring in and scarce a ship arrives from the slaveholding states [countries] that does not come freighted with a living cargo of vices and crime, to be disgorged upon our shores and incorporated into our domestic establishments."

—W.G.C.

Tregle, Joseph G., Jr. "Henry S. Thibodaux, Governor, 1824" and "Henry S. Johnson, Governor, 1824–1828." *The Louisiana Governors: From Iberville to Edwards*. Joseph G. Dawson III, ed. Baton Rouge: Louisiana State University Press, 1990.

Judith F. Gentry. "Pierre Auguste Bourguignon Derbigny, Arnaud Julie Beauvais, Jacques Dupre, Governors, 1828–1831." *The Louisiana Governors: From Iberville to Edwards*. Joseph G. Dawson III, ed. Baton Rouge: Louisiana State University Press, 1990.

Andre Bienvenu Roman

1831–1835; 1839–1843

The cruel, confused politics of Louisiana after it evolved into an American state became the prototype of what developed in the nineteenth and twentieth centuries, even into the twenty-first. A political gumbo-land, no less, led to a showdown in the election 1831.

Disarray marked the ranks of the Creoles as they split their support between Bernard Marigny, who violently opposed the Anglo-Americans, and the more moderate former governor, Jacques Philippe Villere, who was induced to try for a comeback. Meanwhile, Martin Duralde, son-in-law of Kentucky senator Henry Clay, regarded as the most powerful Creole in the state and thought to be poised to run for the office, declined in the face of a possible squabble with the followers of Andrew Jackson, hero of the Battle of New Orleans and future president of the United States. Duralde and forces supporting Clay's expected bid for the presidency in 1832 sought to avoid splitting his support along ethnic lines in the governor's race, fearing it would be costly later to Clay.

But Clay played a pivotal role in the 1831 race. State government had been thrown into confusion by the death of Derbigny, after which the legislature called a special election in 1830 while the current term had two

Andre Bienvenue Roman. Courtesy of Special Collections, Tulane Libraries.

years left. Andre Bienvenu Roman, speaker of the House of Representatives, entered the race against William S. Hamilton, an Anglo-American, who had come to prominence in Florida; Armand Julie Beauvais, a Creole who had become acting governor but resigned to make the race for a full term; and David Randall, another Anglo-American.

Clay moved to New Orleans to coordinate the campaign, and his efforts were credited with winning the election for Roman, who served one term from 1831 to 1835, and another from 1839 to 1843, the break occasioned by the law prohibiting successive terms. Roman received 3,638 votes compared with 2,701 for Hamilton, 1,478 for Beauvais, and 463 for Randall.

While Roman was not personable, he was well educated and disciplined. The Creole population was convinced that he was capable of matching the political mastery of the Anglo-Americans, a big issue of the times, and could fend off the advancing political fortunes of the Virginia immigrants, who had won the governorship in 1820 and 1824.

Born in the Opelousas district of the state on March 5, 1795, Roman became a state representative, speaker of the House on two occasions, and a parish judge. The son of Jacques Etienne Roman and Marie Louise Patin, he was married to Aimee Francoise Parent, and they had eight children. As he took office in 1831, the state was hit by a devastating epidemic of cholera and yellow fever, which again ravaged the area in 1833.

But Roman pushed ahead, increasing the number of banks from five to eleven, starting a penitentiary system, and broadening state support for education. While his first term was hailed as a big success, his second was marred by the Panic 1837, highlighted by bank failures and the worst economic depression of the pre-Civil War years.

In his first term Roman saw the opening of the Pontchartrain Railroad, the first line west of the Allegheny Mountains, and the New Basin Canal, each built to move commerce within the port of New Orleans. Colleges were built in St. James and St. Landry Parishes. These successes, plus his efforts in bringing about a more modern banking system, led Roman to run for the U.S. Senate as his governorship ended; he was beaten by Alexandre Mouton, a popular young Creole.

Nevertheless, Roman remained well-liked and, in 1839, was the choice of the Whigs to succeed the man who had selected him, Edward Douglass White. In the race for a second term, Roman was opposed by the mayor of New Orleans, Denis Prieur, a follower of Andrew Jackson and a Democrat. The Panic 1837 had cast gloom over the business community, yet Roman managed to eke out a victory over Prieur, who proved to be a poor campaigner and brought public criticism by openly living with a quadroon mistress. The vote was 7,590 for Roman to 6,682 for Prieur.

In the wake of the 1837 economic downfall, Louisiana's banking system was shattered. Roman brought about more restrictive monetary policies through the Bank Act 1842. Although he experienced few successes in his second term, Roman established himself as a leader in Creole political circles, heading off the threat of a Virginia dynasty in the state.

Roman's service extended beyond his terms as governor. He initially opposed the secession of Louisiana from the Union in 1861, but had second thoughts later and supported the Confederacy. In 1861 the Confederacy appointed him, John Forsyth, and Martin Crawford to seek a peaceful compromise with the United States. The effort ended with Secretary of State William Seward's refusal to see them.

Roman was appointed by Governor James Madison Wells in 1866 as recorder of mortgages in New Orleans but died before taking office. He is buried on the family estate in St. James Parish.

—W.G.C.

Gayarré, Charles. *A History of Louisiana. Vol. IV: The American Domination.* Gretna, LA: Pelican, 1965.

Martin, Francois-Xavier. *A History of Louisiana from the Earliest Period.* Gretna, LA: Pelican, 1975.

Edward Douglass White

1835–1839

Edward Douglass White, governor from 1835 to 1839, found himself in a crossfire as campaigns became factionalized and issue-oriented, portending the everlasting culture of gubernatorial races in Louisiana.

He endured a term marked by quarrels over patronage, his vote to authorize a gradual reduction in the sugar tariff when he was a congressman, and public hysteria generated by fears of slave insurrection and supposed plotting by subversive abolitionists. The native American movement, founded to protect the rights of native-born Louisianians, became a vehicle of hatred and antagonism toward any group not traditionally Anglo-American Protestant, and led to the division of New Orleans into three municipalities in 1836.

Soon after being elected, White had to fight off charges that he was anti-American in his appointments of officeholders; his supporters thought they could demand appointment and, when they did not get jobs, turned against him. He had been elected with the support of Alexander Porter, the powerful lawyer under whom he had studied, but opposed by Martin Gordon, federal collector of customs, who was aligned with supporters of General Andrew Jackson. Gordon and his group charged that White, a Whig, was delivering Louisiana to the domination of foreigners, claiming that he was the tool of the "hated" Irishman Porter.

White's term as governor coincided with the rise in influence of the "foreign French," immigrants from France following the Louisiana Purchase, who became a substantial force. His appointment of several to state positions led the *Louisiana Advertiser* to say it did not object to selection of Creoles, but that this view did not extend to the foreign French "who neither knew or cared particularly for American institutions." Public protests resulted, and federal troops were called upon to monitor them for fear of trouble.

Nevertheless, the first two years of White's governorship were acclaimed a success. His administration aided in establishment of six new banks, two railroads, and two hotels in the New Orleans area. Also, it supported establishment of the Lafourche Canal Company to encourage commerce along the waterway, and White signed the charter creating the Medical College of Louisiana, forerunner of Tulane University.

The Panic 1837 brought a setback for White. While his administration supported a strong and regulated banking system, it became a victim of the panic, in which several banks failed during a plunge in the economy.

Prior to his race for governor White had established himself as a member of the United States Congress, where he served before and after his governorship. There he became a supporter of Senator Henry Clay, and because of his tie to Clay, voted for reduced protection of Louisiana's sugar industry in furtherance of Clay's plan to run for president.

In his first race for Congress in 1828, White defeated Edward Livingston, the pioneer Louisiana lawyer. In seeking two terms after being governor, he had little trouble in reclaiming the congressional job.

Born on March 3, 1795, in Maury County, Tennessee, White was the son of James White and Mary Wilcox. In 1834 he married Catherine Sidney Lee Ringgold, daughter of Tench Ringgold, a U.S. marshal under Presidents James Madison and James Monroe. The Whites had five children: Susan, James, Eliza, Edward Douglass Jr., and Mary Sidney. Edward Douglass White Jr. became a justice of the U.S. Supreme Court in 1894 and chief justice in 1910.

White launched his career as a city court judge in 1825, but left that job to become a Bayou Lafourche sugar planter three years later. He died on April 18, 1847, and is buried in Thibodaux.

—W.G.C.

Tregle, Joseph G. "Edward Douglass White, Governor, 1835–1839." *The Louisiana Governors: From Iberville to Edwards*. Joseph G. Dawson III, ed. Baton Rouge: Louisiana State University Press, 1990.

Alexandre Mouton

1843–1846

Alexandre Mouton became Louisiana's first Democratic governor in 1843 during economic times so tough he had to sell state properties, even the state-owned slaves, to balance the budget.

Because of the times, Mouton opposed expenditures for internal improvement and leased the penitentiary in order to reduce expenses. He supported legislation to limit state borrowing, and at the same time advocated using income to pay off the state debt, except in the sale of public lands, whose revenue went to public education.

Mouton and the Democratic Party supported calling a new constitutional convention, which resulted in revising the state's basic law in 1845. The new constitution provided for direct election of governors by voters and regular reapportionment of election districts. The change had the effect of reducing the power of French-speaking Catholics, who were in the majority when the Constitution 1812 became law.

Mouton's role in Louisiana's secession from the Union gained him especial prominence after he served as governor. When the Secession Convention met in Baton Rouge on January 23, 1861, Mouton was elected president. After a 113 to 17 vote to secede, Mouton proclaimed: "In vir-

Alexandre Mouton. Courtesy of Special Collections, Tulane Libraries.

tue of the vote just announced, I now declare the connection between the state of Louisiana and the Federal Union dissolved; and that she is a free, sovereign and independent power."

For almost two months, January 26 to March 21, 1861, Louisiana was a republic. Governor Moore, the sitting chief executive, became president of the republic and the legislature continued in session as a congress, with state courts serving in place of federal courts. In March, Louisiana joined the Confederate States of America.

After the war, Mouton became a sugar planter and vice-president of the New Orleans, Algiers, Attakapas and Opelousas Railroad. The Union army used his 1900-acre plantation, Ile Copal, near Carencro, as its headquarters and arrested him. His sugar mill was burned and his 120 slaves freed.

Mouton was born on November 19, 1804, in what is now Lafayette Parish. He was elected by the legislature to the United States Senate in 1837 and he served there for five years, resigning to run for governor. Mouton was a banker before his political career and he was one of the organizers of the Union Bank of Louisiana, founded to provide credit to rural areas. He died on February 12, 1885, in Lafayette.

—W.G.C.

Davis, Edwin Adams. *Louisiana: A Narrative History*. Baton Rouge: Claitor's Publishing Division, 1971.

Gayarré, Charles. *History of Louisiana*. Gretna, LA: Pelican, 1965.

Gentry, Judith F. "Alexandre Mouton, Governor, 1843–1846." *The Louisiana Governors: From Iberville to Edwards*. Joseph G. Dawson III, ed. Baton Rouge: Louisiana State University Press, 1990.

Isaac Johnson

1846–1850

Isaac Johnson, Democratic governor from 1846 to 1850, was a different kind of politician. He believed in appointing the most qualified men to public office, and in doing so incurred the wrath of his party by appointing numerous Whigs. Within two years of his election, he was out of favor in the Democratic party, which had experienced a rise in popularity under the leadership of John Slidell.

Johnson was attracted to politics in 1833, when he won a seat in the Louisiana State Assembly, after which he was appointed judge of the Third District. He and a brother, William, and an uncle had established a law firm, which prospered. In 1845 he was nominated by the Democrats for governor and defeated the Whig candidate, William DeBuys.

A champion of public education, Johnson faced opposition in appropriating public money for the cause, but by the time his term expired he could point to increased enrollment in the public schools. Among other issues, the war between the United States and Mexico drew attention to Louisiana. Johnson became involved because he advocated annexing Mexico, sanctioning the expansion of slavery. He denounced the Wilmot Proviso, a congressional resolution that would have prohibited slavery in any territories obtained from Mexico.

During Johnson's term the capital and principal state offices were moved from New Orleans to Baton Rouge, as provided in the Constitution 1845. This move brought criticism and resurrected the feud between city and country. Johnson's retirement from public life on January 28, 1850, was short-lived because his successor appointed him attorney general, a post he held for two years.

Johnson was born on his family's plantation at Troy in West Feliciana Parish, on November 1, 1803. He was married to Charlotte McDermott, who died in 1847, leaving three children. His second marriage was described as a union of convenience.

When Johnson retired to his plantation, it appeared his political career had ended. However, in early 1853 he announced as a candidate for associate justice of the Louisiana Supreme Court. Before the election he suffered a heart attack in his room at the Verandah Hotel in New Orleans, and died on March 15, 1853. His two sons died of yellow fever shortly thereafter.

—W.G.C.

DeLatte, Carolyn. *The Louisiana Governors*. Baton Rouge: Louisiana State University Press, 1990.

www.enlou.com. State Governors of Louisiana: Isaac Johnson. Baton Rouge, 2004.

Joseph Marshall Walker

1850–1853

State constitutional problems confronted Joseph Marshall Walker after he was elected governor in 1850. Commercial interests in Louisiana were unhappy with the Constitutional Convention 1845 and mounted a campaign to expand its reforms.

Principal objections included the limited right of the legislature to borrow money, a prohibition against public loans, chartering new banks and restrictions on licensing of corporations to twenty-five-year terms. Walker supported the restrictions, but the populace wanted a freer hand in play for business. The regulations were proposed in the Constitutional Convention 1845, which Walker chaired.

Walker and most of the Democrats favored changes voted by specific constitutional amendments. The new constitution also had the effect of shortening Walker's term by a year, because of a change in the date of elections. Walker's objections were so strong that when his term ended, he refused to be nominated for other offices, including the United States Senate.

However, Walker did bring about some changes, including improvement of public schools, election rather than appointment of judges, and the constitutional requirement to apportion the House of Representatives by total population, which in effect transferred control of the legislature from property to the people.

Walker described himself as a Southern Rights Democrat who advocated equality for the South within the Union. Actually, he went further in his support of the South by declaring in a public speech that if the South should not receive its rights, "we are prepared to make common ground with our neighbors of the slaveholding states and pronounce the Union at an end." Louisiana seceded from the Union nine years after Walker's pronouncement.

Walker was born in New Orleans' French Quarter in July of 1786 and died in Rapides Parish on January 26, 1856. He served as a state legislator (House and Senate), state treasurer, and governor. In his youth he joined the Spanish military service in Mexico, was commissioned a lieutenant of the dragoons, and for a time headed the military school at Chihuahua. Coming back to Louisiana, he enlisted in the state militia, served with Andrew Jackson at Chalmette in the Battle of New Orleans, and was promoted to brigadier general of the First Brigade of the state militia. He was married to Catherine Carter of Adams County, Mississippi; after settling in Rapides Parish, they raised three daughters and seven sons.

—W.G.C.

Carriere, Marius M., Jr. *The Louisiana Governors.* Baton Rouge: Louisiana State University Press, 1990.

thefreedictionary.com/governor/Louisiana. Encyclopedia article on Joseph Marshall Walker. 11/14/04.

Paul Octave Hebert

1853–1856

Slavery resurfaced as a national issue by the mid-1850s, and its cross-currents touched upon Louisiana when the conservative Whig party gave way to the Native American or Know-Nothing party, throwing the political landscape into turmoil. Such was the climate in 1853, when Paul Octave Hebert defeated a Whig candidate, Louis Bordelon, for governor by 2,000 votes.

Actually, change had set in during the administration of Joseph Marshall Walker, who served from 1850 to 1853. Two new parties came into being, the Know-Nothings and the Republicans. Resistance to slavery in the northern tier of states brought on the politics of secession. A new state constitution, adopted in 1852, required a new election for governor in 1853 in which the new term would be shortened—as well as the term of the sitting governor, in order to make calendar adjustments.

While no Republican candidate appeared on a ballot in Louisiana prior to the Civil War, the Know-Nothings caught on. (The name came from a secret order with a ritual of the Native American party, in which members, when questioned about their affiliation, would answer, "I know nothing.") When Hebert announced for governor in 1853, he and other Democrats denounced the new constitution as a "Whig document." Newspapers affiliated with the Whig and Know-Nothing parties charged that Hebert had grown disenchanted with the Democratic party and was poised to defect to the Know-Nothings. He did not, but he proved to be quite a maverick, naming Whigs and Know-Nothings to office over loyal Democrats.

Stirring the concern over the status of slavery, Congress adopted the Kansas-Nebraska Act, which broke a fragile truce on the slavery issue that had followed the Missouri Compromise 1820. The Missouri Compromise had provided for Maine to enter the Union as a free state, and for Missouri to come in with no restrictions regarding slavery. Missouri came in as a slave state, but the Compromise also prohibited slavery north of the southern border of Missouri, at latitude 36-30. The Kansas-Nebraska Act nullified that prohibition by providing that those two new territories, both above the line established by the Missouri Compromise, could decide for themselves whether or not to allow slavery within their borders. In Kansas, warfare broke out between pro- and antislavery forces, two opposing territorial governments were established, and the period of violence known as "Bleeding Kansas" helped lead to the Civil War.

The demands of the Whigs and the rise of the Republican party committed the United States to the containment of slavery and convinced the South that abolitionists were on a course of action to abolish slavery where it already existed. Concern in Louisiana ran high, with slave labor integral to the economy of a substantial part of the state. The Know-Nothings won control of New Orleans in 1854, in a reaction to the influx of immigrants that prompted this nativist political movement. While they engaged in anti-immigrant activities, the Know-Nothings played down their anti-Catholic stand in New Orleans in light of the large number of Irish and German immigrants to the city who were Catholics.

Hebert as governor brought about improvements in education and transportation, strengthening water commerce and chartering four railroads. Also, he was a strong supporter of public education. He suffered a major setback at the outset of his term, as yellow fever returned, claiming 9,000 lives in New Orleans alone.

Hebert was born in Iberville Parish on December 12, 1818. He graduated first in his class from Jefferson College near New Orleans, and first in his class in 1842 at the United States Military Academy at West Point. He was an assistant professor of engineering at West Point for a time and later an engineer at the port of New Orleans. He married Cora Wills Vaughn.

Governor Mouton appointed Hebert state civil engineer in 1845; he resigned in 1847 to fight in the Mexican War, and served as lieutenant colonel of the U.S. 14th Infantry Regiment until April 1848, when he returned to Louisiana. Governor Moore named Hebert to a military board to reorganize the state's militia in 1860; he became a colonel of the First Louisiana Artillery in 1861, and later a brigadier general in the Confederate army in charge of Louisiana troops. He aided in the defense of Vicksburg and took part in the Battle of Milliken's Bend in June 1863.

Hebert returned to political activity in New Orleans during Reconstruction, supporting the Liberal Republican Party and later Henry Clay Warmoth, the Republican governor of Louisiana. He also supported General Ulysses S. Grant in 1872 and urged a third term for him as president. Governor William Pitt Kellogg named Hebert to the Mississippi River Commission, a position for which he was well qualified. He died in New Orleans on August 29, 1880.

—W.G.C.

Wall, Bennett H., ed. *Louisiana: A History*. Wheeling, IL: Harlan Davidson, 1997.

Robert C. Wickliffe

1856–1860

Louisiana moved steadfastly toward its Civil War destiny with the election of Robert C. Wickliffe as governor in 1856. He set the tone of his administration in his inaugural address, in which he denounced congressional interference with domestic policy of the states. He remained preoccupied with southern rights, proposing that the nation annex Caribbean territories, obviously in an effort to spread slavery, and later he attempted to act as an intermediary between the Confederacy and the Union.

But Wickliffe had more immediate problems after he won the Democratic party's nomination and, carrying 31 of the state's 43 parishes, defeated Charles Derbigny, the Know-Nothing candidate. He was in a continual battle with the Know-Nothings, who controlled New Orleans. Twice he had the General Assembly strengthen the voter registration laws in an attempt to rein in violence at the polls. There was so much ballot-box stuffing and violence in New Orleans in 1857 that Wickliffe called out the militia to suppress it.

Wickliffe's accomplishments as governor included strengthening banking laws, greater support for building railroads, and stricter management of the currency, requiring banks to make weekly statements on their operations. As a state senator Wickliffe had advocated reform for basic education, but did little as governor to upgrade it. Instead, he paid more attention to improving higher education.

For much of his career, Wickliffe was locked in a battle with U.S. Senator John Slidell over leadership of the Democratic party, and refused to support Democratic candidates in some elections. In 1857 Wickliffe opposed Slidell's choice of a candidate in the Third Congressional District, but lost. He backed Stephen A. Douglas in the 1860 presidential race, while Slidell supported John C. Breckinridge, who carried Louisiana but lost nationally to Abraham Lincoln.

After his term as governor, Wickliffe was elected as a representative to Congress from the Third District, but Congress refused to seat him because of his stand on slavery.

Wickliffe kept up his political activity following his term and the Civil War but did not seek office.

As can be gleaned from the writings of the time, slavery was the hottest national topic in politics, or generally. The strengthening of proslavery attitudes in the South grew fast after invention of the cotton gin and the open-kettle process of making sugar from Louisiana cane. Planters who owned slaves made handsome profits and, with their business allies, dominated state government.

Born on January 6, 1819, in Bardstown, Kentucky, Wickliffe died there on April 18, 1895. He graduated from Centre College in Kentucky and studied law in Washington, D.C., under Hugh Legare, attorney general of the United States in the administration of John Tyler. He returned to Kentucky in 1843 and married Anna Dawson, daughter of Louisiana congressman John B. Dawson and niece of former governor Isaac Johnson. During the Mexican War, Wickliffe served with the army of General Winfield Scott, winning the rank of colonel.

—W.G.C.

Carriere, Marius M., Jr. "Robert C. Wickliffe, Governor, 1856–1860." *The Louisiana Governors: From Iberville to Edwards*. Joseph G. Dawson III, ed. Baton Rouge: Louisiana State University Press, 1990.

Davis, Edwin Adams. *Louisiana: A Narrative History*. Baton Rouge: Claitor's Publishing Division, 1971.

Wall, Bennett H., ed. *Louisiana: A History*. Wheeling, IL: Harlan Davidson, 1997.

Thomas O. Moore

1860–1864

Louisiana's Civil War–era governor, Thomas O. Moore, took office in January 1860 as the winds of secession blew across the South, the threat of slave rebellions was being felt, and state politics were in an upheaval.

Moore was thrust into a chaotic situation at the start of his administration. Chosen to run for the office by the politically powerful United States senator John Slidell, leader of the regular faction of the Democratic party, Moore defeated Thomas J. Wells, who had the endorsement of the Know-Nothing party, a group formed from the remnants of the Whigs. Both Moore and Wells were from Rapides Parish; Moore moved there from North Carolina at age twenty-five to live with an uncle, Walter H. Overton, and Wells grew up there.

Louisiana's future lay in the presidential election of 1860, when Abraham Lincoln of Illinois, a Free Soiler who favored giving government land to settlers and was opposed to the expansion of slavery in the new territories and states formed from them, defeated a staunch slavery supporter, Vice-President John C. Breckinridge of Kentucky. Lincoln was not even on the ballot in Louisiana, but there were two pro-Union candidates, John Bell and Stephen A. Douglas. Bell received 20,204 votes and Douglas 7,625 against Breckinridge's 22,681, totals that showed that Union sentiment in Louisiana outweighed secession.

Louisiana was faced with a choice, however, as a feeling for secession swept the state. A general convention was called to reach a decision on what to do about it. The gathering adopted an Ordinance of Secession on January 26, 1861, and ten days later six Louisiana delegates to a meeting in Montgomery, Alabama, helped form the Confederate States of America. Moore did not wait for secession to be declared before acting, immediately ordering seizure of Forts Jackson and St. Philip, seventy-five miles downriver from New Orleans; the arsenal in Baton Rouge; and other installations in the state, including the U.S. Mint and Custom House in New Orleans. After secession became official, Moore named General Braxton Bragg to form a militia and encouraged the organization of local companies to bolster the state's defense against attack.

Jefferson Davis, president of the Confederacy, called on Moore to supply 3,000 men for the Confederate army, and Moore asked for an additional 5,000 to serve until regular Confederate troops arrived. The governor moved the state capital from Baton Rouge to Opelousas to distance his headquarters from a possible invasion by Union forces, and ordered cessation of trade with the enemy along with an order to burn all cotton that was in danger of falling into enemy hands. Also, he had the legislature create a state guard and approve use of slave labor to build fortifications.

Moore warned the Confederate high command that Louisiana was highly vulnerable to attack from the sea as well as by land, but his pleas went unheeded. A naval attack directed by Captain David Farragut was launched against the Mississippi River forts in April 1862. A series of fierce battles ensued, with both sides unleashing firepower that lit up the skies and lasted for five days and nights. At 2 a.m. on the 24th of April, Farragut's fleet of 17 wooden warships and 20 mortar boats, which had been moored at the mouth of the Mississippi, moved upstream to the forts. The Union attackers ran past the forts in a continuous bombardment and captured New Orleans.

Six ships of the Confederate River defense fleet fled during the battle, but three others fought with valor, among them one named *Governor Moore*, which after the other Confederate vessels pulled away, stood to fight, engaging the Federal *Varuna* in a running battle and sinking it. Ironically, down with the *Varuna* went any hope of the governor and his administration surviving the Union invasion, causing New Orleans to capitulate on April 25 and bringing on attacks against Baton Rouge and other points.

To all practical purposes, Louisiana had fallen to the Union forces after the capture of New Orleans and Baton Rouge, but the state did not officially fall until the surrender of the Trans-Mississippi Department of the Confederate Army by General Edmund Kirby Smith, at Shreveport, after Lee's surrender at Appomattox. Elsewhere in Louisiana, Union forces under General Nathaniel P. Banks captured Alexandria, but almost lost their river fleet to low water and only saved it by building Bailey's dam. Banks's Red River campaign was defeated by General Richard Taylor in the Battles of Mansfield and Pleasant Hill.

As the war wore on, Moore moved the state capital from Opelousas to Shreveport, and after the war ended and Reconstruction was imposed, it was moved again to New Orleans, from whence it later returned to Baton Rouge.

Defeated, and with no power remaining, Moore resigned the governorship in January 1864, but his troubles were not over. Moore retired to Rapides Parish; his home and other buildings had been burned by Union soldiers. Raids along the Red River above Rapides Parish threatened Moore and his family, and at the end of the war, he fled to Mexico and later to Havana to avoid arrest by Union forces. President Andrew Johnson pardoned him, and he returned to Rapides Parish, near Alexandria, where he had gotten his start in Louisiana.

Born on April 10, 1804, in Sampson County, North Carolina, he had a bright career in public office before becoming governor, serving on the police jury, in the state legislature (both House and Senate), and eventually succeeding to leadership of the Democratic party in central Louisiana. In 1830 he married Bethial Jane Leonard, and the couple had five children. Moore became a leading planter with an avid interest in politics as Louisiana grew into statehood. He died on June 25, 1876.

—W.G.C.

Davis, Edwin Adams. *Louisiana: A Narrative History*. Baton Rouge: Claitor's Publishing Division, 1971.

Dufour, Charles L. *Ten Flags in the Wind: The Story of Louisiana*. New York: Harper & Row, 1967.

Wall, Bennett H., ed. *Louisiana: A History*. Wheeling, IL: Harlan Davidson, 1997.

George F. Shepley

1862–1864

George F. Shepley, who was appointed commandant (acting mayor) of New Orleans when the city fell to the onslaught of the Union forces that stormed up the Mississippi River during April 1862, became U.S. military governor little more than a month later. He did not seem to be up to the job: in the words of chroniclers of the time, he was a mere functionary.

At the outbreak of the war, Shepley received a commission as a colonel in the 12th Maine Infantry Volunteers, and because of his friendship with General Benjamin F. Butler his regiment was included in the federal expedition against New Orleans. Shepley became an acting brigadier general in command of the Third Brigade. Later he was elevated to brigadier general and played the role of a buffer between Butler and foreign diplomats, who complained that Butler dealt with too heavy a hand in his relations with consuls.

The job of trying to appease or silence citizen groups fell to Shepley, who became the principal spokesman for the higher authorities, locally and in Washington.

When General Nathaniel Banks took command in Louisiana, an elec-

George F. Shepley. Courtesy of Special Collections, Tulane Libraries.

tion was held in fourteen parishes of southeastern Louisiana on February 22, 1864, and Michael Hahn was elected the first civil governor since secession. Shepley was transferred to Virginia and placed in command of the Eastern District of that state. When Richmond fell, he was made military commander there.

Shepley resigned from the army in June 1865 and moved to Portland, Maine, where he had started his career. He was offered a seat on the U.S. Supreme Court, but declined. Later, he became a federal judge in the First District of Maine.

Shepley was born in Saco, Maine, on January 1, 1818, and died in Portland on July 20, 1878. He graduated from Dartmouth College in Maine, and read law at Harvard and with his father. He was United States Attorney for Maine, but lost that post when Zachary Taylor was elected president. In 1853 he was reappointed by President Franklin Pierce. He was married first to Lucy Ann Hayes in 1844, and when she died, to Helen Merrill in 1872.

—W.G.C.

Taylor, Joe Gray. *Louisiana Reconstructed, 1863–77*. Baton Rouge: Louisiana State University Press, 1975.

Michael Hahn

1864–1865

Michael Hahn, an orphan who grew up with a penchant for politics and matured in the Civil War era, served Louisiana in a wide spectrum of high offices: as governor, United States senator, twice as a U.S. congressman, and thrice in the state legislature. Along the way, he became a confidant of President Abraham Lincoln and, during and after the war, advised Washington on Louisiana developments.

Hahn had strict Unionist views, and to disseminate them he bought, took over, or created four newspapers, obviously to promote his and the Union cause. But Hahn, who walked with the aid of a crutch because one leg was shorter than the other, was frustrated by the turn of events as often as he was successful. He associated himself with the military commanders as soon as they took over New Orleans. When Lincoln pushed a plan to restore civil government, congressional elections were ordered for the First and Second Districts, which were under the control of the Union army. Hahn ran for the Second District seat and was elected with the backing of German immigrants, his family being among them. His term in Congress lasted only a month because it adjourned after that period. However, in that short span Hahn struck a close friendship with

Michael Hahn. Courtesy of Special Collections, Tulane Libraries.

Lincoln, and it continued when he returned to Louisiana. The president came to rely on him for guidance in political intelligence and patronage.

Hahn, short and dark with a broad face and curly hair, and Lincoln, tall with sharp, elongated facial features, made a spectacular pair as they moved about the capital. Their interests merged when Lincoln, unhappy with the slow pace of civil government restoration in 1863, directed Major General Nathaniel Banks to assume control of affairs in the Union-held part of Louisiana. Banks called elections for February 22, 1864, and Hahn became a candidate for governor. He swept to victory over the conservative candidate, J. Q. A. Fellows, who came in second, and Benjamin Franklin Flanders, who ran third. During the campaign, Hahn bought a pro-slavery newspaper, the *New Orleans Delta*, and converted it to Unionism.

Lincoln, impressed with Hahn's victory, extended his authority by making him military governor. As governor, Hahn had a leading role in the state constitutional convention of 1864 and worked with the legislature. However, he ran into a roadblock when Major General Stephen A. Hurlbut, commander of the Army Department of the Gulf, refused to act on Reconstruction plans until Congress approved Lincoln's plan. An impasse developed; Hahn appealed to Lincoln, but got no relief. Angered, he resigned and accepted nomination to the U.S. Senate.

Hahn was elected to the Senate in January 1865 and resigned as governor on March 3, 1865. Lincoln was assassinated on April 14, and Congress refused to seat senators from the South. Thus, Hahn did not serve in the Senate.

Back in Louisiana, Hahn joined the Louisiana Radical Party and helped set up a new constitution for the state, supporting black rights and voting privileges. This was a tough time in state politics, because the ex-Confederates opposed efforts to enfranchise the blacks. Conservatives stood by, doing nothing, during a race riot on July 30, 1866.

To promote the blacks' cause, Hahn became editor of the *New Orleans Republican* in 1867, and continued in that role until 1871. The next year he retired to his sugar plantation in St. Charles Parish and founded the village of Hahnville. Also, he started another newspaper, the *St. Charles Herald*. He turned his attention to education, becoming a director and later president of a state convention on education. Still interested in government, he ran for the legislature and served three terms, 1872 to 1876. For a time after that, he was superintendent of the U.S. Mint in New Orleans and was appointed a federal district judge. When state elections took place in 1880, he started another newspaper, the *New Orleans Ledger*, to promote Republicans. In 1884 he was again elected to Congress, running in the heavily Democratic Second District but winning by a margin of 1,300 votes.

Hahn, little known in the twenty-first century, played a vital role in state politics in the latter half of the nineteenth century. A bachelor, he was born Georg Michael Decker in Klingemunster, Germany, on November 24, 1830, the son of Mrs. Hahn (nee Decker), who had been widowed two years. His mother and her five children emigrated to America and eventually settled in the German community of New Orleans. Hahn's mother died of yellow fever in 1841, and Hahn became an orphan at the age of eleven. He managed to attend public schools and, at the age of nineteen, began reading the law under Christian Roselius, a prominent Whig politician, and attended the University of Louisiana (now Tulane). He first joined the Democratic Party's faction headed by Pierre Soulé. In the secession crisis, he switched to the Union party and served on the state committee that supported Stephen A. Douglas for president.

Hahn died at the age of fifty-five of a ruptured blood vessel in a Washington hotel on March 15, 1886. He is buried in Metairie.

—W.G.C.

Davis, Edwin Adams. *Louisiana: A Narrative History*. Baton Rouge: Claitor's Publishing Division, 1971.

Henry Watkins Allen

1864–1865

Douglas Southall Freeman, the Southern historian, described Henry Watkins Allen, governor of Louisiana in 1864–65, as "the single great administrator produced by the Confederacy." There were ample reasons for the laudatory remark, for Allen was not only a fierce fighter; he moved resolutely to shore up the infrastructure of the crumbling Confederacy, especially in the latter stages of the Civil War.

At the outset of the war Allen aided in the formation of several military companies, volunteering as a private in the Delta Rifles Company in 1860. Then he took part in the seizure of the federal arsenal at Baton Rouge in 1861. His regiment occupied Ship Island off the Mississippi Gulf Coast, a Union stronghold, and took over Berwick Bay in Louisiana before being sent to Tennessee, where he took part in the Battle of Shiloh in April 1862, suffering a bullet wound in the face. Promotions came rapidly, and he was a colonel in the Confederate army when he commanded a brigade in the Battle of Baton Rouge in August 1862. He was again wounded, this time severely in both legs, as his group attacked a Union battery.

Henry Watkins Allen. Courtesy of Special Collections, Tulane Libraries.

Allen resigned his colonelcy in January 1863; he was named to a military court at Jackson, Mississippi, after which the Confederate Congress promoted him to brigadier general and sent him to Shreveport to organize paroled prisoners of war. He ran for governor in the fall of 1863 and was elected. After being inaugurated on January 25, 1864, Allen devoted his attention to helping the suffering civilian population.

His administrative ability blossomed as he sought to aid the war effort and the civilian population. He set up a state factory to manufacture cotton cloth, a commodity sorely needed by the troops as well as civilians. He established stores to provide household goods and food at reduced prices, giving them to the needy when possible. He established a state laboratory at Minden to manufacture and distribute low-cost medicines and extended this service to Shreveport as well.

One of his biggest efforts was to supervise a program to collect cotton for trade outside the United States. This meant he had to find a way to evade the Union blockade. He did it by transporting the cotton through Texas and Mexico. And early in 1864, when the war was going badly for the Confederacy, he formed two battalions of state guards to assist the regular Confederate military. When General Lee surrendered, Allen wanted to continue the fight, but gave up the idea and went into exile, fleeing with other Confederate leaders to Mexico, where he published a newspaper, the *Mexican Times*. Friends placed his name on the ballot for governor of Louisiana again in November 1865, and he carried five parishes even though he had disavowed the race.

Born in Farmville, Virginia, on April 27, 1820, Allen died in Mexico on April 2, 1866. He was buried in the American Cemetery in Mexico City, but his remains were moved to New Orleans in 1867 and to the state capitol grounds in Baton Rouge in 1885.

Allen got to Louisiana via Missouri, where his father had moved to Ray County following the death of his mother in the early 1830s. He attended Marion College in Philadelphia, Missouri, and moved to Grand Gulf, Mississippi, in 1837. He was tutored in law and was elected to the Mississippi House of Representatives, serving one term. In 1844, he married Salome Ann Crane, who died in 1851. Allen moved to West Baton Rouge Parish in 1852 and became a sugar planter. He won a seat in the Louisiana legislature in 1857 as a member of the Know-Nothing party but switched to the Democratic party in 1859. His farming experience in West Baton Rouge Parish led him to build a railroad from West Baton Rouge (Port Allen) to Rosedale on Bayou Grosse Tete.

—W.G.C.

Davis, Edwin Adams. *Louisiana: A Narrative History*. Baton Rouge: Claitor's Publishing Division, 1971.

Freeman, Douglas Southall. "Henry Watkins Allen." *Dictionary of American Biography*, vol. 3. New York, 1971.

James Madison Wells

1865–1867

James Madison Wells, who became governor of occupied (Southern) Louisiana upon the naming of Governor Michael Hahn to the United States Senate, found himself in a crucial role in momentous times as the Civil War ended. The Union victory attracted many opportunists from both within and without the conquered states. Natives who supported the Reconstruction military and civil authorities were called "scalawags." Those who came to take advantage of the situation were called "carpetbaggers," for the valises in which they carried their belongings. Both were regarded as fortune-seekers and scoundrels by the general population.

Wells, the lieutenant governor under Hahn, helped to relieve the shock of Reconstruction by making good appointments to local offices, and by acts of kindness to the returning Confederates. He opposed, however, granting voting rights to Negroes because, he stated, he believed the emancipated slave had a lot to learn. Wells, a scalawag himself, was quoted as telling an army officer carpetbagger: "The truth is, sir, that we're very much obliged to you for all you Northern gentlemen have done, but now that you are successful, you had better go home. Louisiana must be governed by Louisianians."

While Wells identified himself as a scalawag, he was not typical of the breed because he had been a Unionist from principle and conviction prior to the Civil War rather than from opportunism after it.

It would be a long time before the race factor was quieted or moderated. But it was not long before Wells was accused of exceeding his authority as governor and leaning toward the Radicals, causing him to lose support among white citizens. A bloody riot took place in New Orleans on July 30, 1866, in which thirty-four Negroes were killed, with many Negroes and whites wounded.

Bennett Wall, historian and professor, wrote in his book, *Louisiana: A History*: "If Louisianians had deliberately set out to antagonize the people of the North, the state could not have done a better job of it. In the first place, violence against African-Americans, no longer protected by their status as valuable property, began with the end of the war and grew in frequency as Reconstruction continued. Furthermore, the actions of the new legislature engendered despair among the African-Americans, as lawmakers attempted to regain control over the former slaves' labor, and reestablish the system of race relations that existed before the war."

Under the condition created by Congress in 1867, the United States army's orders could supercede those of civil officials. As Wells took steps to implement President Andrew Johnson's lenient plan to reinstate citizenship rights to the returning Confederates, he ran into political animosity, with the result that General Philip H. Sheridan, the military commander, relieved him as governor.

Actually, the legislature attempted to reestablish a lighter form of slavery through enactment of new "Black Codes." The new codes required ex-slaves to hire themselves out for yearlong terms at fixed prices. This made them wards of the people who hired them. The state also established a convict lease system and made it possible to lease the convicts to plantation or farm owners.

Harsh treatment of ex-slaves and the opportunities of Unionists led to organization of what became the Republican party of Louisiana. The New Orleans race riot, known as the Battle of Liberty Place, convinced Congress that African Americans in the South needed special protection. Louisiana refused to ratify the Fourteenth Amendment, which guaranteed former slaves "equal protection of the laws." Violence caused Congress to adopt the Reconstruction Act of 1867, which divided the South into five districts. It gave General Sheridan power to register all adult males, black or white, to vote, providing they took an oath they had not voluntarily aided the Confederacy. This disenfranchised most white males in Louisiana.

Wells, born near Alexandria on January 8, 1808, died February 18, 1899, in Lecompte. He received his schooling at St. Joseph's College in Bardstown, Kentucky, and at Partridge's Academy in Middletown, Connecticut. He studied law at the Cincinnati Law School. Returning to Louisiana in 1830, he operated three plantations. Despite his strong Union sympathies, he became a large slaveholder. Originally a Whig in Louisiana politics, Wells opposed secession, remaining loyal to the Union during the Civil War. In 1864, he was nominated for lieutenant governor by both factions of the Free State (Union) party, the radicals led by Benjamin Flanders and the moderates led by Hahn.

As lieutenant governor and governor, Wells played a key role in Louisiana politics.

—W.G.C.

Davis, Edwin Adams. *Louisiana: A Narrative History*. Baton Rouge: Claitor's Publishing Division, 1971.

Dawson, Joseph G. III. "James Madison Wells, Governor, 1865–1867." *The Loui-*

siana Governors: From Iberville to Edwards. Joseph G. Dawson III, ed. Baton Rouge: Louisiana State University Press, 1990.

Wall, Bennett H., ed. *Louisiana: A History*. Wheeling, IL: Harlan Davidson, 1997.

Benjamin Franklin Flanders

1867–1868

Benjamin Franklin Flanders was military governor of Louisiana for only six months (June 6, 1867, to January 1, 1868), but his influence in state and New Orleans city government extended over several years during Reconstruction. Ironically, his enthusiasm for the Union cause shortly before New Orleans fell in April 1862 got him run out of town—fleeing so rapidly he had to leave his family behind.

His vice: raising an American flag amid fields of Confederate banners.

Flanders went first to Cairo, Illinois, where he offered his services to Union authorities, and then to New York City. After New Orleans was captured, he reappeared and found himself in a number of roles in support of federal forces. His rise to prominence was spectacular. Major General Benjamin Butler, who directed the occupation, tapped him for New Orleans city treasurer, and he served in that capacity from July 20 to December 10, 1862. President Lincoln wanted to get civil government back in operation as soon as possible in order to heal the wounds of war. The United States army had been placed in control of the state through its congressional districts, and special elections were called for the First and Second districts in December 1862. Unionists endorsed Flanders for the First District post, and he defeated John Bouligny. Michael Hahn won in the Second. They were seated in the 37th Congress, which adjourned only a month after being convened.

Flanders began his governmental service in the early 1850s, when he was selected alderman of the Third Municipal District of New Orleans. A native of Bristol, New Hampshire, he had come to New Orleans to

Benjamin Franklin Flanders. Courtesy of the Louisiana Secretary of State.

join an older brother, Wardwell Flanders, a sea captain. His service as alderman, and later as superintendent of public schools in the Third District, apparently brought him to the attention of the military command. In May 1863, Flanders was appointed a special agent of the U.S. Treasury to oversee regulations covering financial activities between the government and occupation forces in Louisiana, Texas, Mississippi, Alabama, and Western Florida. At the same time, he was placed in control of freed slaves (freedmen), some 63,000 of whom found themselves without jobs when the war ended.

In 1864 Flanders lost a race for governor as a Radical Unionist, and in 1868 was defeated in a race for state treasurer, this time as a Republican. On June 9, 1867, he was named military governor by Major General Philip Sheridan, and served under two other military commanders until January 1, 1868, when Major General Winfield Scott Hancock, a conservative Democrat, took command of the district. Flanders resigned because of Hancock's removal of Radical Unionists from state offices.

In May 1870 Flanders was appointed mayor of New Orleans by carpetbag governor Henry Clay Warmoth, and subsequently was elected to a two-year term. President Grant later named him assistant treasurer of the United States at New Orleans.

After graduation from Dartmouth in 1842, Flanders moved to New Orleans and read law under Charles M. Emerson. He never practiced law, however, becoming a teacher and principal of public schools in 1844–45. He returned to Bristol to marry Susan Sawyer in 1847, and they had six children. Flanders died on March 13, 1896, on his plantation near Youngstown, Louisiana. His widow survived until August 12, 1908.

Flanders was one of five persons who won a charter for the New Orleans, Opelousas, and Great Western Railroad, a line that eventually became part of the Southern Pacific Railroad linking Louisiana to California.

In addition to his wartime service, Flanders is considered a leader in creation of the Republican party in Louisiana.

His crowning glory came in 1872 when, as mayor of New Orleans, he welcomed the first Rex, king of New Orleans' famous Carnival, and the Grand Duke Alexis of Russia, a guest.

—W.G.C.

Dawson, Joseph G. III. *Army Generals and Reconstruction: Louisiana, 1862–1877.* Baton Rouge: Louisiana State University Press, 1982.

Jewel's Crescent City Illustrated. *Biographical Sketches of Distinguished Citizens of New Orleans.* January 1, 1873.

Wetta, Frank J. *The Louisiana Scalawags.* Ph.D. dissertation. Baton Rouge: Louisiana State University, 1977.

Woolfley, H. L. D. Personal interview, citing family papers written by a cousin, Ada DePass Patterson. March 2004.

Joshua Baker

1868

Joshua Baker, named military governor to succeed Benjamin Franklin Flanders, was caught in the switches, so to speak, in the four months he served. He won appointment through his support of President Andrew Johnson's policy of leniency toward the South during Reconstruction, but soon found himself in the middle between the theories of competing generals.

General Winfield Scott Hancock, commander of the Fifth Military District, encompassing Louisiana and Texas, set out to remove Radical Republicans from state and local offices, in an effort to establish a conservative restoration of the civil government. In doing so, he was reversing the policies of General Philip H. Sheridan, who followed a stern policy under provisions of the Congressional Military Reconstruction Acts of 1867. The law gave Hancock the power to override Baker on any action. But when Hancock ordered nine New Orleans city councilmen from office, even he was overridden. Ulysses S. Grant, then commander-in-chief of the United States army, countermanded the order, frustrating Hancock, who asked to be reassigned. His replacement called new elections in April 1868, and this is when Henry Clay Warmoth won election as governor.

Historians accord Baker no more than a footnote in the lineup of Louisiana governors, but he did provide an example of the chaos brought on by the upheaval in politics after the Civil War.

Baker, born on March 23, 1799, in Mason County, Kentucky, died in Lynn, Connecticut, April 15, 1885. His family had moved to Oak Lawn Plantation in St. Mary Parish in 1811. Baker was a graduate of the United States Military Academy. After studying law, he served in a number of positions in Louisiana. He also had credentials in engineering and served in that capacity in St. Mary and Terrebonne Parishes. He owned three sugar plantations. He aligned himself with the Conservative Democrats, opposing secession and collaborating with the federal occupation forces.

He was married twice, first to Fanny Assherton of Opelousas and then to Catherine Patton of Fairfax, Virginia. He fathered five children.

—W.G.C.

Davis, Edwin Adams. *Louisiana: A Narrative History*. Baton Rouge: Claitor's Publishing Division, 1971.

Henry Clay Warmoth

1868–1872

The people of Louisiana and the South generally were a defeated, impoverished mass of humanity who had suffered through four years of excruciating pain as the Civil War ran its course. Poorly clad soldiers came home in the spring of 1865 to a war-ravaged, desolate state, where they found humiliation, poverty, and despair. It was thus a land ripe for exploitation by unscrupulous men from the North, who came to be known as carpetbaggers.

Imagine, then, the arrival of Henry Clay Warmoth, exploiter and adventurer from Illinois, who seized the opportunity at age twenty-six to become governor and in essence dictator.

A political enigma for sure, Warmoth nevertheless had a lot going for him. He was described as "young, tall, slender and handsome with a large nose full at the nostrils, keen measuring eyes, a superb mustache and well-cut brows and chin" who personified dignity, graceful manners, and a charm of conversation. Indeed, he was an attractive newcomer with an ambition that would carry him to great heights in the history of Louisiana.

Henry Clay Warmoth. Courtesy of Special Collections, Tulane Libraries.

Born on May 9, 1842, in McLeansboro, Illinois, the son of a saddle and harness maker, Warmoth received an irregular early education, after which he read the law books of his father, a justice of the peace. At age eighteen he went to Lebanon, Missouri, where a month before turning nineteen he began the practice of law. He joined the Missouri militia and soon became lieutenant colonel of the Thirty-Second Missouri Infantry Regiment. Then General John McClernand, involved in the campaign against Vicksburg, made him a member of his staff.

Following the Vicksburg campaign, General Ulysses S. Grant removed McClernand from his command and ordered a dishonorable discharge for Warmoth for circulating false battle reports. But Warmoth, injured in the fighting, went to Washington and talked President Lincoln into reinstating his commission. Warmoth returned to Louisiana and saw action in the Red River campaign. Late in the war General Nathaniel P. Banks appointed him judge of the provost court in New Orleans, and by the end 1864 he was out of the army and practicing law in New Orleans.

Warmoth saw the possibilities of running for office and was elected a delegate to Congress, but the House of Representatives refused to recognize him. Political turbulence developed when returning soldiers took advantage of the constitution and elected a Democratic legislature in 1865, an election totally unacceptable to Washington and the Republican party. Attempts to reconvene the 1864 constitutional convention in 1866 led to a bloody riot on Canal Street in New Orleans on July 30, in which eighteen men were killed and 147 wounded.

Clearly, race was the problem. Even though President Lincoln had said, "I do not and never have been in favor of bringing about in any form the social and political equality of the black and white races," the Radical Party leaders (who favored strict enforcement of laws upholding black rights) did not agree with him. Many wanted revenge.

When the midterm congressional elections 1867 went against President Johnson, who favored light restrictions on the Confederacy, the victorious Radicals proceeded to pass the Reconstruction Acts of 1867. Military commanders in Louisiana at that point decided to give the state the kind of constitution the Radical Republicans sought. On November 23, 1867, they produced a document that destroyed the Southern tradition of white supremacy and set the stage for the emergence of Warmoth to become the dominant force in Louisiana politics. Warmoth already had built a following among black citizens and he was favored by most of the Radical Republicans. Louisiana was, in fact, an occupied territory, and Warmoth was ready to begin his offensive to capture its governmental machinery.

The 1867 constitution provided for election of new state officers, as well as ratification of the convention's articles. Warmoth had done his homework, for one provision eliminated the age limit for a candidate for governor and permitted successive terms. A compliant legislature promptly passed acts which put registration and election machinery in the governor's hands. Warmoth came up with the idea of creating an Election Returns Board and invested it with the power to check the vote of any parish and throw out any ballots that, in the board's judgment, had been invalidated because of bribery or intimidation at the polls.

In the election 1868, the twenty-six-year-old Warmoth and his black lieutenant governor running mate, Oscar J. Dunn, swept to victory, taking with them a legislature composed of nearly 50 percent blacks in the House of Representatives and some 20 percent in the Senate. Laws establishing extraordinary police power also passed. Through his control of the legislature and police powers, Warmoth, the first governor after Reconstruction and the youngest ever, became a virtual dictator, a role some historians claim influenced Huey P. Long to follow in the next century.

Warmoth buttressed his position by encouraging the establishment of Republican newspapers throughout the state and giving them a monopoly in the printing of laws and public announcements.

Historian Edwin Adams Davis said that the worst evils of the Reconstruction period began with Warmoth. Factional politics ensued, said Davis, and each faction stole as much money as possible. Confronted with such charges, Warmoth is reputed to have said, "I don't pretend to be honest . . . I only pretend to be as honest as anybody in politics."

The Warmoth legislature appropriated large sums of money, ostensibly to finance public projects, but much of it found its way into the pockets of Radical politicians. When the session adjourned, the *New Orleans Times* wrote: "The crime of its life was only equaled by the wickedness of its acts. Its death leaves the state plundered and bankrupted, with a people so shackled mentally, morally, and socially as to evoke the pity of all more fortunate Americans."

Toward the end of his term Warmoth's popularity faded, because of factional quarrels within his party and the outbreak of race riots. His followers in the legislature deserted him, mainly because of his veto of a social equality bill, failure to sign a civil rights bill, and failure to enforce the public education law. The House of Representatives, on December 9, 1872, voted 57 to 6 to impeach him, but his term ended before he could be tried by the Senate. However, because it had immediately resolved itself into a court of impeachment, Warmoth was suspended from office. Lieutenant Governor Dunn had died unexpectedly on November 22, and the president of the Senate, P. B. S. Pinchback, a black legislator, was declared governor on the day Warmoth was suspended. Davis noted that Warmoth refused to answer charges made against him, and he was not brought to trial by the succeeding Senate.

Pinchback, whose term lasted little more than a month, and Warmoth became stars in a vignette that again showed the ingenuity of Warmoth. The Republican party called upon Pinchback to speak in the New England states. At the same time, Warmoth decided to go to New York to consult with Liberal Republican colleagues. Warmoth, out for a walk in New York, ran into Pinchback and invited him to his hotel that night. Pinchback did not appear. The next morning it dawned on Warmoth that Pinchback may have caught a train back to Louisiana in order to sign the bills Warmoth had refused to sign. The law stipulated that Pinchback, as acting governor, could sign bills at any time before the next legislative session.

At the thought, Warmoth went into action, telegraphing a political crony and manager of the Illinois Central Railroad at New Orleans, Major E. A. Burke, that he did not want Pinchback back in New Orleans before he could get there. Burke commandeered a rail car and engine for Warmoth, then ordered Pinchback's train to be held at the Canton, Mississippi, terminal until Warmoth arrived. Warmoth was right; his nemesis was on that train and destined to arrive before he did.

Said Pinchback later, "I shall never forget that triumphant expression upon his [Warmoth's] face as I saw him standing upon the front platform of the special car as it came lumbering into Canton that morning, and the haughty, taunting manner in which he exclaimed, 'Hello, old fellow, what are you doing here?' I replied with the best grace I could command, 'I am on my way home, and if you have no objection I will go with you the rest of the journey.'"

Warmoth became a sugar plantation owner upon his retirement in 1877, after President Rutherford B. Hayes removed federal troops from Louisiana, ending the occupation. He married nineteen-year-old Sally Durant of Newark, New Jersey, in 1877, and the couple honeymooned in Europe. He was elected to the legislature in 1876 and remained Republican party boss. In 1888, he ran for governor again but was hopelessly beaten. Through his Washington ties he won appointment as collector of customs in New Orleans, serving from 1890 to 1893; he also wrote his memoirs. A familiar figure in New Orleans until the last, Warmoth died September 30, 1931, at eighty-nine years of age, in New Orleans. The old governor's funeral was well-attended, which would have pleased him.

—J.B.McG.

Davis, Edwin Adams. *Louisiana: A Narrative History*. Baton Rouge: Claitor's Publishing Division, 1971.

The Times-Picayune and predecessor newspapers.

Warmoth, Henry Clay. *War, Politics and Reconstruction: Stormy Days in Louisiana*. New York: Macmillan, 1930.

P. B. S. Pinchback

1872–1873

While the governorship of Pinckney Benton Stewart Pinchback spanned parts of two years, from the end 1872 until the beginning 1873, it lasted only thirty-five days, and gave him the distinction of being the only black who has ever held the office.

On November 22, 1871, the lieutenant governor, Oscar Dunn, died. As Governor Henry Clay Warmoth was threatened with impeachment by his enemies in the Custom House Gang, Dunn's successor became a crucial issue. If a Custom House Gang man became the lieutenant governor, he would succeed Warmoth if the governor was removed. Warmoth, wanting an ally in the position, convened a special session of the Senate to elect a new president, who would then become the acting lieutenant governor. Pinchback, a Negro and state senator, was his candidate, but the forces were evenly matched. A 17–17 tie between Pinchback and a Custom House Gang member was broken when Warmoth persuaded a senator to change his vote. Charles L. Dufour wrote that the governor's request "was backed by a $15,000 bribe" and that "offers of bribes by both sides were general."

Warmoth denied purchasing votes, but in his memoirs acknowledged that he had worked the floor and was able to elect Pinchback by his "presence, cheerful conversation, pleasant manners, and so on." Presumably the "so on" covered a multitude of sins, just as Huey Long's tactics in obtaining the votes for the "Round Robin" to prevent his conviction on charges of impeachment fifty-seven years later included bribes and job offers.

In the aftermath of the disputed election of 1872, Governor Warmoth was impeached. The constitution required the suspension of impeached officials pending the outcome of their trials. The legislature declared Warmoth suspended from office and Pinchback took the oath as acting governor on December 9, 1872. With a proclamation from President Grant recognizing him as the lawful executive, backed by the metropolitan police and federal troops, Pinchback held office until William Pitt Kellogg was inaugurated on January 13, 1873. Edwin Adams Davis wrote that "little of importance occurred" during Pinchback's brief tenure, and that he "never succeeded in opening the safe containing the records of the governor's office."

Pinchback was born in Georgia on May 10, 1837, the mulatto son of a white planter and a freed mulatto woman. The family was moving from Virginia to Mississippi when he was born near Macon while they were en route. Pinchback attended school in Cincinnati but returned home to a Mississippi plantation after his father died. He went to Ohio with his mother and brothers because they feared that without his father's protection, they would be seized as slaves. He worked on steamboats on the Mississippi River and went to New Orleans after its fall to the Union, where he joined the 1st Louisiana Volunteer Infantry, a white unit. General Benjamin F. Butler gave him authority to raise a company of black volunteers, and he became captain of a company in the Louisiana Native Guards. When white officers refused to accept him as an equal, he resigned his commission.

When the Civil War ended, Pinchback moved to Alabama for two years. He returned to New Orleans in 1867, determined to take advantage of the political opportunities offered by Reconstruction. He became active in Republican politics, served as a delegate to the 1867 constitutional convention, and is credited with authorship of its civil rights article. Pinchback was elected a state senator from a New Orleans district in 1868, serving until that body elected him the acting lieutenant governor following Dunn's death.

Warmoth maintained that he was still governor after his impeachment and suspension from office by the House of Representatives, and that Pinchback had no legal authority to serve as governor, but Pinchback broke into the governor's office and functioned there, sending messages to the legislature and signing acts into law.

Following Kellogg's inauguration, Pinchback was elected a U.S. senator by the legislature, but the senate declined to seat him in the confusion over the political situation in Louisiana—with two governors and two legislatures, each claiming legitimacy. He continued to play an active political role, serving as a delegate to the 1879 constitutional convention and as a member of the state board of education. He also held federal patronage appointments as an Internal Revenue agent and as Surveyor of Customs in New Orleans. Pinchback is also credited with establishment of Southern University, having proposed that a college to educate blacks be built.

Pinchback moved to Washington, D.C., in 1883 and in 1895 to New York, where he was a U.S. marshal. He had studied law in New Orleans and was admitted to the bar, and he returned to Washington, D.C., and practiced law there from 1909 to his death in 1921.

He was the only black to serve as governor of a Southern state during Reconstruction; only one Southern state, Virginia, has elected a black as governor since then. For many years the impression was given that Pinchback was a mere product of carpetbag rule, and that he had risen above his abilities as a stooge of the Reconstruction administrations. In truth, he was well-educated, possessed astute political instincts, and left a lasting mark in the political history of the state.

—J.B.McG.

Davis, Edwin Adams. *Louisiana: A Narrative History*. Baton Rouge: Claitor's Publishing Division, 1971.

Dufour, Charles L. *Ten Flags in the Wind: The Story of Louisiana*. New York: Harper & Row, 1967.

Grosz, Agnes Smith. "The Political Career of Pinckney Benton Stewart Pinchback." *Louisiana Historical Quarterly* XXVII (1944).

Lonn, Ella. *Reconstruction in Louisiana after 1868*. New York: G. P. Putnam and Sons, 1918.

McGinty, Garnie W. *Louisiana Redeemed: The Overthrow of Carpetbag Rule, 1876–1880*. New Orleans: Pelican, 1941.

Vincent, Charles. "P. B. S. Pinchback, Governor, 1872–1873." *The Louisiana Governors: From Iberville to Edwards*. Joseph G. Dawson III, ed. Baton Rouge: Louisiana State University Press, 1990.

Wall, Bennett H., ed. *Louisiana: A History*. Wheeling, IL: Harlan Davidson, 1997.

Warmoth, Henry Clay. *War, Politics, and Reconstruction: Stormy Days in Louisiana*. New York: Macmillan, 1930.

John McEnery

1873

John McEnery and his brother, Samuel Douglas McEnery, were one of three pairs of brothers to serve as governor; the others were Iberville and Bienville, and Huey and Earl Long. While much is known about Samuel, information about John McEnery focuses on his political activity, and the confusion about his background extends to his place of birth. Joseph G. Dawson III, in *The Louisiana Governors*, said that McEnery was a "native son," while Edwin Adams Davis, in his *Louisiana: A Narrative History*, wrote that he was "Virginia-born," in Petersburg, in 1833, according to another source.

McEnery's family moved to Monroe, Louisiana, in 1835, and he received a law degree from the University of Louisiana. He was elected to the Ouachita Parish police jury, and with onset of the Civil War became a captain in the Fourth Louisiana Infantry Regiment, serving in battles in Virginia, and winning promotion to lieutenant colonel. He was elected to the state legislature in 1867, but was removed from office by General William T. Sherman, then commanding in Louisiana.

McEnery was the Democratic candidate for governor against the Radical Republican William Pitt Kellogg in the 1872 state election. The Re-

John McEnery. Courtesy of Special Collections, Tulane Libraries.

publicans split between the Warmoth faction, calling themselves Liberal Republicans; the Custom House Gang, led by the U.S. marshal, Stephen B. Packard; and black Republicans, led by P. B. S. Pinchback. The Pinchback and Custom House Gang factions joined forces with Kellogg as their standard bearer for governor and C. C. Antoine, a black, for lieutenant governor. The Democrats were split between the regulars, led by McEnery, and a new reform group. In a strange turn of events, Warmoth, breaking with the Custom House Gang that was allied with the Grant administration, supported McEnery. They put forth a fusion ticket, with McEnery for governor, Davidson B. Penn, a Liberal, for lieutenant governor, and a black for secretary of state.

The election was marred by fraud on all sides. The official State Returning Board, controlled by Governor Warmoth, declared McEnery the winner over Kellogg, 65,579 to 55,973. Kellogg obtained an injunction from a friendly federal judge prohibiting the canvass of its returns. The Custom House faction produced its own returning board, a rump group from the Warmoth board, which proclaimed Kellogg the victor. U.S. District Judge E. H. Durell did not wait for that result to declare Kellogg the victor.

The Custom House Gang's returning board awarded 77 House seats to Republicans and 32 to Democrats. The Warmoth board gave 75 seats to Democrats and Liberals and 35 to Republicans. When Warmoth called his new legislature into special session, Judge Durell pronounced it an "unlawful assemblage" and ordered U.S. marshal Packard to prevent its meeting. The U.S. attorney general in Washington authorized Packard to employ federal troops to assist in enforcing the orders of the court if necessary.

When the legislature met in New Orleans at the Mechanics Institute, serving as the state house, federal marshals refused entry to the members certified by the Warmoth board whose seats were disputed. The House proceeded to impeach Governor Warmoth, suspending him from office pending a Senate trial. Pinchback, the acting lieutenant governor, immediately took the oath of office as governor. In a flurry of telegrams concerning the situation in Louisiana, McEnery pleaded with Grant to withhold judgment until a citizens' committee could present the facts to him, but the president declined. Grant issued a declaration recognizing Pinchback as the duly installed governor and ordered U.S. troops to support him.

On January 13, 1873, two men took the oath of office as governor of Louisiana: Kellogg at the Mechanics Institute, McEnery at a ceremony in Lafayette Square. Both installed their own legislatures and prepared for a fight. On March 5, 1873, despairing of a fair hearing from Washington,

McEnery sent his militia against Kellogg's police at their Cabildo headquarters. Three men were killed and eight wounded in the battle, which McEnery called off after U.S. troops arrived on the scene.

The Kellogg forces struck back, sending the metropolitan police to evict the McEnery legislature from its meeting place at Odd Fellows Hall.

Congress investigated the Louisiana election. Its majority report found that Judge Durell's actions were illegal and said that, while fraud was committed by all parties, the McEnery ticket should be recognized as the legal government; failing that, a new election should be held. With no means to install McEnery or order a new balloting, Congress left the matter in Grant's hands. While he considered the report, news came of a bloody race riot in the Grant Parish town of Colfax. Estimates of the dead varied widely, but it appears that seventy or more blacks were killed. Determined to have law and order in Louisiana, on May 22, 1873, Grant issued a proclamation declaring the Kellogg administration the legally constituted government of the state.

McEnery and his group continued to function as a government, and he made several trips to Washington to press his claims to recognition. He was absent from the state when the Crescent City White League called for an end to Reconstruction and overthrow of Kellogg. After a mass meeting, several thousand White Leaguers, most of them respectable citizens and Confederate veterans, engaged in a pitched battle with the metropolitan police on Canal Street. The White Leaguers lost 16 killed and 45 wounded; the metropolitan police had 11 dead and 60 wounded. Encouraged by the failure of U.S. troops in the Custom House to intervene in support of the police, the White Leaguers surrounded the state house, where the police and Negro militia were barricaded. The Kellogg forces surrendered, and the McEnery-Penn officials were declared the legitimate government by the insurgents.

Apprised of events, President Grant issued a proclamation ordering the White Leaguers to disperse and demanding that all citizens recognize the Kellogg government. Grant sent reinforcements to General Emory, as well as three warships to place the city of New Orleans under their guns if necessary. Fearing a bloodbath, McEnery, who had returned to New Orleans, submitted rather than fight.

McEnery later served as Register of the State Land Office, and in 1879 was one of a group of leading citizens of the state who asked General Frederick N. Ogden, who had organized the White League, to allow his name to be placed before a convention of the state Democratic party as a candidate for governor. McEnery practiced law in New Orleans, where he died in 1890. While he was unable to secure recognition as the legitimate governor of Louisiana, he saw his brother, Samuel Douglas McEnery, serve as governor for seven years, from 1881 to 1888.

—J.B.McG.

Conrad, Glenn R. *A Dictionary of Louisiana Biography*. New Orleans: Louisiana Historical Association, 1988.

Davis, Edwin Adams. *Louisiana: A Narrative History*. Baton Rouge: Claitor's Publishing Division, 1971.

Dufour, Charles L. *Ten Flags in the Wind: The Story of Louisiana*. New York: Harper & Row, 1967.

Lonn, Ella. *Reconstruction in Louisiana after 1868*. New York: G. P. Putnam and Sons, 1918.

McGinty, Garnie W. *Louisiana Redeemed: The Overthrow of Carpetbag Rule, 1876–1880*. New Orleans: Pelican, 1941.

Wall, Bennett, ed. *Louisiana: A History*. Wheeling, IL: Harlan Davidson, 1997.

Warmoth, Henry Clay. *War, Politics, and Reconstruction: Stormy Days in Louisiana*. New York: Macmillan, 1930.

William Pitt Kellogg

1873–1876

William Pitt Kellogg bore little resemblance to his distinguished namesakes, William Pitt, Earl of Chatham, who guided as prime minister Great Britain through the Seven Years' War with France, and his son, William Pitt the Younger, who became prime minister at twenty-four and died in 1805 during another war with France. Rather, Kellogg had more in common with their ancestor, "Diamond" Pitt, an official who managed to make a fortune on a meager salary in India during turbulent times.

Kellogg was born in Orwell, Vermont, in 1831, and attended Norwich Military Institute. His family moved to Peoria, Illinois, when he was seventeen, and he taught school, read law, and, after passing the bar, opened an office in Canton. Kellogg became active in Republican politics, was a delegate to the 1860 national convention that nominated Lincoln, and was an Illinois elector for him.

Kellogg was favored by a grateful Lincoln on several occasions. The president appointed him chief judge of the Nebraska territory shortly after taking office. With the outbreak of war, Kellogg returned to Illinois and raised a regiment of cavalry that he commanded until ill health forced him to leave the army. He resumed his territorial judgeship until Lincoln, in one of his last appointments prior to his assassination, issued him a commission as Collector of Customs in New Orleans on April 13, 1865.

The St. Louis *Republican* dismissed him as "a worn out political bummer from Illinois," but Kellogg's political career prospered in Louisiana. In July 1868 the legislature elected him a U.S. senator, and on November 1, 1872, he received the Republican nomination for governor, with C. C. Antoine, a black, as his running mate for lieutenant governor. The Republican party split into two factions, one headed by Governor Henry Clay Warmoth and his supporters, and the other, known as the Custom House Gang, led by Kellogg and U.S. marshal Stephen B. Packard.

Warmoth's "Liberal Republicans" joined the "Reformers" and Democrats in supporting a ticket of Democrats John McEnery for governor and Davidson B. Penn for lieutenant governor. In an election marked by widespread fraud and voter intimidation on all sides, both Kellogg and McEnery claimed victory. With Warmoth's State Returning Board expected to certify McEnery the winner, Kellogg obtained an injunction to halt promulgation of the returns and had a rival returning board that he organized name him the victor.

The Warmoth returning board reported that McEnery won, 65,579 to 55,973, but federal judge E. H. Durell ordered that Kellogg be seated. Both men, and the legislatures each claimed to have elected, were inaugurated in separate ceremonies on January 13, 1873. After months of turmoil and a congressional investigation, President Grant issued a proclamation that recognized the Kellogg administration.

The outraged Democrats denounced Kellogg as a "usurper" and many citizens outside of New Orleans refused to pay taxes. Federal troops supported Kellogg's regime, but McEnery and Penn continued to maintain they were the duly elected officials. Riots occurred in several towns, and violence was widespread. Kellogg survived an assassination attempt.

"Kellogg's authority never extended much beyond New Orleans," according to *Louisiana: A History*. "Much of the time near-anarchy or guerrilla warfare existed in the countryside." When supporters of rival sheriffs appointed by McEnery and Kellogg fought in Colfax, in Grant Parish, sixty to one hundred blacks were killed. In Coushatta, in Red River Parish, the newly organized White League demanded the resignations of Radical Republican parish officials. After a brief gun battle, the Republicans surrendered when the White Leaguers guaranteed their safety. The next day, while they were being escorted to Shreveport under guard, another band of White Leaguers apprehended them and hanged all five. After the Colfax riot, Grant issued a proclamation that ordered "turbulent and disorderly persons to disperse."

The armed disputes came to a head with the Battle of Liberty Place, in New Orleans, on September 14, 1874, when the White League and the Carpetbag regime's metropolitan police clashed on Canal Street. The battle was brought on by the police's seizure of a shipment of rifles and ammunition that Kellogg suspected was destined for the Crescent City White League, which was organized by General Frederick N. Ogden.

The White League called for a mass meeting at the Henry Clay statue, then on Canal Street at Royal Street, and several thousand citizens responded to the summons. With McEnery traveling out of state, his lieutenant governor, D. B. Penn, and General Ogden took charge. Penn read a proclamation calling on all able-bodied men to drive the usurpers from power; significantly, he pledged that black rights would be upheld. They sent a message to Kellogg demanding his immediate resignation, and when he refused, they called for citizens to arm themselves and reassemble that afternoon.

Kellogg left the statehouse in the St. Louis Hotel for refuge in the

Custom House. When the White Leaguers threw up barricades on Poydras Street, between St. Charles and the river, the Metropolitan Police, 500 strong, opened fire on them with six cannon. The White Leaguers outflanked the police, who broke ranks and sought safety in the Custom House. The sharp battle lasted only fifteen minutes. Eleven police were killed and sixty wounded; the White League counted sixteen killed and forty-five wounded. A detachment of federal troops took no part in the battle, and the White League did not assault the Custom House, as they did not want war with U.S. troops.

The next day, the metropolitan police and the Negro militia in the state house surrendered. The White League declared vacant the offices held by Radical city officials and replaced them with Democrats elected with McEnery and Penn, but the celebration of the overthrow of Carpetbag rule was short-lived. President Grant ordered all illegal groups of armed men to disperse and sent additional federal troops and three naval vessels to enforce his edict. McEnery, who had returned to New Orleans, threw in the towel. He was prepared to fight Kellogg's police and militia, but not the armed might of the U.S. government.

There was widespread voter fraud in the legislative election 1874. After one month of canvassing, the State Returning Board said that the Republicans and Democrats had each won fifty-three seats, with five disputed ones to be resolved by the legislature itself. When the House met on January 4, 1875, Louis A. Wiltz, a Democrat, was quickly nominated for temporary speaker by his party. Wiltz took the gavel, bypassing a vote, and had a waiting justice of the peace swear him in. Overriding protests by the Radicals, Wiltz then swore in the members, seated a clerk, appointed sergeants-at-arms who were waiting at the rear of the chamber, seated five Democrats in the challenged seats, and then called for a vote that saw the Democrats, now holding a majority, elect him speaker.

The Republicans stormed out, returning with federal troops who threw out the five Democrats. Wiltz responded by leading his members out, and they organized their own legislature in a nearby building. At the height of the turmoil, General Philip Sheridan, sent on a tour of the South by Grant, arrived in New Orleans. Sheridan took command of the troops and sent a telegram to Grant, stating that "if Congress would pass a bill declaring them banditti," he would arrest the ringleaders of the White League and try them before a military commission.

Sheridan was denounced in the North as well as in New Orleans. A congressional subcommittee of two Republicans and one Democrat that came to New Orleans to investigate matters, held that "If Louisiana were a country by itself, McEnery and his associates would at once be installed in power; but the Conservatives in Louisiana do not intend to fight the federal government." The subcommittee brokered a compromise by which Kellogg held his governorship until the expiration of his term in 1877, setting the stage for a battle in the 1876 election. Democrats were given the disputed seats; once in the majority they impeached Kellogg, but the Senate refused to convict him.

Kellogg advised the Republican state convention that he would not seek renomination. Henry Clay Warmoth and P. B. S. Pinchback were both candidates, but Stephen B. Packard, the U.S. marshal, won the nomination, with C. C. Antoine renominated for another term as lieutenant governor. The Democrats nominated General Francis T. Nicholls, a Confederate hero who had lost both an arm and a leg in battle, with Wiltz as his running mate. Nicholls won, carrying a Democratic legislature in with him. The Democrat, Samuel J. Tilden, captured Louisiana's electoral vote for president.

The State Returning Board, controlled by Kellogg, manipulated the canvass and certified the election of Packard and Antoine, a Republican majority in the legislature, and an electoral victory for the Republican, Rutherford B. Hayes. Grant sent a committee to New Orleans to investigate the vote, and it affirmed the Republican sweep.

On January 8, 1877, the state again saw two inaugurations. Kellogg sealed all doors to the state house except one, at which he stationed policemen who admitted only those legislators holding credentials he had issued. The situation remained volatile, but was resolved through the Compromise 1877, when an electoral commission of Congress had to determine who should be president. Nicholls and his adherents entered into an agreement through which Louisiana's electoral vote was awarded to Hayes in return for acceptance of the election of Nicholls and an end to Carpetbag rule. The Packard legislature had elected Kellogg to the U.S. Senate, and despite the bad feeling against him, his election was reaffirmed by the Democrats in the legislature, and he served until 1883.

Kellogg followed his Senate service with one term in the U.S. House of Representatives. He held no further public offices, but remained active in Republican politics until moving to Washington, D.C., where he died in 1918.

Corruption was rampant in Reconstruction Louisiana under Warmoth and Kellogg—although, unlike Warmoth, Kellogg's personal honesty was not questioned. In assessing the Louisiana legislature in 1872, a congressional committee said that "the world has rarely known a legislative body so rank with ignorance and corruption."

In evaluating Kellogg, *Louisiana: A History* said: "White Louisianians made Kellogg the most despised chief executive in Louisiana history. The fact that he reduced the state debt, lowered taxes, and maintained his personal honesty did not endear him to the Democrats, who looked upon him as a usurper." C. Howard Nichols wrote he faced "electoral disputes, legal controversies, an assassination attempt, civil insurrection, and finally, impeachment."

Henry Clay Warmoth outlived all of his enemies and then wrote his memoirs. While Kellogg lived to an old age, dying fifty-seven years after Abraham Lincoln appointed him a territorial judge, he remained a despised figure in Louisiana. He was an object of ridicule during his term, with one bit of doggerel expressing the views of many citizens:

The other day, in a swampy bog
A serpent bit William Pitt Kellogg.
Who was poisoned, do you say?
The snake; it died that very day.

—J.B.McG.

Davis, Edwin Adams. *Louisiana: A Narrative History*. Baton Rouge: Claitor's Publishing Division, 1971.

Dufour, Charles L. *Ten Flags in the Wind: The Story of Louisiana*. New York: Harper & Row, 1967.

Kendall, John Smith. *History of New Orleans*. Chicago: Lewis, 1922.

Lonn, Ella. *Reconstruction in Louisiana after 1868*. New York: G. P. Putnam and Sons, 1918.

McGinty, Garnie W. *Louisiana Redeemed: The Overthrow of Carpetbag Rule, 1876–1880*. New Orleans: Pelican, 1941.

Nichols, C. Howard. "William Pitt Kellogg, Governor, 1873–1876." *The Louisiana Governors: From Iberville to Edwards*. Joseph G. Dawson III, ed. Baton Rouge: Louisiana State University Press, 1990.

Wall, Bennett, ed. *Louisiana: A History*. Wheeling, IL: Harlan Davidson, 1997.

Warmoth, Henry Clay. *War, Politics, and Reconstruction: Stormy Days in Louisiana*. New York: Macmillan, 1930.

Francis R. T. Nicholls

1877–1880; 1888–1892

Confederate general Francis R. T. Nicholls, who lost his left arm and left foot in Civil War battles, had little interest in politics when the fighting ended but emerged as a leader in a political drama that unfolded, winning the governorship of Louisiana and becoming a central figure in the disputed election of Rutherford B. Hayes as president in 1876.

Nicholls planned to return to Napoleonville to resume the practice of law after the war, but his popularity would not be denied. With the general population economically destitute in the wake of the war and Carpetbag corruption rampant, Nicholls, a staunchly conservative Democrat, had a change of heart for politics and accepted a draft to run for governor in 1876. His Republican opponent was Stephen B. Packard, a Maine native who had opened a law practice in New Orleans and was appointed United States marshal during Reconstruction. Packard was a member of the Custom House Gang that had become a powerful force in Louisiana politics. The state and national elections were held simultaneously, and both campaigns were violent and bitter, each ending in dispute.

In the presidential race, Democrat Samuel J. Tilden had 184 undisputed electoral votes, just one short of the number needed for election; Hayes, a Republican, had 165. Twenty were in dispute. Of the twenty, one was in Oregon and the others were spread through Louisiana, Florida, and South Carolina.

The United States Constitution at the time had no provision to resolve such disputes. Louisiana certified its vote for Tilden, and the other three states certified their votes for Hayes. At that point E. A. Burke, Louisiana's state treasurer and a powerful politician, and three members of the state's congressional delegation succeeded in convincing Congress to create an electoral commission to settle the matter. The commission was composed of five members of the House and Senate, and five justices of the U.S. Supreme Court. Of the fifteen members, eight were Republicans and seven Democrats. Each dispute in the recount ended with an 8–7 vote in favor of Republican Hayes. Democrats controlled the House and could have prevented a formal vote, but Southern Democrats agreed not to obstruct the formal vote if Nicholls were allowed to become governor. Thus

Nicholls was proclaimed the winner, even though the state's Republicans had contested the election.

Actually, Louisiana had two governors for three and a half months in 1877. Packard was sworn in as governor and a legislature seated behind closed doors on January 8 at the St. Louis Hotel, the Louisiana statehouse at the time. The current governor, William Pitt Kellogg, telegraphed President Grant seeking federal troops to preserve the peace. Grant refused, saying he would await the action of Congress. A crowd surrounded the statehouse when Packard took his oath of office, and the atmosphere was tense.

A citizens' committee arranged for the inauguration of Nicholls at St. Patrick's Hall, just off Lafayette Square, on the same day. When the group and the carriage in which Nicholls and his lieutenant governor, Louis A. Wiltz, drew up, enthusiasm was running high. The horses were unhitched and gleeful men grabbed the carriage and pulled it up Camp Street to the square where some 10,000 people had gathered. Cannons were fired as jubilation spread across the square. Obviously, the people were expressing their pent-up feelings over the war and Reconstruction. The Reverend Benjamin Morgan Palmer, the same minister who delivered an emotional speech defying the Union in the First Presbyterian Church that fronted Lafayette Square prior to the declaration of secession, offered prayers. A judge administered the oath to Nicholls, and the new governor addressed the crowd, urging demonstrators to conduct themselves peacefully.

The next day, Nicholls ordered the metropolitan police to duty to patrol the city. Packard and his group remained in the statehouse, while armed patrolmen and a militia of mostly black men stood guard with Winchester rifles. United States army troops gathered in the area, but the peace held without bloodshed.

Nicholls's first act was to appoint a new Supreme Court. He took a number of precautionary steps to assure that his people would maintain authority, but resolved not to undertake any move that would embarrass the federal government because, at the time, the presidential election had not been fully resolved.

President Hayes withdrew most of the federal troops from Louisiana and other Southern states, ending Reconstruction; there was no way an administration that depended on black votes could survive. As a result, Packard's bid for the governorship collapsed, and Nicholls gained solid control, with heavy Democratic majorities in both houses of the legislature. Thus, the same class of men who had controlled the state prior to the war was back in power!

Nicholls had promised to respect the Fourteenth and Fifteenth Amendments of the U.S. Constitution, the amendments guaranteeing the end of slavery and granting voting rights to blacks. He also vowed to continue support of public education and to stop the use of public funds for private purposes. But he had to give up the final year of his term because a new state constitutional convention had rewritten the basic law and changed the dates for election of state offices.

The 1879 rewriting of the constitution was chaired by the lieutenant governor, Wiltz, who had been elected on the Nicholls ticket. Wiltz engineered his own nomination for governor and won in the general election. Along with his lieutenant governor, Samuel McEnery, they operated a corrupt regime tied to the Louisiana lottery, which had been chartered for twenty-five years in 1868 during a Radical Republican administration. By 1887 the lottery was in great disfavor among voters, to the extent that Nicholls was called upon again to run for governor.

Henry Clay Warmoth, the Carpetbagger, tried to recapture the office in the election of April 17, 1888, but Nicholls won easily. The lottery by that time had become the biggest political issue in Louisiana history.

In seeking extension of its charter beyond 1893, the lottery offered to pay the state $1,250,000 annually, a healthy increase when compared with the $40,000 a year it had been paying. To win favor, the lottery made frequent donations for public and charitable purposes, and spent some $2 million yearly on advertising in friendly journals, using its resources against unfriendly newspapers. In its struggle for survival, it managed to get the legislature to adopt a proposed constitutional amendment extending its charter, but in 1890 Congress adopted a law banning the use of the mails for selling and delivering lottery tickets. This was the lottery's death knell. It moved to Honduras, but failed after a few years there. Still, it had not been eliminated, and the issue would continue into the following administration.

Nicholls, son of District Judge Thomas C. Nicholls and Louise Hannah Drake, was an honor graduate of the United States Military Academy at West Point. He also attended Jefferson College in New Orleans and studied law at Tulane University but did not graduate. He married Caroline Guion in 1860, fathering one son and five daughters. He joined a Confederate infantry company at the start of the Civil War, losing his left foot in the Battle of Chancellorsville and his left arm in the Battle of Winchester.

The battle wounds brought widespread sympathy to candidate Nicholls, as in the case of the fellow Confederate veteran who also had lost an arm and leg in the war and sidled up to him, saying, "General, all what's left of me is going to vote for what's left of you."

Others chided Nicholls, saying he was "too one-sided to be a judge," but he wound up his career by being appointed chief justice of the Louisiana Supreme Court, retiring in 1911. At his death in 1912, the New Orleans *Picayune* editorialized that Nicholls was "without doubt the most truly eminent, the most highly esteemed and the most deservedly honored citizen in Louisiana." Nicholls State College in Thibodaux was named for him, a lasting tribute.

—W.G.C.

Dawson, Joseph G. III. "Francis R. T. Nicholls, Governor, 1877–1880, 1888–1892." *The Louisiana Governors: From Iberville to Edwards*. Joseph G. Dawson III, ed. Baton Rouge: Louisiana State University Press, 1990.

Casso, Evans J. "Francis T. Nicholls, A Biographical Tribute." Thibodaux: Nicholls State Foundation, 1987.

Hair, William Ivy. *Bourbonism and Agrarian Protest*. Baton Rouge: Louisiana State University Press, 1969.

Jackson, Joy J. *New Orleans in the Gilded Age: Politics and Urban Progress, 1880–1896*. Baton Rouge: Louisiana State University Press, 1969.

Lathrop, Barnes F., ed. "An Autobiography of Francis T. Nicholls, 1834–1881." *Louisiana Historical Quarterly* XVII (1934).

McGinty, Garnie W. *Louisiana Redeemed: The Overthrow of Carpetbag Rule, 1876–1880*. New Orleans: Pelican, 1941.

Taylor, Joe Gray. *Louisiana Reconstructed, 1863–1877*. Baton Rouge: Louisiana State University Press, 1974.

Wall, Bennett H., ed. *Louisiana: A History*. Wheeling, IL: Harlan Davidson, 1997.

Louis Alfred Wiltz

1880–1881

Samuel D. McEnery

1881–1888

Louis Alfred Wiltz, Governor Nicholls's lieutenant governor, was well-positioned to make the race for governor in 1880. He set the stage in 1879 while presiding as president of the constitutional convention of that year. The Democratic party, tired of functioning under the Constitution of 1868, which was written by the Radical Republicans, mustered the strength to revise the state's basic law.

The new document, however, turned out to be an instrument fashioned by an alliance between the Bourbon and Lottery forces, and had the effect of strengthening the hand of Major Edward A. Burke, Louisiana's

Samuel D. McEnery. Courtesy of Special Collections, Tulane Libraries.

strongman in the 1880s. Editorialized one newspaper, "[I]t has served as the anchor of a regime remarkably powerful, backward and corrupt."

Wiltz's tenure as governor was shortened, however, as he became seriously ill of tuberculosis and died October 16, 1881, after serving less than two years of his four-year term.

Speaker of the House in the legislature and mayor of New Orleans prior to seeking the governorship, Wiltz had built a reputation as a good public speaker and presiding officer. As governor he established a bureau of agriculture and immigration, built a number of public schools, improved public health facilities, and encouraged the building of new railroads throughout the state.

Samuel D. McEnery of Monroe moved up from lieutenant governor to chief executive upon Wiltz's death. He served out Wiltz's term and then was elected to a four-year term that ended in 1888.

The Wiltz-McEnery years were marked by an epidemic of yellow fever; some 4,999 persons died from it in New Orleans and more in the Louisiana countryside.

The election of Wiltz marked another turning point in Louisiana gubernatorial elections. He was the last Catholic elected to the office for almost a century, until Edwin W. Edwards won the office in 1972. The first governors following Louisiana's joining the Union were Virginia-bred; next, a number of Creole Americans claimed the office, and following the Civil War came men of various affiliations. Black men, enfranchised during Reconstruction, were not just slaves anymore, but a symbol of election victory. Politicians turned to appealing for racial harmony and began luring Negro voters with parades and barbecues instead of pistols and other forms of intimidation.

McEnery called for greater levee protection when he took office and, as a supporter of the 1884 Cotton Centennial Exposition, tried to attract new business and industry. He was often referred to as "McLottery" or "McLevee," in deference to his main interests.

Edward A. Burke, the veteran state treasurer, held the greatest power by his manipulation of state funds. McEnery was seen as a weak governor with no checks on Burke's authority. Burke arranged to pay off certain bondholders and, in an economic crunch, paid state employees in warrants they had to sell to brokers at a discount.

Burke reveled in the fact that people knew he ran the capitol. "I hear it from one end of the state to the other that this poor weakling of a governor . . . is under the control and domination of Burke and some others," Burke remarked in public. The "others" included three powerful businessmen, Charles T. Howard and John A. Morris of the Louisiana

Lottery Company, and S. L. James, chief lessee of the state penitentiary convicts and a former large slaveholder.

When suggestions were made that McEnery be given a raise from his $4,000 annual salary, the *Daily Picayune* responded: "[T]he quality of the article paid for should take primary consideration, and viewed this way Louisiana's governor was the most expensive in existence."

Despite low approval ratings McEnery sought renomination by the Democratic party, but was blocked by a move to bring back Nicholls in 1888.

McEnery was appointed an associate justice of the Louisiana Supreme Court after his term ended, and again ran for governor in 1892 on a pro-lottery ticket but was defeated. The legislature elected him to the U.S. Senate in 1897, where he served until 1910. He died on June 28th of that year.

—W.G.C.

Hair, William Ivy. *Bourbonism and Agrarian Protest*. Baton Rouge: Louisiana State University Press, 1969.

Jackson, Joy J. "Samuel D. McEnery, Governor, 1881–1888." *The Louisiana Governors: From Iberville to Edwards*. Joseph G. Dawson III, ed. Baton Rouge: Louisiana State University Press, 1990.

Reeves, Miriam G. *Governors of Louisiana*. Gretna, LA: Pelican, 1976.

Uzee, Philip D. "Louis A. Wiltz, Governor, 1880–1881." *The Louisiana Governors: From Iberville to Edwards*. Joseph G. Dawson III, ed. Baton Rouge: Louisiana State University Press, 1990.

Murphy J. Foster

1892–1900

The Louisiana lottery was the paramount issue in the 1892 governor's race, a year in which the Democratic party chose two candidates for the state's top office. Competing groups—pro- and anti-lottery—were so hostile to each other they did not meet in the same building at Baton Rouge, and each group claimed the other was but a rump organization.

This was the era in which Louisiana men described themselves as Bourbon Democrats—men who held propertied interests and upheld Southern ideals, conservative Democrats who lived mostly where cotton had made fortunes for them.

The pro-lottery group chose former governor and Supreme Court justice Samuel D. McEnery to head the "regular" Democrats. The anti-lottery faction, known as the reform group, chose Murphy J. Foster. There were five candidates for governor that year, with both the Democrats and Republicans offering two tickets each.

The Louisiana Farmers' Union was destined to play a leading role in the election, and its president, Thomas S. Adams, surprisingly was offered the nomination for governor. But lottery politics and general lean

Murphy J. Foster. Courtesy of the *Times-Picayune*.

times of the era intervened. Adams declined to run and swung his support to Foster. This occurred after Adams was advised that he could not possibly beat McEnery in the general election.

The motivating factor in the move to Foster was the effort to eliminate the lottery from Louisiana. By 1890 it had receipts of between twenty and thirty million dollars annually. Approximately 47 percent was retained as profit; the rest went for bribes to state legislators, prizes, advertising, and other expenses. It was a cancer eating at Louisiana's economic life.

The lottery had a key operative within state government, Edward A. Burke, the state treasurer who had managed Governor Nicholls's campaign. Louisiana's lottery was created in 1868 by a New York gambling syndicate whose operators bribed Governor Warmoth's legislature into granting a twenty-five-year charter for the payment of $40,000 per year to the state.

By 1877 the Louisiana lottery had become the most lucrative venture of its kind in the nation. To extend the charter another twenty-five years the syndicate offered $1,250,000 annually, but the proposal was finally rejected.

The Louisiana version of the People's Party came to life in 1890–91, born of frustration of farmers who subscribed to a federal treasury plan to set up warehouses to provide low-cost loans to allow farm products to be held until a more favorable selling time. Democratic congressmen of the area refused to support the warehouse plan, and in the meantime the Farmers' Union had been captured by the Nicholls administration.

The People's party nominated Robert L. Tannehill of Winn Parish for governor, along with a slate of candidates for lesser offices. The Republicans nominated Albert H. Leonard of the pro-lottery or Kellogg faction and John E. Breaux as the anti-lottery or Warmoth faction candidates. With the state firmly controlled by the Democratic party at the time, Foster swept to an easy victory over Warmoth, polling 79,270 votes to his opponent's 47,046. Other candidates were also-rans.

Foster served two terms, beating John N. Pharr, a fusion candidate of the Republican and Populist parties, in 1896. This time he won with 116,216 votes against his opponent's 87,698. His accomplishments included support for the creation of Louisiana Technical University at Ruston and abolishing the lottery. During his term the legislature established the "separate but equal" facilities law, which demanded different facilities for white and black railroad travelers, and expanded that doctrine to include schools and institutions as well, establishing a system of segregation of the races that survived court attacks for some fifty years.

Barred from seeking a third term as governor by the Constitution of 1898, Foster was elected by the legislature to the United States Senate and served until 1906. In 1912 he was appointed collector of customs at New Orleans, serving until his death in 1921.

Born on Dixie Plantation near Franklin on January 12, 1849, Foster graduated from Cumberland University in Tennessee and gained a law degree from Tulane University, at that time the University of Louisiana. He was married twice, first to Daisy Hine in 1877 and then, after her death shortly after their wedding, to Rosa Rosetta Ker. They had ten children.

—W.G.C.

Hair, William Ivy. *Bourbonism and Agrarian Protest*. Baton Rouge: Louisiana State University Press, 1969.

Jackson, Joy. *New Orleans in the Gilded Age: Politics and Urban Progress, 1880–96*. Baton Rouge: Louisiana State University Press, 1969.

William Wright Heard

1900–1904

The first governor of the twentieth century, William Wright Heard, was born in Union Parish on April 28, 1853. He spent much of his long career in a succession of public offices: clerk of court for Union Parish, state representative, and state senator.

Heard was a strong supporter of Murphy J. Foster and was tapped as the Foster slate's candidate for state auditor in 1892. He was reelected with Foster in 1896, "in what may have been the most hotly contested and fraudulent election Louisiana had yet endured," according to Mark Carleton, who wrote: "Although much evidence suggests that Foster's Popular-Republican fusion opponents had the support of a statewide voter majority, the Fusionists were 'counted out' in the Democrat-controlled cotton parishes of north Louisiana."

Considered a reformer, at least in the context of his time, Heard was a staunch opponent of the lottery and the infamous convict lease system. Close to Foster personally as well as politically, Heard was viewed as the "outgoing administration's crown prince." With Foster unable to succeed himself, he selected Heard as his heir, and Heard became the standard bearer of the Bourbon Democrats in the 1900 election.

William Wright Heard. Courtesy of the *Times-Picayune*.

He was nominated for governor at the party convention that was controlled by Foster, and in the ensuing election he won easily, with 78 percent of the vote. The day after his inauguration, he repaid his mentor for his support by endorsing Foster's election as U.S. senator by the legislature.

With the lottery banished from Louisiana and the convict lease system terminated in 1901 by the state Constitution 1898, Heard did not have to deal with those difficult problems. The same constitution required proof of ownership of property or passage of a literacy test for a citizen to register to vote. These mandates struck both black Republicans and white Populist Democrats from the voting rolls and erected insurmountable barriers for many prospective registrants, insuring Bourbon ascendancy in what has been called "a legal disenfranchisement." The only exception to the literacy and property ownership requirements (and the property had to be valued for at least $300, a substantial sum then) was the notorious "grandfather clause." It extended the suffrage to those whose fathers or grandfathers had been registered to vote in 1867, thus enfranchising many whites while excluding most blacks and many illiterate whites. The statewide vote in gubernatorial elections dropped from 206,354 in 1896 to 76,780 in 1900, due largely to the restriction placed on the franchise.

Louisiana historian Mark Carleton wrote that, with the severely reduced registration rolls and lack of a viable opposition, "Heard enjoyed a relatively tranquil administration from 1900 to 1904, having to deal with no major political confrontations or crises. In the relatively calm aftermath of the turbulent 1890s, Louisiana Democrats apparently felt no need for continued aggressive, decisive leadership. An administrator-custodian in the governor's office was the order of the day, and Heard, with his clerical and accounting background and bland, stable disposition, filled the role admirably."

Heard died in New Orleans on May 31, 1926, after a long post-gubernatorial career in banking and accounting. His administration may have been as colorless as he was, but he achieved solid gains for the state during his tenure. His greatest accomplishment was the creation of a properly managed state penal system. He also established the first Oyster Commission and persuaded the legislature to authorize funding for a black insane asylum in Alexandria. Education of rural children was one of his major concerns. The first state board of education was established in his administration, and the legislature, acting on Heard's request, passed the first law that established parish school boards.

When the boll weevil scourge struck Louisiana in 1903, Heard called the legislature into special session to deal with the problem, and established the State Board of Pest Control. The oil industry, soon to outstrip cotton as a major economic engine, had its beginnings in the Heard governorship, although he was not involved with its start. The official state seal, with its "Union, Justice, Confidence" motto, was chosen by Heard.

While Heard may have conducted "an efficient but quite modest gubernatorial administration," he was well-regarded by his contemporaries, noteworthy for his integrity, and content to have his record speak for itself.

—J.B.McG.

Carleton, Mark T. *Politics and Punishment: The History of the Louisiana State Penal System.* Baton Rouge: Louisiana State University Press, 1971.

"William Wright Heard, Governor, 1900–1904." *The Louisiana Governors: From Iberville to Edwards.* Joseph G. Dawson III, ed. Baton Rouge: Louisiana State University Press, 1990.

Conrad, Glenn R. *A Dictionary of Louisiana Biography.* New Orleans: Louisiana Historical Association, 1988.

Davis, Edwin Adams. *Louisiana: A Narrative History.* Baton Rouge: Claitor's Publishing Division. 1971.

Dufour, Charles L. *Ten Flags in the Wind: The Story of Louisiana.* New York: Harper & Row, 1967.

Wall, Bennett H., ed. *Louisiana: A History.* Wheeling, IL: Harlan Davidson, 1997.

Newton Crain Blanchard

1904–1908

Newton Crain Blanchard served as congressman, United States senator, associate justice of the State Supreme Court, governor, and president of the Louisiana Constitutional Convention of 1913. He held so many high public offices that it is no wonder that friends as well as political enemies regarded him as a "stuffed shirt" with a condescending manner that in his day was known as "strutting."

Blanchard was born near Boyce, in central Louisiana's Rapides Parish, on January 29, 1849. His family home was Rosedale Plantation, and he had the manner of a plantation aristocrat throughout his life, a trait that came to him naturally.

In 1870 Blanchard received a law degree from Tulane's predecessor, the University of Louisiana, and opened a law office in Shreveport. Active in Democratic politics in the Reconstruction era, he was indicted on charges of intimidating black Republicans in an 1878 election, but was not convicted. The charges probably increased his political stature, as he was elected a delegate from Caddo Parish to the Constitutional Convention 1879, where he emerged as an articulate spokesman for the Bourbon Democrats.

Newton Crain Blanchard. Courtesy of the *Times-Picayune.*

Blanchard was elected to Congress from the Fourth District in 1880, serving until 1894. He used his chairmanship of the influential Rivers and Harbors Committee to promote flood control projects in the Lower Mississippi Valley, but gave up his seat in the House of Representatives when Governor Murphy J. Foster appointed him to the U.S. Senate to complete the term of Edward Douglass White, whom President Grover Cleveland had appointed to the U.S. Supreme Court.

Blanchard served as an associate justice of the state Supreme Court from 1897 until 1903. He was the Bourbon choice for governor in 1904, defeating Leon Jastremski in the Democratic primary. In the general election he defeated W. J. Behan, a former Confederate officer and mayor of New Orleans who had defected to the Republican party. In defeating Jastremski, Blanchard effectively ended the political career of one of the most colorful characters of his era. Of French and Polish descent, Jastremski served in the Confederate army and was later mayor of Baton Rouge and state adjutant general. He took time off from state politics to serve as the U.S. consul in Lima, Peru. In his campaign for governor, Jastremski, at a loss for any issue on which to attack Blanchard, accused him of being a slacker when the Southern cause needed him. Mark Carleton wrote that Jastremski's claim that Blanchard was a coward was "a ridiculous accusation in light of the fact that Blanchard had been only twelve years of age when the Civil War began and was barely sixteen at its conclusion."

Blanchard's administration enacted strong new state banking laws in the wake of the Panic of 1907. Edwin Adams Davis said that the Blanchard administration represented a "four year reform period," noting: "By the end of his administration, Governor Blanchard could point with pride to his achievements in reducing executive patronage, more than doubling appropriations for education, securing the passage of a new primary-election law, and other progressive measures."

Blanchard had defeated Jastremski in a party primary that they entered voluntarily, although Blanchard would have received the nomination had he insisted on a party convention. Party primaries replaced the state nomination conventions in his administration; while viewed as a "democratic" reform, institution of the primaries probably relegated the Republican party to a minor role, as the primary system encouraged registration as a Democrat in order to vote for local officials as well as candidates for state offices.

Blanchard strongly supported the efforts of State Superintendent of Education James B. Aswell to improve the elementary and secondary school systems. He reduced his own powers by making elective a number of offices that had been appointive, including justices of the Supreme

Court, parish assessors, and school board members. When Blanchard learned that many properties were not on the tax rolls and others were greatly undervalued, he backed creation of a State Board of Equalization to place all property on the tax rolls and set fair assessments. Appalled by the incarceration of minors in the state penitentiary because of the lack of appropriate facilities for them, he supported creation of a state reform school.

Mark T. Carleton characterized Newton C. Blanchard as "the most experienced and perhaps best qualified gubernatorial winner in the state's history," based on his service in both houses of Congress and on the state Supreme Court. Partisans of Edwin Edwards can rightfully assert the same claim for him, pointing to his service as a city councilman, state senator, and congressman prior to his election as governor, and his brief service in 1980 as an associate justice of the state Supreme Court between gubernatorial terms, making him the only governor to serve in all three branches of the state government.

Following his term as governor, Blanchard was elected a delegate to the Constitutional Convention of 1913 and was the unanimous choice to serve as its president. The last of the Old Bourbons, Blanchard died in Shreveport in 1922, probably viewing with disdain the rise of his neighbor, Huey P. Long, to political prominence as a member of the State Railroad Commission.

Carleton wrote that Blanchard was "the first Louisiana Democratic governor to have a hint of progressivism in his administration." While this view fails to take into account the genuine enlightenment of Heard on some issues, particularly penal reform, Blanchard was ahead of his time on social issues. He made it clear that he did not favor social equality or voting rights for blacks, but he denounced lynching and strongly supported adequate funding for black schools and institutions. In his 1904 inaugural address, Blanchard said, "The Negro is here. He is a man and a citizen." His candor was remarkable in the era of Jim Crow; it would be fifty-five years before another governor, Earl K. Long, would tell the legislature, at the height of the segregation hysteria, "The Negro is human, too!"

—J.B.McG.

Carleton, Mark T. *Politics and Punishment: The History of the Louisiana Penal System*. Baton Rouge: Louisiana State University Press, 1971.

"Newton Crain Blanchard, Governor, 1904–1908." *The Louisiana Governors: From Iberville to Edwards*. Joseph G. Dawson III, ed. Baton Rouge: Louisiana State University Press, 1990.

Davis, Edwin Adams. *Louisiana: A Narrative History*. Baton Rouge: Claitor's Publishing Division, 1971.

Dufour, Charles L. *Ten Flags in the Wind: The Story of Louisiana*. New York: Harper & Row, 1967.

Wall, Bennett H., ed. *Louisiana: A History*. Wheeling, IL: Harlan Davidson, 1997.

Jared Y. Sanders

1908–1912

When J. Y. Sanders and Huey P. Long squared off in the lobby of the Roosevelt Hotel in New Orleans on November 15, 1927, it was probably the only time that a former governor and a future governor came to blows during a state campaign. Long, running for governor, had attacked Sanders repeatedly in the campaign, dismissing his opponents, Congressman Riley Joe Wilson and Governor O. H. Simpson, as mere tools of Sanders.

Sanders, two dozen years older than Long, was seething at Long's slurs when he encountered him outside the hotel's dining room. Accounts of what followed depended on who was telling the story, but it appears that Sanders called Long a liar, and that Long struck him while another man held the old governor. Huey ran for the elevator, followed by Sanders, who hit him once or twice in the elevator, until they were separated by onlookers. Regardless of who said what, or struck a blow, there is no doubt that Long was seen running through the lobby with Sanders in pursuit.

Described by T. Harry Williams, Long's biographer, as a "spellbinding orator," Jared Young Sanders was born on his father's sugar plantation in St. Mary Parish on January 29, 1869. He was editor of the St. Mary *Banner*, a weekly newspaper, but turned to the law, receiving a degree from

Jared Y. Sanders. Courtesy of the *Times-Picayune*.

Tulane Law School in 1893. He opened offices in Franklin and New Orleans.

While still a newspaperman, at the age of twenty-three Sanders was elected to the state House of Representatives on the anti-lottery ticket in 1892. He served ten years in the House, which elected him its speaker in 1900. As a delegate to the 1898 constitutional convention, he was one of the authors of the infamous "grandfather clause" that effectively disenfranchised blacks. He ran for lieutenant governor with Blanchard in 1904, but soon broke with him and positioned himself as a leading candidate for governor in 1908.

Sanders defeated former congressman Theodore Wilkinson of Plaquemines Parish, an anti-lottery leader, in the Democratic primary, and beat a Republican, Henry N. Pharr, in the general election. Martin Behrman, who had been elected state auditor when Sanders was elected lieutenant governor, said that it was plain that "Sanders would be in the campaign for governor or in his grave" when the 1908 race started. Behrman said that the Sanders camp "paid poll taxes in bunches" to secure his election. Sanders, known as J.Y. throughout Louisiana, aroused strong feelings from both supporters and opponents. Governor Blanchard vigorously opposed his election, while former Governor Foster was a supporter. Behrman, who was elected mayor of New Orleans five times, was a sometime ally.

Behrman said that the largest crowd he ever saw at an inauguration attended the Sanders event, some 5,000 spectators. To the city boss's surprise, Sanders denounced gambling in his inaugural address and pledged to rid the state of betting on horse races. Since there were two tracks in New Orleans, Behrman said that Sanders's statement was "a shock." The legislature enacted the Locke law, which made racetrack gambling illegal.

Sanders's greatest ambition was to crown his political career with election to the United States Senate. When Senator Samuel D. McEnery died in 1910, the legislature elected Sanders to complete the unexpired term. He was preparing to take the seat when he was importuned by business interests to give it up. New Orleans was in a hotly contested competition with San Francisco for selection as the site of the Panama Canal Exposition, and the directors of the city's exposition company asked Sanders to remain as governor to support their bid. Sanders reluctantly announced that, if the exposition was of such importance to Louisiana that he could best serve the state's efforts to secure it by continuing as governor, he would do so. Sanders worked diligently on behalf of the New Orleans bid, but the fair went to San Francisco, where it was billed as the Panama-Pacific Exposition.

Sanders was a conservative and insisted that state government be operated on a "pay-as-you-go" basis rather than incur debt by issuing bonds. Despite this, he was the father of the "Good Roads" movement, and was known as "Gravel Roads" Sanders. He continued to champion good roads after leaving the governorship, serving as attorney for the state's first highway commission in the Parker administration. As a delegate to the 1921 Constitutional Convention, he maintained his position against bonded debt but proposed that auto and truck license fees be raised and a tax of one cent per gallon be placed on gasoline, in order to have enough funds annually to build a statewide system of gravel roads without going into debt. His ideas were adopted in the final document.

During the Sanders administration and with his support, the legislature created the Conservation Commission to oversee the state's developing natural resources and adopted the first severance taxes. He also established a separate highway fund for construction of roads and bridges and surfaced several thousand miles of state roads with gravel.

Edwin Adams Davis wrote in his history of the state that Sanders "accomplished little" as governor, contending that while J.Y. was "mildly progressive," his legislation was "lukewarm to fundamental reforms." Another historian said he "failed to keep abreast of Progressive tendencies in Louisiana and the nation at large" during his term. A differing view was taken by one who wrote that his governorship was "marked by the passage of progressive reform legislation in such areas as conservation, child labor, gambling, and prohibition." Louis Vyhnanek, in a sketch of Sanders, concluded that "his significance as governor lies in his pioneering efforts toward passage of a number of pieces of mildly progressive reform legislation reflecting some aspects of the so-called progressive movement in vogue nationally." T. Harry Williams characterized Sanders as "a thorough conservative" who had little sympathy for governmental reforms.

Sanders sought the Senate seat he coveted in 1912, but trailed Robert Broussard and withdrew from a runoff after accusing Behrman and others of double-crossing him. He told supporters that he was "ambushed."

Sanders moved to Bogalusa, in the Sixth Congressional District, was elected to the U.S. House of Representatives in 1916, and served two terms in Congress from 1917 to 1921. He lost another race for the Senate in 1920 against Edwin Broussard, who had followed his brother Robert in the seat. Sanders wanted to run against incumbent Senator Joseph E. Ransdell in 1924, but Behrman was committed to Ransdell and wanted to uphold an unwritten rule that one senator should come from North Louisiana and one from South Louisiana. He told Sanders that if he waited until 1926, the city machine of Behrman's Old Regulars would back him against Broussard, and Sanders reluctantly agreed to do so.

In the 1926 Senate race Sanders expected strong support from South Louisiana, where he was popular, even though "Coozan Ed" Broussard was a Catholic and he was a Protestant, and the southern parishes were Broussard's backyard. Sanders reasoned that if he could poll a respectable vote there, his election would be assured with a heavy vote for him by North Louisiana Protestants. Martin Behrman had died after being returned to City Hall for a fifth term, but the Old Regulars kept his promise to Sanders and supported him.

There were many crosscurrents in the race. Broussard supported repeal of Prohibition, while Sanders was anti-saloon, which was expected to help solidify his standing with North Louisiana "drys." The city machine "Ring" was "wet," but endorsed Sanders nonetheless. A splinter Ring group, calling itself the "New Regulars," campaigned for Broussard, and former governor Ruffin Pleasant endorsed him. Governor Henry L. Fuqua, whom Sanders had backed in 1924, repaid the favor by declaring for him and throwing state administration support behind him.

Sanders appeared to be the favorite until Huey P. Long endorsed Broussard and toured the state for him. The flamboyant Public Service Commissioner, who had run a strong third for governor in 1924 and was already planning a race in 1928, extracted a promise of support from Broussard then in return for his help now.

Sanders was attorney for the Watson-Williams Syndicate, which proposed a toll bridge across Lake Pontchartrain, and Long attacked him viciously, promising that he would build a free bridge that would make the toll span a "buzzard roost." With his talent for colorful invective, Long called Sanders, who had become stoop-shouldered as he aged, "Old Buzzard Back." Williams wrote that "Sanders said later that if there was anything Huey didn't say against him, it was an oversight." Sanders, responding to Long, said: "When it comes to arousing prejudice and passion, when it comes to ranting and raving, when it comes to vituperation and vilification, when it comes to denunciation and demagoguery, there is one who stands out by himself alone. He has many imitators but no equals."

Broussard won a narrow victory, dashing Sanders's dream of a Senate seat. It is ironic that he gave up the seat to which the legislature elected him, and which he would have been favored to hold onto in the next election, only to lose three elections for the Senate in following years.

In the 1928 state election, Huey Long castigated Sanders for his support of toll bridges and said that it did not matter to Sanders whether

Simpson or Wilson was elected, because both were his stooges. Long claimed that Sanders controlled the city and state machines and was spokesman for the big corporations. Their enmity for each other was passionate, and it is no wonder that they came to blows.

J. Y. Sanders Jr., known as "Little J.Y.," was elected to the state House of Representatives from East Baton Rouge Parish, and was a member of the "Dynamite Squad" of legislators who opposed Long. He was a ringleader in the impeachment of Long. A former Long bodyguard, Representative Battling Bozeman of Caddo Parish, said that Long told him to kill Sanders, although "Little J.Y." believed Long was drunk and did not mean his threat to be taken literally. Sanders was elected to Congress from the Sixth District, the seat his father, J. Y. Sanders Sr., once held, and participated in the DeSoto Hotel conference of anti-Longs in 1935, at which Long claimed a plot to murder him was discussed.

The elder Sanders supported impeachment as well, and when the legislature convened, joined former Governor Parker in lobbying House members to unseat Long's ally, John B. Fournet, as speaker, an effort that failed. Sanders opposed Long during the following years and felt no remorse when his bitter enemy was assassinated. Two former governors, Sanders and Parker, were mourners at the funeral of Dr. Carl Austin Weiss, who shot Long.

Sanders continued to practice law and follow state politics until his death in Baton Rouge on March 23, 1944, at age 75. While historians have widely differing views of him, J. Y. Sanders was one of the truly "big men" of state politics. The best assessment of his achievements was made by Louis Vyhnanek, who said, "He was a strong executive who knew how to take charge and a skilled politician who knew how to gain passage of his legislative program. The position of chief executive in Louisiana was certainly strengthened during his term."

—J.B.McG.

Conrad, Glenn R. *A Dictionary of Louisiana Biography*. New Orleans: Louisiana Historical Association, 1988.

Davis, Edwin Adams. *Louisiana: A Narrative History*. Baton Rouge: Claitor's Publishing Division, 1971.

Dethloff, Henry C. "The Longs: Revolution or Populist Retrenchment." *Louisiana History* (Fall 1978).

Dufour, Charles L. *Ten Flags in the Wind: The Story of Louisiana*. New York: Harper & Row, 1967.

Kemp, John, ed. *Martin Behrman of New Orleans: Memoirs of a City Boss*. Baton Rouge: Louisiana State University Press, 1977.

Sindler, Allan P. *Huey Long's Louisiana: State Politics, 1920–1952*. Baltimore: The Johns Hopkins Press, 1971.

Vyhnanek, Louis. "J. Y. Sanders, Governor, 1908–1912." *The Louisiana Governors: From Iberville to Edwards*. Joseph G. Dawson III, ed. Baton Rouge: Louisiana State University Press, 1990.

Wall, Bennett H., ed. *Louisiana: A History*. Wheeling, IL: Harlan Davidson, 1997.

Williams, T. Harry. *Huey Long*. New York: Alfred A. Knopf, 1969.

Luther E. Hall

1912–1916

For most governors of Louisiana, election to that office represented the capstone of their political ambitions. Some went on to the United States Senate, others served as senator prior to their elections as governor; but as a general rule, with the exceptions of Claiborne, who aspired to national office but died before he could seek it, and Huey Long, whose threatened third-party campaign for the presidency was stilled by an assassin's bullet, the governorship was the culmination of their political ambitions.

Luther E. Hall is unique in that regard. He may have been the only governor who wished that he had never run for the office, much less won it, and who was happier to serve as an assistant attorney general after leaving the office than he ever was when he held it. Mayor Martin Behrman, the longtime machine boss of New Orleans, wrote that Hall was the only governor he had known "who was elected to that office without desiring it in the least."

Hall was born in Bastrop, in Morehouse Parish, on August 30, 1869. He received an undergraduate degree from Washington and Lee University and a law degree from Tulane, and after opening a law practice that served clients in Ouachita and Morehouse Parishes, completed an unex-

Luther E. Hall. Courtesy of the *Times-Picayune*.

pired term in the state senate from that area. He was subsequently elected a district court judge, and then a judge of the Court of Appeal.

Hall won the Democratic nomination to a seat on the state Supreme Court in 1911, and eagerly anticipated his associate justice's position the following year. Fate intervened in the person of John M. Parker and a split in the Democratic factions that dominated the state.

The Regular Democratic Organization—known as the RDO, the Old Regulars, or the Choctaw Club—and its great chief Martin Behrman, the longtime mayor of New Orleans, had previously allied with courthouse gangs at parish seats and cotton planters to install a succession of governors. Their bargain was a simple, strictly political one: the urban organization delivered a heavy city vote for the agreed-upon candidate as well as support for the Bourbons from the city's legislative delegation, and the country politicians took a "hands-off" policy toward the machine's rule in New Orleans, while awarding the Regulars the state patronage there.

As Matthew J. Schott noted, "Such an alliance made it quite difficult for any rival or reform faction within—or without—the Democratic party to come to power as long as the city machine and country Bourbons worked in close harmony and delivered their votes." That alliance elected three governors between 1908 and 1924: J. Y. Sanders (1908–12), Ruffin G. Pleasant (1916–20), and Henry Fuqua (1924–26). Its hold on the statehouse was broken in 1912 and 1920, and in both instances, John M. Parker was the agent of its defeat, first by backing Luther E. Hall in 1912, and then running for governor himself in 1920.

In the 1912 election the Choctaw Club wanted John T. Michel, the incumbent secretary of state, while the courthouse machines and cotton planters favored James B. Aswell, who had a distinguished tenure as state superintendent of education. The Good Government League, based in New Orleans but with support in some southern parishes, called for "businesslike" administration of state government. Its leader, John M. Parker, who had made a fortune from family cotton plantations in Mississippi, persuaded Hall to enter the race as a reform candidate.

The Choctaws carried Michel in New Orleans, but Hall won 43 percent of the statewide vote, and Michel withdrew from the runoff. Hall took office on May 20, 1912, with mixed feelings, as he had to give up the Supreme Court seat prior to assuming it in order to take the governorship.

In another study of the state's governors, Matthew J. Schott contended that "Hall's governorship was characterized by weak leadership, albeit the enactment of some reforms identified with progressivism, including passage of a workmen's compensation law, the first enacted in the South." The Hall administration was considered unspectacular, but he did have accomplishments and was able to increase tax revenues through a reorganization of assessments. He also secured legislative approval of a commission council form of municipal government for New Orleans, a goal of the reform element, but Behrman and his allies won a resounding victory in the next city election. Hall's plans for a constitutional convention in 1915 were thwarted by feuding between the Old Regulars and the reformers. When Mayor Behrman (in expectation of serving as its chairman) supported the call for the convention, John M. Parker, who was disenchanted with Hall, opposed it.

After he left office, Hall sought support from both the reformers and the Regulars for the U.S. Senate seat held by Robert Broussard, who had died with his term unexpired. Behrman supported Edward J. Gay, and Hall was rebuffed.

Hall was appointed an assistant attorney general in 1918, a position that he professed to enjoy holding more than governor. He was defeated in a contest for the state Supreme Court in 1921. Hall died of a heart attack in New Orleans on November 6, 1921. Behrman, who liked him personally, said that Hall died of a broken heart after losing the Supreme Court race.

Behrman said that when Luther Hall gave you his word he could be absolutely depended on, but "he was very slow about making up his mind to do anything." The mayor thought Hall's "slow deliberation over matters" was an admirable quality in a judge but hindered his success as governor. Hall told Behrman that he never liked being governor and should have passed on that race and taken his seat on the Supreme Court. Instead, Behrman wrote, "The queer tricks and turns of our politics placed a good, clean, hard-working man, mentally trained and by character a judge, in the position of an administrator. He took it because he thought it was his duty to take it, and he was always sorry he did."

In evaluating Hall's administration, Schott said that he was "apparently honest, well meaning, and conscientious," but did not have the necessary leadership or legislative support to achieve his most important goals, including constitutional revision and tax reform to refinance the state debt.

—J.B.McG.

Conrad, Glenn R. *A Dictionary of Louisiana Biography*. New Orleans: Louisiana Historical Association, 1988.

Davis, Edwin Adams. *Louisiana: A Narrative History*. Baton Rouge: Claitor's Publishing Division, 1971.

Dufour, Charles L. *Ten Flags in the Wind: The Story of Louisiana*. New York: Harper & Row, 1967.

Kemp, John, ed. *Martin Behrman of New Orleans: Memoirs of a City Boss*. Baton Rouge: Louisiana State University Press, 1977.

Schott, Matthew J. *Louisiana Politics and the Paradoxes of Reaction and Reform*. Vol. VII of the Louisiana Purchase Bicentennial Series in Louisiana History. Lafayette: Center for Louisiana Studies, 2000.

———. "Luther E. Hall, Governor, 1912–1916." *The Louisiana Governors: From Iberville to Edwards*. Joseph G. Dawson III, ed. Baton Rouge: Louisiana State University Press, 1990.

Wall, Bennett H., ed. *Louisiana: A History*. Wheeling, IL: Harlan Davidson, 1997.

Ruffin G. Pleasant

1916–1920

Several Louisiana governors have been distinguished by their ardent support of the LSU football team, notably Huey Long and John J. McKeithen, but Ruffin Golson Pleasant was the only governor who was captain of the Tigers, in Louisiana's first intercollegiate game, a 34–0 drubbing by Tulane.

Pleasant was born in Shiloh, in Union Parish, on June 2, 1871. Following graduation from LSU he studied law in the East, at both Harvard and Yale. He was lieutenant colonel of the First Louisiana Infantry Regiment in the Spanish-American War, after which he opened a law office in Shreveport. He was city attorney for Shreveport from 1902 to 1908. He was defeated for attorney general in 1908, but served as an assistant attorney general from 1908 to 1912, when he was elected attorney general.

In the 1916 state election J. Y. Sanders persuaded Pleasant to declare for governor, and he won the influential support of Robert Ewing, a political power in New Orleans, who was publisher of the *Daily States* there and the *Times* in Shreveport. To the surprise of many, Pleasant was also anointed as the candidate of New Orleans Mayor Martin Behrman and the Regular Democratic Organization. Their hearts were with Lieutenant

Ruffin G. Pleasant. Courtesy of the *Times-Picayune*.

Governor Thomas O. Barret, who had served sixteen years in the state Senate, but their heads were with Pleasant.

Behrman said that the city political machine (or "Ring") "followed their usual policy of going to the candidate who apparently had a majority of votes in the parishes outside Orleans. It had sometimes turned out that the Regulars did not show accurate judgment in picking a candidate, but they always preferred to back a man who had the country folks with him. In this instance they decided on Ruffin G. Pleasant."

Outgoing governor Hall supported Barret, but was taken aback when his lieutenant governor, who had previously supported local option on liquor, came out for a statewide ban. Pleasant was for local option, and the only issue left in doubt after Barret's announcement was how big Pleasant's majority would be. Behrman explained in his disarmingly candid memoir, "There are thousands of voters who are devoted to prohibition at home so long as they may take a train to Alexandria, Eunice, or New Orleans and go wet for a few hours. They are strictly local option. Their option is to be dry at home and wet when off on a visit."

Pleasant rolled over Barret 84,407 to 30,112. He carried New Orleans 29,557 to 3,758, and in the general election defeated John M. Parker, running on the Progressive party ticket, 80,801 to 48,068. While Behrman could claim much credit for Pleasant's huge majority in the city, he feared that Sanders, for whom he had no love, would wield enormous influence over him at the expense of the Regulars. In this he was pleasantly surprised, as the governor gave the state patronage in New Orleans to the Ring. Matthew J. Schott said that Pleasant was "the closest thing to what reformers called a tool of the Ring than [*sic*] any other governor." Behrman wrote, "I certainly did not expect Governor Pleasant to appoint any of our enemies to office. On the other hand, I did not expect to come so near to having one hundred per cent of our recommendations go through." The mayor said that the Regulars had more influence with Pleasant on jobs than they had ever received from Governors Foster, Heard, Blanchard, and Sanders.

Behrman said that as attorney general, Pleasant was "neither conspicuously able nor bad enough to deserve any unqualified condemnation," with a record that "gave no reason to believe he would not be a good governor." The Pleasant administration was largely uneventful. The governor was energetic in mobilizing support for American entry into World War I and encouraging the war effort, but he failed to gain passage of his proposals for a constitutional convention and refunding of the state debt. Characterized as "ever the opportunist" in politics, he shocked even Behrman when he endorsed the national Prohibition amendment in 1919, after being elected governor with the support of local option forces.

Pleasant supported the call for a constitutional convention in 1920 and was elected a delegate to it. When the call was issued, Pleasant suggested that the delegate qualifications should rule eligible every citizen "whose ancestry immediately previous to the discovery of America by Christopher Columbus in the year 1492 inhabited any part of the earth north of the 20 degree north latitude, as shown by historical and anthropological evidence." The line Pleasant drew excluded Africa and made all blacks ineligible for election as delegates.

Pleasant was very active in the deliberations of the convention, which produced the 1921 Constitution. Pleasant and State Railroad Commissioner Huey P. Long had both supported John M. Parker in his successful election as governor in 1920, but they joined in opposition to Parker's convention proposals for severance taxes on the state's mineral resources. In the 1924 election, Pleasant, J. Y. Sanders, and Behrman all supported Henry L. Fuqua in his successful race for governor, when Huey Long ran a strong third. Pleasant supported Long in the 1928 election but, after Long took office, became a vocal opponent of the Kingfish.

Pleasant died in Shreveport on September 12, 1937, remembered more for his reversals on local option and on Huey Long, and his characterization as a "creature" of the Ring in New Orleans, than for any substantial achievements as governor.

—J.B.McG.

Conrad, Glenn R. *A Dictionary of Louisiana Biography*. New Orleans: Louisiana Historical Association, 1988.

Davis, Edwin Adams. *Louisiana: A Narrative History*. Baton Rouge: Claitor's Publishing Division, 1971.

Dufour, Charles L. *Ten Flags in the Wind: The Story of Louisiana*. New York: Harper & Row, 1967.

Kemp, John, ed. *Martin Behrman of New Orleans: Memoirs of a City Boss*. Baton Rouge: Louisiana State University Press, 1977.

Schott, Matthew J. "Ruffin G. Pleasant, Governor, 1916–1920." *The Louisiana Governors: From Iberville to Edwards*. Joseph G. Dawson III, ed. Baton Rouge: Louisiana State University Press, 1990.

Wall, Bennett H., ed. *Louisiana: A History*. Wheeling, IL: Harlan Davidson, 1997.

John M. Parker

1920–1924

John M. Parker, in his long and distinguished life, battled such diverse enemies as the Ku Klux Klan, the Mafia, and Huey Long, according to historian William Ivy Hair. There is no doubt that, while he regarded them as equally evil, he reserved his greatest contempt for Long. For recreation, Parker enjoyed hunting and killing snakes on his farm at Bayou Sara; he probably associated the Kingfish with those creatures.

"He was in many ways the antithesis of Huey Long," Hair wrote. "Parker was dignified, honor-bound, and taciturn; Huey was indecorous, devious, and loquacious. Parker thought first about principles, Huey of results. Parker actually was indifferent about his political future; Huey pretended not to care, but in fact nothing was more important. Parker thought leadership meant pointing the way and setting a good example; Huey believed a leader should compel. Parker lacked imagination but had integrity; Long possessed imagination without integrity. Unavoidably, the two were fated to become the worst of enemies."

John Milliken Parker was born in Bethel Green, Mississippi, near Port Gibson, on March 16, 1863. He attended several private academies and business schools, but passed up college to enter his father's firm. The

John M. Parker. Courtesy of the *Times-Picayune*.

elder Parker, also John M., had moved the family to New Orleans in 1872, where he became a prosperous merchant and cotton factor, while retaining his plantation holdings in the Delta.

Parker's father was a member of the Crescent City White League. He answered the call to meet at the Clay statue to overthrow Carpetbag misrule, and participated in the Battle of Liberty Place on September 14, 1874. The White League gained a victory over the reconstruction administration of Governor William Pitt Kellogg and its metropolitan police, but could not take over the state government after President Grant sent troops and warships to support Kellogg. In 1924 Governor Parker was the principal speaker at the ceremonies marking the fiftieth anniversary of the Battle of Liberty Place.

Parker eventually took over his father's businesses and sold the cotton plantations in Mississippi. He became one of the wealthiest men in Louisiana, served as president of the New Orleans Cotton Exchange and the Board of Trade, and married into a prominent family. Matthew J. Schott, in an evaluation of Parker for *The Louisiana Governors*, wrote that Parker "disliked the social demands of his wife and the obligations of his status in the city, and he submitted only once, and with distaste, to ruling as king of Comus, New Orleans' most prestigious Mardi Gras krewe." Parker preferred hunting and fishing to parties and balls. He "regarded the formal debut as snobbish and the Carnival as a frivolous waste," in the belief that the energy and money spent on those pursuits should be directed to civic betterment.

Parker became a leader in reform politics and good government initiatives. He looked down on professional politicians and supported candidates for mayor and governor who were opposed to the Ring, the Regular Democratic Association that dominated New Orleans politics for fifty years.

In 1888 he was one of the organizers of the Young Men's Democratic Association, a reform group opposed to the Old Regulars.

In March 1891 Parker was a ringleader of the lynch mob that killed eleven Sicilian immigrants accused of belonging to the Mafia and implicated in the assassination of Chief of Police David C. Hennessey. When a jury that the public believed had been coerced or purchased acquitted the men, a mass meeting was called at the Clay statue on March 14, 1891. Its purpose was to "remedy the failure of justice," and citizens were told to "come prepared for action." Parker was one of the sixty-one signers of the newspaper notice. Thousands responded and marched on the Parish Prison, where they shot or hanged the Sicilians. While Parker did not kill any of the men personally, he had no apologies for his part in the lynching, then or later, because he believed that justice had been done.

Although a Democrat, Parker was an admirer of Theodore Roosevelt, whom he met in 1898 when the Rough Riders passed through New Orleans en route to Cuba. He tried to enlist with them, but was turned down because of a lifelong asthmatic condition. Parker and Roosevelt became fast friends, making hunting and fishing trips together in following years. The most memorable one was in 1907, when he accompanied the president on a lengthy hunting trip in the Tensas swamp. When they cornered a bear, Roosevelt could not get a clear shot at him, so Parker leaped forward and killed the animal with a Bowie knife.

Parker's reform credentials included his leadership in the Citizens' League in 1896, the Good Government League in 1912, the Progressive Party in 1916, and the Orleans Democratic Association in 1920.

Mayor Martin Behrman, longtime boss of the Old Regulars, dismissed Parker as one of the "outs wanting in," but Parker's career reflects a commitment to what he saw as his duty. He was the embodiment of a gentleman, although his dignified bearing made many think him aloof and lacking in a common touch. T. Harry Williams, in his biography of Huey Long, wrote, "Louisianians did not always agree with John M. Parker, but they could not ignore him, and they felt a perverse pride in him even when they disagreed with him or when he violated some of the most respected tenets of Louisiana and Southern politics."

Those taboos included supporting his friend Teddy in Roosevelt's "Bull Moose" campaign against Taft and Wilson in 1912 and running for governor in 1916 as a Progressive. Roosevelt elected Wilson by splitting the Republican party, and Parker went down to defeat by Ruffin G. Pleasant in the state election. Parker had been an early and influential supporter of Governor Luther E. Hall in 1912, and after he received 38 percent of the vote as a Progressive in 1916, he was viewed as the frontrunner for 1920.

After his loss for governor, the national Progressive party nominated Parker for vice president in 1916. When Roosevelt declined the nomination for president and endorsed the Republican, Charles Evans Hughes, the Progressive party folded, and Parker returned to the Democratic party and supported Wilson's re-election.

Parker was on good terms with Wilson despite his friendship with Roosevelt. He joined Teddy in petitioning Wilson to allow them to raise a "Rough Rider Division" of middle-aged men to fight in France, with T.R. as its general and Parker as colonel of a Louisiana regiment, but the president turned them down. Instead, Parker was appointed food administrator for Louisiana by Federal Food Administrator Herbert Hoover, and served in that post during 1917–18. When U. S. senator Robert Broussard died in 1918, Governor Pleasant offered Parker appointment to the vacancy. Parker declined because he thought he had a duty to continue in his job as food administrator.

Parker, William Ivy Hair said, "attained something that, for anyone involved in state politics, was almost as rare as gold in Louisiana—national respectability."

Parker ran for governor in 1920 as a Democrat, against Colonel Frank P. Stubbs of Monroe, the standard-bearer of the Old Regular–planter alliance. Stubbs had served with distinction in France as colonel of the First Louisiana regiment. Parker won the Democratic primary 77,686 to 65,685 and had an easy victory over a Republican opponent in the general election.

Parker was elected with the support of the Good Government League, the Orleans Democratic Association (a breakaway group from the Old Regulars), and Governor Ruffin G. Pleasant, who had defeated him in 1916. Pleasant dismissed hundreds of state patronage employees in New Orleans who were Ring men supporting Stubbs, and replaced them with men who pledged support to Parker. In a strange twist, J. Y. Sanders also backed Parker. He had been elected governor with Behrman's support in 1908 but was angered at the Ring's failure to support him for U.S. senator, and he now stumped for Parker, attacking the Ring as "the Hun that is ever thundering at our gates."

The most interesting member of the Parker coalition was Huey P. Long, described as "the crusading young railroad commissioner from the third district" in North Louisiana. Long said he backed Parker after receiving his commitment to support regulation of pipelines to protect small, independent oil and gas production from Standard Oil and other large companies. Long stumped tirelessly for Parker, delivering votes for him in North Louisiana and claiming credit for the victory.

In a terse inaugural address, Parker said, "We have played too much politics and too little common sense."

The authors of *Louisiana: A History* wrote that Parker's election "formed the most promising break yet with Louisiana's slowly decaying Bourbon past." With a businesslike approach and absolute integrity, Parker was very different from many of his predecessors. He pushed through the Constitution of 1921, the first state severance tax on natural resources, and created a new campus for LSU, moving the university to its present site from one near the capitol. He had previously opposed women's suffrage, but supported it in the 1920 election. He retained his paternalistic view toward blacks and did not favor their right to vote. He had originally opposed women's suffrage on the grounds that giving women the right to vote would set a precedent for enfranchisement of blacks.

Allan Sindler, a keen student of state politics during the Huey Long era, characterized Parker as "a gentlemanly reformer elected largely on his pledge to end Ring rule of the state." Parker first had to destroy the Ring hold on New Orleans, and he used his power as governor to defeat it in the 1920 city election. He backed the reformer, Andrew McShane, who beat Behrman for mayor by only 1,450 votes, with the support of Parker's Orleans Democratic Association. Behrman found it ironic that Parker, a longtime supporter of civil service, fired those Ring members still on the state payroll and replaced them with men pledged to vote for and support McShane. Parker supported a provision in the 1921 constitution that authorized the legislature to enact a merit system for the city government, but did nothing to implement it, to allow McShane to build reform support with patronage. William Ivy Hair wrote that "Parker hated the Ring so much that he was willing to cooperate with a new machine trying to take its place." The reform victory lasted for only one term, and Behrman stormed back into office for a fifth term as mayor, dying soon after taking office. Sindler wrote that both Parker and the reform administration in New Orleans "were as blind to city vice and gambling as the Ring had been."

When Parker sponsored the severance tax in the 1921 constitution, he expressed his views that business and industry should pay their fair share of the tax burden. He wanted to use the additional revenue to expand LSU, particularly in its agricultural college. He was far ahead of his time in proposing that the tax be based on the value of the resource severed rather than its quantity. The constitution allowed the legislature by statute to tax either the value or the quantity.

Believing that government and business should be conducted by gentlemen, Parker allowed Standard Oil's attorneys to advise him during the convention and to assist in drafting the legislation. Huey Long wanted to declare pipelines common carriers, giving small producers access to them. Parker shared that goal, but the major companies that owned the pipelines fought them furiously. A compromise was effected, brokered by the governor, that gave the independent producers most of what they wanted. They were satisfied but Long was not. Parker spoke of "gentlemen's agreements" to resolve the pipeline issue and pass the severance tax; Long attacked him as a tool of Standard Oil and issued circulars denouncing him for turning the governor's office over to the company. Parker, claiming that Long had attacked his "character," swore out a warrant against him on charges of criminal libel.

Parker said that if Long's charges were true, then he was not fit to be governor, but if they were false, then Long should be removed from office as a public service commissioner, the designation the constitutional convention had given the old railroad commission.

At Long's trial Parker denounced him as a liar, but unwittingly acknowledged that he had in fact allowed Standard Oil's legal department to write the severance tax law. Long was found guilty, but the judge, deciding that Long should have his comeuppance but the penalty should not be too great for what was essentially a political dispute, gave him a suspended sentence on the first count. On the second count Long was fined one dollar or one hour in prison. He refused to pay, and his attorney put up the dollar.

Parker also dealt with the legislature as a gentleman presenting matters to a board. He did not try to force some parts of his program on them, to the regret of some supporters. He was a vigorous opponent of the rejuvenated Ku Klux Klan. In a sensational case, two Klan opponents were murdered. Parker asked the legislature to enact an anti-masking law, but it failed to receive consideration, with opponents contending that an old statute forbidding masking except at Mardi Gras was sufficient to deal with the modern Klan as it had with the Reconstruction organization.

In the 1924 election, Henry L. Fuqua, general manager of the state penitentiary, was supported by former governors Sanders and Pleasant. While Parker had reappointed Fuqua to his post at Angola, his choice for governor was his lieutenant governor, Hewitt Bouanchaud, a French Catholic from Pointe Coupee Parish. Huey Long, in his first race for governor, denounced them as the "Parker Gold Dust Twins."

Long ran a strong third. Fuqua won the election but died two years later, and was succeeded by his lieutenant governor, Oramel H. Simpson. Some observers viewed Fuqua's victory as a rejection of Parker, but Bouanchaud had an uphill battle, handicapped by his Catholicism, and Parker stood by him on principle.

With the 1928 election shaping up as a contest between Simpson and Long, some state politicians asked Parker to run again to stop Long, but he refused, stating that when he left office in 1924, he had vowed never to run for any office again. Parker did render further public service in 1927, when Secretary of Commerce Herbert Hoover, who had named him federal food administrator for Louisiana in 1917, appointed him director of flood relief. Parker worked heroically to relieve the widespread suffering caused by the massive destruction of the Great Flood of 1927.

After Long's election as governor in 1928, in the controversies that followed, anti-Longs and businessmen formed the Constitutional League and elected Parker its president after the Senate failed to convict Long on House articles of impeachment. He was one of Long's most outspoken foes, and forsook his plans for retirement to his farm to oversee investigations of corruption in the Long administration. When the Constitutional League published a list of twenty-three of the governor's relatives on the state payroll, Long dismissed the report with the observation that they had missed several. He ridiculed Parker's organization as the "Constipational League."

Long controlled the party machinery in the state, but the anti-Longs sent their own delegation to the 1932 Democratic Convention, headed by three former governors: Sanders, Pleasant, and Parker. Long ridiculed the group as "just a bunch of exes." The convention upheld the decision of the credentials committee to seat Long's delegation after he made a masterful oration on its behalf.

Parker opposed Long's election to the U.S. Senate in 1930, denouncing him as "a creature devoid of every element of honor and decency." In the 1932 election he made statewide radio addresses, opposing the "Complete the Work of Huey P. Long" slate. When Long's candidate, John H. Overton, defeated U.S. Senator Edwin S. Broussard in 1932, Parker joined other anti-Longs in claiming vote fraud by the Long machine and asking for a Senate investigation. After hearings held in New Orleans, a subcommittee of the Senate concluded that there had been fraud, but it would not have altered the outcome, and Overton was seated. The anti-Longs continued to demand that both Long and Overton be expelled from the Senate for their election tactics.

In supporting one petition seeking Long's expulsion from the Senate, Parker wrote a covering letter to Vice President John N. Garner stating: "Senator Huey Long knows neither truth, honesty, or decency. His black record in our state is nationally known. Psychiatrists in my presence have stated that he is a dangerous paranoiac. The Senate should have him examined by experts and to save certain trouble and probable future killing have him permanently incarcerated in the criminal insane hospital in Washington."

By 1934 Parker and Sanders were leaders for President Roosevelt in the state. They embraced the president because they had concluded that only the powers of the national government could bring the Kingfish to heel. Roosevelt, fearing that Long would lead a third-party movement that would split the vote and elect a Republican in 1936, was determined to destroy Long politically. Federal patronage was channeled through several anti-Long congressmen, as well as Parker and Sanders, and an investigation of income tax returns of Long and a number of his political supporters was opened.

Parker supported overthrow of the Long dictatorship by the ballot box, but feared that the regime was too entrenched and its power too great. The Square Deal Association, formed in 1934 with chapters in many parishes, proposed to overthrow the Kingfish and his state administration, headed by the compliant Governor Oscar K. Allen, by armed revolt if necessary. Parker was a member, but did not participate in the "Battle of the Airport" in Baton Rouge, in which the state guard dispersed several hundred Square Dealers with only minor injuries.

In July 1935 Sanders, Parker, Mayor T. Semmes Walmsley of New Orleans, and congressmen opposed to Long met with anti-Long political figures from throughout the state in a two-day conference at the DeSoto Hotel in New Orleans to decide on a ticket for the 1936 state election and to plot strategy. Long charged on the floor of the Senate that they met to plot his murder as well, claiming that a dictograph recording from a microphone that one of his allies planted by an open window caught references to killing him with "one man, one gun, and one bullet." Participants responded that it was a public meeting, that a few men in one room might have talked about killing Long, but many people thought that was the only way to remove him from power. Parker told friends that whenever anti-Longs talked, someone always said that "the only way to get rid of the S.O.B. is to kill him."

Parker was one of the most respected men in Louisiana and had friends throughout the state. One was Dr. Carl Adam Weiss in Baton Rouge. Parker was a patient and friend of Dr. Weiss (who also treated Huey Long for an eye irritation on one occasion) and was an occasional dinner guest at the Weiss home. When Carl Austin Weiss shot Huey Long in the capitol building on September 8, 1935, and was riddled with bullets by Long's bodyguards, Parker comforted the grieving father. Carl Weiss was buried before Huey Long died from his wound, and the aging former governor, thin and frail, who had been called "Old Sack of Bones" by Huey, stood in the rain at the cemetery among a large gathering of mourners. Parker did not live to see Sam Jones elected as a reform governor in 1940, ousting the heirs of Huey Long and defeating the Kingfish's younger brother, Earl K. Long. He died at his summer home in Pass Christian, Mississippi, on May 20, 1939.

T. Harry Williams wrote that, while Parker was praised by some as the first chief executive to recognize the need for social change and take positive steps to advance it, "judged in a larger context, he was a failure, a prime example of the tragedy of the progressive reformer limited by his own vision. His most serious error, say some commentators, was that he did not destroy the New Orleans Ring and build his own organization." In that sense, Williams said, Parker's problems as governor were not the result of a failure to use political means, but rather a reluctance to "use them with enough frequency and ruthlessness."

He was "a significant transitional figure, bridging the chasm between Louisiana's reactionary planter–Old Regular oligarchy and the explosive populism of Huey Long," Bennett H. Wall and his colleagues said. Sindler agreed that Parker made Huey Long possible through his failures to destroy the Ring, bring natural gas to New Orleans, and oppose the J. Y. Sanders "pay-as-you-go" program for road construction as it became clear that the only way to bring the state out of the mud was through a massive highway program funded by bonds. Williams called Parker "a very special figure in state politics, the most compelling personality to appear in the first twenty years of the century." Williams believed that Parker was the precursor to Long, however, stating that "Politicians like Parker prepare the way for revolutionary change. They improve conditions somewhat, enough to arouse desires for more change but not enough to satisfy existing needs. They sow the seeds, but bolder men have to do the harvesting."

John M. Parker felt that Louisiana paid a terrible price for the harvest brought in by Huey Long. He would have been satisfied with this epitaph: "One of the state's most admired men; his reputation for honesty, independence, and sincerity of purpose stood in shining contrast" to most politicians of his era.

—J.B.McG.

Davis, Edwin Adams. *Louisiana: A Narrative History*. Baton Rouge: Claitor's Publishing Division, 1971.

Dethloff, Henry C. "The Longs: Revolution or Populist Retrenchment." *Louisiana History* (Fall 1978).

Dufour, Charles L. *Ten Flags in the Wind: The Story of Louisiana*. New York: Harper & Row, 1967.

Kemp, John, ed. *Martin Behrman of New Orleans: Memoirs of a City Boss*. Baton Rouge: Louisiana State University Press, 1977.

Schott, Matthew J. "John M. Parker, Governor, 1920–1924." *The Louisiana Governors: From Iberville to Edwards*. Joseph G. Dawson III, ed. Baton Rouge: Louisiana State University Press, 1990.

Sindler, Allan P. *Huey Long's Louisiana: State Politics, 1920–1952*. Baltimore: Johns Hopkins Press, 1971.

Wall, Bennett H., ed. *Louisiana: A History*. Wheeling, IL: Harlan Davidson, 1997.

Williams, T. Harry. *Huey Long*. New York: Alfred A. Knopf, 1969.

Henry L. Fuqua

1924–1926

It has been reported that when Governor Henry Luse Fuqua died at the executive mansion in Baton Rouge, inmates of the Louisiana State Penitentiary shed tears at his loss. Fuqua was appointed general manager of the prison by Governor Pleasant and was reappointed by Governor Parker. He was described as a kindly man who won the trust of convicts by improving conditions at the facility.

Born in Baton Rouge on November 8, 1865, the son of a veteran of both the Mexican and Civil Wars, Fuqua attended LSU, worked on construction projects, and started his own hardware company after clerking in another store. A good businessman, he expanded into farm supplies and sugarcane, cotton and rice growing. His skills at large-scale farming operations attracted Pleasant's attention, as the penitentiary used convict labor for its farms, and he accepted the governor's invitation to take over the prison operation. Fuqua was very successful in his administration of the prison. Louis Vyhnanek, in his essay about Fuqua for *The Louisiana Governors: From Iberville to Edwards*, said that under his direction "the penitentiary's vast agricultural resources began to turn a profit." He also

Henry L. Fuqua. Courtesy of the *Times-Picayune*.

abolished the traditional striped uniforms of prisoners and began use of inmate trusties as guards.

Fuqua had demonstrated no prior interest in elective office and was literally drafted by friends and admirers to run for governor in 1924. T. Harry Williams wrote that "heavily built and paunchy, with a pudgy face and sparse hair, he was not a particularly dynamic figure or a very impressive public speaker. But he had an affable and friendly manner that stood him well in individual contacts, and he looked like a solid, safe small-town businessman who could be depended on to do nothing rash."

The principal candidates in the 1924 race were Fuqua, a Protestant from South Louisiana; Hewitt Bouanchaud, a French Catholic from Pointe Coupee Parish in South Louisiana; and Huey P. Long, a Protestant from North Louisiana.

Bouanchaud was an early favorite as the incumbent lieutenant governor under Parker, who supported him. Former governors Sanders and Pleasant supported Fuqua, as did the New Orleans Ring led by former Mayor Martin Behrman, who was maneuvering for a comeback at City Hall. Behrman, explaining his preference for Fuqua over Bouanchaud, said that a Catholic had "practically no chance of being elected" governor.

Several historians believe that Parker supported Bouanchaud solely out of loyalty to his lieutenant, but it is likely that Parker welcomed the opportunity to elect his own chosen successor over the opposition of the Ring. Parker also thought that Fuqua and Long were waffling on the Klan issue, while Bouanchaud denounced it as a hooded menace. All three candidates were publicly against the Klan, but Bouanchaud pledged to support a strong anti-masking law and to require secret societies to file lists of their members with the secretary of state's office.

The Klan and religion were major issues in the election, with Prohibition a sideshow. Fuqua said that he was a "theoretical prohibitionist." Behrman said that most people were in that class: "They advocate the theory and they practice it whenever they have no opportunity to do otherwise."

Long, public service commissioner from the North Louisiana district, claimed that the real issues facing the state were being neglected in the controversies over the Klan and liquor, and he promised an extensive program of public improvements. He ridiculed Fuqua and Bouanchaud as the "Gold Dust Twins" of John M. Parker.

Bouanchaud led in the primary vote, with 84,162 to Fuqua's 81,382. Long finished a surprisingly strong third, with 73,985 ballots. Long did not make an endorsement in the runoff, but the great majority of his supporters went for Fuqua, who won 125,880 to 92,006.

Fuqua served as governor from May 19, 1924, until October 11, 1926. At his instigation, the legislature passed strong anti-Klan laws. "The most important of the measures, passed in 1924, made it a misdemeanor to wear a mask in a public place except on Mardi Gras and a felony for a masked person to commit an assault," Vyhnanek noted.

The legislature authorized the state highway commission to contract with private investors to build a toll bridge across Lake Pontchartrain near the eastern boundary of New Orleans. The franchise to build the bridge was awarded to the Watson-Williams syndicate, represented by Sanders. The controversy over the toll bridge provided a ready-made issue for Huey Long, who promised a free bridge in his 1928 campaign for governor.

Fuqua was a strong supporter of LSU and Southern University in Baton Rouge. He ran an honest, respectable administration as a businessman-governor, operating behind the scenes but "capable of forceful leadership when necessary, as when he moved quickly to implement anti-Klan legislation."

—J.B.McG.

Conrad, Glenn R. *A Dictionary of Louisiana Biography*. New Orleans: Louisiana Historical Association, 1988.

Davis, Edwin Adams. *Louisiana: A Narrative History*. Baton Rouge: Claitor's Publishing Division, 1971.

Dufour, Charles L. *Ten Flags in the Wind: The Story of Louisiana*. New York: Harper & Row, 1967.

Hair, William Ivy. *The Kingfish and His Realm: The Life and Times of Huey P. Long*. Baton Rouge: Louisiana State University Press, 1991.

Kemp, John, ed. *Martin Behrman of New Orleans: Memoirs of a City Boss*. Baton Rouge: Louisiana State University Press, 1977.

Sindler, Allen P. *Huey Long's Louisiana: State Politics, 1920–52*. Baltimore: Johns Hopkins Press, 1971.

Vyhnanek, Louis. "Henry L. Fuqua, Governor, 1924–1926." *The Louisiana Governors: From Iberville to Edwards*. Joseph G. Dawson III, ed. Baton Rouge: Louisiana State University Press, 1990.

Wall, Bennett H., ed. *Louisiana: A History*. Wheeling, IL: Harlan Davidson, 1997.

Williams, T. Harry. *Huey Long*. New York: Alfred A. Knopf, 1969.

Oramel H. Simpson

1926–1928

Governor Oramel Hinckley Simpson and General Andrew Jackson had one thing in common: they both saved the city of New Orleans, Jackson from the British invasion in 1815, and Simpson from invading floodwaters in 1927. At the height of the Great Mississippi Flood, when raging waters threatened to inundate New Orleans, Simpson ordered the levee at Caernarvon, below the city, dynamited. The crevasse created by dynamite preserved the levees protecting New Orleans from being topped by diverting floodwaters to the Gulf of Mexico through a temporary outlet. Later historians said the dynamiting was not necessary, but at the time Simpson was hailed as a hero.

Born in Washington, Louisiana, on March 20, 1870, Simpson graduated from Centenary College and Tulane Law School. After practicing law in New Orleans for several years, he was appointed assistant secretary of the state Senate in 1900. He became the secretary in 1908 and held that post until election as lieutenant governor in 1924. He also served as secretary of the Constitutional Convention of 1921.

Simpson was elected lieutenant governor as Henry L. Fuqua's run-

Oramel H. Simpson. Courtesy of the *Times-Picayune.*

ning mate and was sworn in as governor following Fuqua's death on October 11, 1926.

Described by T. Harry Williams as "short and dumpy," Simpson "functioned as a transitional figure between the old days of Old Regular dominance and the new era of Huey Long."

When Simpson took over as governor, he tried to use state patronage to organize his own group for the 1928 election, in which he was eligible to seek a full term. He was an activist governor, providing funds for construction of buildings at the new Louisiana State University campus and taking a leading role in calling for federal flood control projects. He also called for a free bridge across Lake Pontchartrain in New Orleans, in opposition to the toll bridge of the Watson-Williams syndicate.

The Old Regulars had supported the Fuqua-Simpson ticket in 1924, but in the 1928 election they sought another candidate, in the belief that Simpson could not win. With Huey Long already in the field, the Regulars were determined to defeat him.

Martin Behrman had won an unprecedented fifth term as mayor of New Orleans in 1925, but died shortly thereafter, and his successor, Arthur J. O'Keefe, viewed Huey Long as "a wild radical who should be crushed before he became dangerous." Simpson, according to Williams, "had no personal magnetism and was a poor speaker." He was also reported to be overly fond of liquor and racetracks.

The Regulars settled on Congressman Riley J. Wilson of Ruston as their candidate for governor. His fourteen-year career in Congress had been lackluster, but his chairmanship of the House Committee on Flood Control put him in the spotlight when the Great Mississippi River Flood of 1927, the greatest natural disaster the nation had thus far experienced, changed the dynamics of the election.

Fed by torrential rains that saturated the Midwest for months and overflowed tributaries that emptied into it, the Mississippi reached flood stage at Cairo, Illinois, on New Year's Day of 1927, the earliest it had ever done so in memory. It crested at levels never previously seen on every gauge from there to New Orleans, and in many places remained at flood stage for 153 straight days. It broke through or over levees in 145 places, as levees actually forced the floodwaters higher, making the river pile up on itself, increasing its speed and force. At Memphis, an area sixty miles wide was flooded. Three million cubic feet of water raced past Greenville, Mississippi, every second.

On April 21, 1927, the levee broke at Mounds Landing, Mississippi, flooding the rich land of the Delta region. Before it was through, the raging river flooded 27,000 square miles, covering land from Illinois and Missouri to the Gulf of Mexico and leaving water thirty feet deep in places. In some areas the water did not recede for weeks. Up to a million people were homeless, the Red Cross fed 700,000 for five months, and hundreds, perhaps several thousand, were killed.

As the torrent roared downstream to New Orleans, the city's power brokers, the business, civic, and social elite, feared that the city would be destroyed. Their committee proposed creating a break in the levee below New Orleans to relieve the pressure on the city's levees. Governor Simpson signed off on their plan, calling the threat to the city a desperate emergency, and the levee at Caernarvon was blown by thirty tons of dynamite. Simpson and the city leaders knew that this crevasse would flood most of St. Bernard and Plaquemines Parishes, and they promised that victims of the dynamiting would be given compensation for their losses. "The crevasse was made," John Barry wrote in *Rising Tide: The Great Mississippi Flood of 1927 and How It Changed America*, "but would prove to have been unnecessary as flood protections continued to crumble elsewhere," removing the threat to the city.

President Calvin Coolidge initially ignored the disaster, leaving the Red Cross to deal with it, but as its magnitude became clear he dispatched Secretary of Commerce Herbert Hoover to coordinate rescue and relief work. Congress recognized the enormity of the problem by passing the 1928 flood control law. As Dr. T. Harry Williams noted in his biography of Huey Long, "demands arose from the Mississippi Valley states for a more effective system of flood controls. The sheer extent of the inundation pointed up an obvious fact—a flood in the Valley was a problem for the whole nation, and to be effective, a control system would have to be constructed by the federal government. It was now evident that levees alone were not enough; spillways, bypasses, and reservoirs would be needed." The federal government took over responsibility for managing the river system through the U.S. Army Corps of Engineers.

The flood helped make Herbert Hoover president and Huey Long governor, and it spawned the migration of blacks to Chicago and elsewhere, as families of both races abandoned the land and never returned to it. The plantation economy of the Delta was changed forever by the exodus of blacks.

Wilson, through his committee chairmanship, played a leading role in passing the flood control act, and he sought to ride the publicity and acclaim he received on that issue into the governor's office, arguing that he was the only man who could head off Huey Long. Simpson declared his candidacy for a full term but put off taking the stump, announcing that his first duty was to see to it that flood victims received assistance. A backlash against him developed when it became evident that dynamiting the levee had been premature; his troubles were worsened when the financiers in New Orleans reneged on their pledge to fully compensate people in the parishes below the city who were ruined, giving them only a pittance instead.

Wilson's supporters hailed him as "an expert on flood control and a champion of Louisiana's welfare, the hero of the hour." They did not reckon with Huey Long's ability to destroy an opponent with a verbal assault. Campaigning throughout the state Long said, "Riley Joe Wilson is running for governor on his flood control record, and I say that record is fourteen feet of higher water than ever before, one foot for each of his fourteen years in Congress."

Long ran first in the primary, with 126,842 votes to 81,747 for Wilson and 80,326 for Simpson. The Old Regulars withdrew their support of Wilson, who had beaten Huey two-to-one in the city, and the *Times-Picayune*, which had supported Simpson, called for Wilson's withdrawal from the runoff. Simpson announced his own endorsement of Long. In the face of these defections, Wilson declined to enter the runoff, and Long became governor with a plurality of the total vote.

Simpson, like Long, had supported a free bridge across Lake Pontchartrain, and following the election complied with Huey's request to place free ferries alongside the Watson-Williams syndicate's toll bridge. Once Long took office, he appointed Simpson a special agent of the State Tax Commission in New Orleans. In 1932, at Huey's behest, Governor O. K. Allen appointed Simpson to the lucrative post of attorney for the State Inheritance Collector for Orleans Parish. Simpson succeeded Earl Long, dismissed for breaking with his brother and running for lieutenant governor against the administration ticket. Simpson's thirty-two-year career in state government ended with his death in New Orleans on November 17, 1932.

Williams said that, with Long's patronage, Simpson "remained in politics, but at the edges of power, a rather pathetic figure whose abilities were not great enough to accomplish his ambitions."

Simpson's knowledge of state laws and the procedures of the legislature, acquired during his two decades of service on the Senate floor, enabled him to pass flood relief legislation quickly in 1927. As Williams noted, he "devised a stratagem to put a bill through the Legislature in five days." The state constitution required that a bill be read in each house on three consecutive days and submitted to members in printed form forty-eight hours before a vote. Under Simpson's process, the legislature suspended its rules, allowing introduction in the House before midnight on the first day of a special session, with initial reading and referral to committee. The committee, just before midnight or early the next morning, reported it back to the House, where it was read again. Then, on the third day, it was read for a final time, adopted, and sent to the Senate, where it was read for the first time and referred to committee that same day. It was read again the fourth day, and then read and adopted by the Senate the following day. As Williams described the procedure, "if everything went off without a hitch, a bill could be enacted and signed by the governor a few minutes after the fourth midnight. Yet it would have had three readings in each house!"

Simpson had devised this expedited procedure for passing bills to address an emergency. Huey Long, who watched it with great interest, utilized it to ram through legislation in a series of special sessions that cemented his control of the state of Louisiana.

—J.B.McG.

Barry, John M. *Rising Tide: The Great Mississippi Flood of 1927 and How It Changed America*. New York: Simon and Schuster, 1997.

Conrad, Glenn R. *A Dictionary of Louisiana Biography*. New Orleans: Louisiana Historical Association, 1988.

Davis, Edwin Adams. *Louisiana: A Narrative History*. Baton Rouge: Claitor's Publishing Division, 1971.

Dufour, Charles L. *Ten Flags in the Wind: The Story of Louisiana*. New York: Harper & Row, 1967.

Hair, William Ivy. *The Kingfish and His Realm: The Life and Times of Huey P. Long*. Baton Rouge: Louisiana State University Press, 1991.

Kemp, John, ed. *Martin Behrman of New Orleans: Memoirs of a City Boss*. Baton Rouge: Louisiana State University Press, 1977.

Sanson, Jerry Purvis. "Oramel H. Simpson, Governor, 1926–1928." *The Louisiana Governors: From Iberville to Edwards*. Joseph G. Dawson III, ed. Baton Rouge: Louisiana State University Press, 1990.

Sindler, Allan P. *Huey Long's Louisiana: State Politics, 1920–1952*. Baltimore: Johns Hopkins Press, 1971.

Wall, Bennett H., ed. *Louisiana: A History*. Wheeling, IL: Harlan Davidson, 1997.

Williams, T. Harry. *Huey Long*. New York: Alfred A. Knopf, 1969.

Huey P. Long

1928–1932

Huey Pierce Long became Louisiana's thirty-eighth governor in 1928 at age thirty-four and the first virtual dictator of an American state as he seized power by whipping the legislature into submission. Two years later, he ran for the United States Senate and was elected but retained the governorship until he could finesse the lieutenant governor, his adversary, out of his job. And, after he took care of that, he established himself as the de facto governor, actually exercising the power of the governor.

The way he did this brought about a fascinating political drama in a state accustomed to tumultuous politics. In order to prevent the duly elected lieutenant governor, Dr. Paul N. Cyr, from succeeding to the governorship, Long delayed taking his oath as senator. Meanwhile, Cyr, a dentist from Jeanerette, was poised to take over the reins of government, even in the face of a vow by Long that he would not allow it. Impatient, Cyr had a friendly court clerk administer the oath in October 1931. This proved to be the mistake of his life, for Long then declared Cyr had abandoned his office.

Long swore in the president pro tempore of the Louisiana senate, Alvin O. King, as governor. Cyr sued to be recognized as the rightful claimant,

Huey P. Long, August 19, 1934. Courtesy of the *Times-Picayune*.

and the action was appealed to the Louisiana Supreme Court, which in a 4–3 decision ruled that only the United States Senate was the proper body to rule on the matter—that is, when Long had become a United States senator, which was not until January 1932.

One of the most remarkable politicians in Louisiana's colorful history, Huey Long swept the state in his race for governor with an "Every Man a King" dogma, calling himself the Kingfish and putting in place liberal reforms that produced free bridges, paved parish roads and state highways, free public school textbooks, and tick eradication, an important problem for cattlemen at the time. As time went on, he expanded the program to include creation of a welfare system, which included building or expanding hospitals, asylums, educational institutions, and other public facilities.

An examination of his record reveals how he took control, beating the legislature into submission through a system of patronage when, because of the Great Depression, jobs were hard to find and the economy generally low.

But as Long moved ahead with his neo-socialist program, the intensity of the time tore Louisiana apart, creating political divisions that lasted for generations. All Louisiana became two parties—Long and anti-Long. Spoils politics, Kingfish style, took over as Long pushed through the legislature laws that gave him control of taxing powers traditionally held by the cities and independent parish and state agencies. He developed a system of employee control through firing or having the legislature vote out of office recalcitrant officials. Less than a month after Long's taking office, the daily newspapers were reporting the ferocity of his attack. Said the New Orleans *Item* on June 1, 1928: "Governor Long's open warfare on every state department where there is a possibility of gaining control, through bills already introduced and statements issued from the executive office, has set members of the Legislature to wondering how far he would go."

They did not have to wait long to find out. Long apparently had set a goal of complete dominance and was building a machine to insure success. First he took control of the highway and tax commissions, reorganizing them through legislative acts. All the state agencies were affected, under the guise of "taking them out of politics." Deadheads and deducts (money withheld from salaries of state workers to provide cash for Long machine expenditures) became common to all departments.

Louisiana did not know what to expect when Long was inaugurated as governor on May 21, 1928. He was a brash campaigner who had made a lot of wild promises in the eyes of many voters, but one who held new hope to the masses.

Long's cunning ways soon surfaced as he took charge. Everybody wanted good roads in that era of few paved roads, but not all members of the legislature favored spending huge sums to pay for them. So, when Long set up legislation for financing them, he had a map made of the roads and highways to be paved. When a legislator would oppose the plan, Long would strike out that legislator's district. It had the effect of changing minds. And in a fight with the city of New Orleans, especially the Old Regular organization, the political group that had put Mayor T. Semmes Walmsley in office, a Long lieutenant suggested he find a way to remove Walmsley as mayor; Long refused, saying, "You always leave a figurehead for your boys to fight . . . Walmsley is a perfect target . . . he's impotent and can't do us any harm." Walmsley refused to resign until full taxing power was returned to the city, which did not come until the administration of Richard W. Leche in 1936, after Long's death.

In his inaugural address Long said: "I am pledged to a platform providing that so far as it is within my power, I will eliminate all means and avenues of waste, extravagance and plunder—that I will attempt to discontinue all barnacles which thrive from the misery of the people, and in doing so I shall show no favor and give no quarter, regardless of whom it may affect or of the consequences which it may bring to my public career which I might be expected to follow in future days."

After saying that, he moved to tax the big corporations, reorganize every state department, fire officials who would not be subservient, and then to appoint members of state boards who would sign resignation letters which had only to be dated and accepted when Huey no longer desired their services. From the outset, he used the National Guard to enforce his edicts.

Long's drive to reorganize the state's departments and to tax big corporations brought fierce opposition from conservative legislators and the state's daily newspapers. Long, as de facto governor after taking his seat in the United States Senate, had the legislature impose a 2 percent tax on gross advertising income of newspapers with circulation of 20,000 or more. It happened that twelve of the thirteen dailies affected had opposed him. The state's press challenged the tax as violating the First Amendment to the United States Constitution, and the U.S. Supreme Court struck it down unanimously.

Long's forces later encountered another bout with freedom of the press issues when seven members of the LSU campus newspaper, the *Daily Reveille*, were expelled when they refused to submit to censorship. The University of Missouri School of Journalism promptly invited the LSU students to complete their education at Missouri, which they did. It was hailed as a bold stroke for freedom of the press.

The *Reveille* Seven included Cal Joseph Abraham of Baton Rouge, Carl

Corbin of Napoleonville, Jesse Cutrer of Kentwood, David R. McGuire Jr. and Sam Montague of New Orleans, Stan Shlosman of Monroe, all in Louisiana, and Rea Godbold of Brookhaven, Mississippi. They were inducted into the LSU Journalism Hall of Fame in 1996.

Long's big push at the outset of his administration as governor was to finance his reforms through taxes on big corporations. He called a special session of the legislature for March 20, 1929, to consider enactment of a five-cents-per-barrel tax on refined oil, an obvious attack on Standard Oil of Baton Rouge.

Suddenly, serious opposition flared into an attempt to impeach Long when a caucus of legislators calling themselves the Dynamite Squad met and made plans to "dynamite" any legislation not considered in the best interest of the conservative group.

Rep. Harney Bogan of Shreveport announced he had an affidavit by a former Huey Long bodyguard, Harry A. (Battling) Bozeman, who claimed Long had tried to get him to assassinate Rep. J. Y. Sanders Jr., one of the Dynamite Squad leaders who had fought Long's legislative programs. The Dynamite Squad decided in a meeting on Sunday, March 24, that Bozeman's charges merited an investigation. The demand for an investigation grew into a call for impeachment of Long the next day. By Monday night when the legislature reconvened, the Long and anti-Long forces squared off in a fight that developed into a wild encounter. Long's opponents called it the "Night of the Hullabaloo."

Rep. Cecil Morgan of Caddo Parish, one of the prime movers in the anti-Long group, was selected by his fellow members to present a resolution calling for an investigation of the Bozeman charges.

Immediately after the House roll call, Rep. Morgan yelled loudly to be recognized by the speaker of the House, Representative John B. Fournet, a Long supporter. Fournet ignored him. Morgan kept talking, shouting that he was introducing a resolution that contained an accusation made under oath to get Bozeman to assassinate Sanders. Fournet continued to ignore Morgan and ordered the sergeant-at-arms to put Morgan off the floor. At that point, Rep. Cleveland Fruge of Evangeline Parish rose and asked recognition. He got it immediately and asked that the House adjourn sine die (indefinitely). Morgan then started walking down the center aisle toward the speaker's platform, disregarding the sergeant-at-arms and his orders.

The procession down that aisle would have been an hilarious comedy had not the circumstances been so tense, Morgan said later.

> Here I came with the sergeant-at-arms plucking at my coattails and my coat sleeves, and making a show of attempting to carry out the orders of the speaker, while 12 of my colleagues from the Dyna-

> mite Squad pushed him aside and formed a semi-circle about me to screen me from him while I continued my approach.
>
> In the midst of this dramatic action, the speaker put the motion to adjourn and the voting machine flashed a large vote for adjournment sine die. It showed 67 votes for and 13 against. The electric voting machine could only be operated when the proper switch was turned on by the clerk; that is, he opened the machine and the vote could be recorded by pushing a button at the desk of each member, green for yea and red for nay.
>
> I differ with T. Harry Williams [author of the Pulitzer Prize–winning biography of Long] as to what happened to the machine, and his description of the machine is in error. The machine showed a clear majority of green votes, including my own, which was impossible as, like many others, I had not pushed my button and so could not have voted as the machine recorded.

At that point pandemonium set in, as Long opposition forces became outraged and fights broke out in the aisles. Morgan continues:

> Just below where I was at the podium and to my left, there was a group of members all attacking one of our friends, Clinton Sayes, a tough and staunch farmer from the parish of Avoyelles, who was limited in education but not in fortitude, and indeed in aggressiveness. While he was being pummeled, others entered the fray until there was a mass of humanity on the floor and all about the area. Harney Bogan tried to reach his friend but was blocked by massed bodies, so he mounted a desk, stepped from one desk to another, and finally—and to this day I have a vision of his leap from the top of a desk and flying through the air—landed headfirst into the melee and pushed some bodies to the left and came up with Clint Sayes, who was bloody, bruised and still fighting. There were three distinct marks down the middle of his forehead, the result of a blow from brass knucks.

Sayes, blood streaming from his forehead, shouted that the House voting machine had been jimmied and accused Fournet of falsely recording the vote. No one knew exactly what had happened, but the Dynamite Squad members said Fournet had manipulated the machine to show a vote for adjournment. Many legislators recorded as voting said they had not.

Fournet, who later was lieutenant governor and for thirty years a justice of the Louisiana Supreme Court, told this writer he had no reason to recognize Morgan. "I was seated on a platform," he recalled, "and Fruge was seated right down there in front of me. Morgan was sitting in the back over to the right side. I always did have a bad eye. I don't say I couldn't have seen him, but he was hard to see."

"But what about the voting machine?" Fournet was asked. His answer:

> The state had bought or leased the voting machine for the House. I didn't know anything about its operation. The clerk operated the machine, and he reported to me that it showed 67 votes for adjournment, which was sufficient. If I had recognized Morgan, he would have had 67 votes for his resolution. If anybody fixed that machine, it was the anti-Long forces. I can't say it was fixed because I never saw it.
>
> They [the anti-Long people] claimed the next day the machine wasn't working, but they didn't say anything that night. If they had I would have called for a voice vote. The key thing is that they did not appeal from the ruling, therefore it was a final decision.

Dynamite Squad members countered that they had no opportunity to appeal the ruling because Fournet had ruled adjournment while Morgan spoke. Morgan later confirmed that.

After the ruling, Fournet left the chair and went to see Long. But the session was not over, after all, as Rep. Mason Spencer of Madison Parish climbed on his desk and bellowed for attention. The crowd was angry, and Spencer pointed out Fournet had abandoned the chair. He said he would appeal the motion to adjourn and he asked Rep. George Ginsberg of Rapides Parish to become temporary speaker. Tellers were appointed to take a voice vote on adjournment. As calm was restored, the vote was taken and it showed a 71 to 9 vote to overturn the previous count. There were 19 absentees by that time. Spencer then made a motion to adjourn until 11 a.m. the following day, March 25.

Impeachment was now on the minds of the anti-Long forces. The Dynamite Squad met through the night and drew up a resolution to do just that. They drew up eight articles of impeachment and then made a tactical error in the drive to possibly unseat Long by adjourning until April 25, giving Long time to rally his forces.

The Louisiana constitution empowers the state Senate to sit as a court in impeachment cases and requires a two-thirds majority to convict in order to remove a governor from office. At the time, the Senate had thirty-nine members, thus it would require at least fourteen votes to block it.

As the trial date neared, Long found himself with thirteen senators pledged to stand by him. He put pressure on New Orleans lawyer Fred Oser, who became the fourteenth. Later, Senator T. A. McConnell was persuaded to join in Long's defense. Bargaining between the Long and anti-Long factions grew intense, and on one occasion a senator was bought off by the anti-Longs and bought back by the Longs. Long held an effective political weapon, the promise of state jobs and contracts.

The Senate prepared for what many thought would produce the greatest political trial in Louisiana history. Stands were erected in the Senate chamber to accommodate as many persons as possible. It was set to begin at noon on Tuesday, May 14. Long had his lawyers ready, including John H. Overton of Alexandria, Leander H. Perez, a St. Bernard Parish figure, and Rep. Allen Ellender of Houma. Louisiana Supreme Court chief justice Charles A. O'Niell presided as the Senate sat as a court of impeachment.

Expectations ran high as a crowd of spectators assembled. At that point, Senator F. H. Gilbert of Assumption Parish arose and offered into evidence a document in which fifteen senators declared that regardless of the evidence against Long, they would not vote to convict him.

Chief Justice O'Niell put the question to each senator who signed the document, which became known as the Round Robin, as to whether he had signed it, and each responded yes. Suddenly, the trial was over before it started, and Long remained in office.

Who really was Huey Long, and how did he develop his philosophies?

Born on August 30, 1893, on a farm in Winn Parish, he grew up in economically tough times. He was put to work on the family farm at age seven, served as a book agent and printer's devil in his early teens in Winnfield, and at sixteen became a traveling salesman. He attended high school in Winnfield and Shreveport but did not graduate. He attended the University of Oklahoma for five months but quit to take a job. At twenty he gained admission to the Tulane University Law School as a special student. He took classes for seven months, passed the bar examination and returned to Winnfield to practice. He moved to Shreveport soon after.

In Shreveport Long met Rose McConnell, a young secretary who had become an expert cake baker. Long had attended baking contests and awarded prizes, one of which went to Rose. That meeting began a courtship and they were married. They had three children: Rose, Russell B., and Palmer Reid Long. Russell followed his father and mother in the United States Senate, where he gained national stature. (Rose Long completed the unexpired term of her husband through appointment by Governor Jimmy Noe.)

In 1918 Long was elected to the Railroad Commission, later renamed the Public Service Commission. In 1924 he ran for governor but lost to Henry L. Fuqua. He ran a surprisingly good race, with a total of 73,985 votes against Bouanchard's 84,162 votes and Fuqua's at 81,382 votes. In the runoff, Fuqua easily bested Bouanchard, picking up most of Long's upstate vote. In 1928 Long won the governorship, defeating O. H. Simpson and Riley Joe Wilson.

In his gubernatorial races Long faced well-financed opponents, but capitalized on his own aggressiveness. He traveled the state stump-speaking, and developed a unique way to get on radio by telephoning selected stations and announcing he would have important announcements at specified times; then he would call friends and ask them to spread the word. Stations favored with Long's announcements liked the exposure. He also plastered telephone poles with his campaign literature. He worked tirelessly to blanket the state with his message.

Long's main campaign device was the stump speech, and his personal appearance helped: approximately five feet eleven, with a full face, a bulbous nose, and reddish-brown hair, Long's appearance was a cartoonist's delight. He was an impassioned speaker: his raucous voice, combined with his looks, made him a movie star–like figure whom the people sought to watch in action.

Long campaigned on his "Every Man a King" slogan, forerunner of his later "Share Our Wealth" program with which he threatened to run for president in an attempt to defeat Franklin D. Roosevelt. He wrote two books, the first an autobiography entitled *Every Man a King*, in which he said he would ride his "Share the Wealth" program to the presidency. Leading politicians of the time doubted he would ever gain the presidency, but he did establish himself as a thorn in the side of the Roosevelt New Deal.

Long's first book told of his early life, his entry into state politics, his election to the Public Service Commission in 1918, and the start of his fight against the Cumberland Telephone and Telegraph Company. His fight against the telephone company set Long on a course of opposition to the big corporations, especially Standard Oil. He wrote that he gained a rebate of $467,000 for telephone users in his first year of opposition to the company, and that rates were reduced by $1 million a year afterward. His major fight, however, centered on Standard Oil.

Long's other book was entitled *My First Days in the White House*, a surprisingly satirical and mythical account of what he might do if elected president. His dreams were fanciful and superficial, judged by the measure of politics then and now. He had a grandiose plan to redirect the nation's water resources to eliminate dust storms, a major problem of the time; reclaim wastelands; control floods; develop navigation and waterpower; improve the lot of farmers; expand transportation facilities; and assure the safety and success of banks.

The ringer was to limit individual wealth to $5 million per person, in line with his highly celebrated Share Our Wealth program, and to create a national Share Our Wealth corporation to handle stock placed by the wealthy in the government's hands.

Long's plan, when publicized, struck J. Pierpont Morgan and other industrial capitalists like a lightning rod, and they vowed to fight it to the United States Supreme Court, if it had come to pass. Long, in his mythical thinking, had it figured out, saying "the laws which Congress enacted not only redistributed wealth and income among the people, but the same laws also levied taxes for support of the government in such a way that the wealth of the country would never again accumulate in a few hands."

The plan would have included appointing the nation's top leaders to his cabinet, such as Franklin Delano Roosevelt as secretary of the navy, Herbert Hoover as secretary of commerce, Frank Murphy as attorney general, James Couzens as secretary of the treasury, Major General Lytle Brown as secretary of the interior, and Edward Keating as secretary of labor.

Long's fantasy, which he envisioned to have been accepted by the Supreme Court, was designed to be a campaign strategy in the 1936 presidential race. Of course, it could not have happened since an assassin's bullet ended his life in 1935. And political wisdom was that Long faced too many obstacles to win the presidency.

All the while, Long continued to run Louisiana as though it was a branch of his Washington office. He would return to Baton Rouge, confer with his legislative lieutenants, and appear at Sunday night sessions of the legislature to steer his pet projects to victory.

One of the projects dearest to Long's heart was the enhancement of Louisiana State University, which he adopted as "his school" after he became governor. He set about improvement of campus facilities and studies, with a keen eye toward developing the football team, the Tigers. His tiff with Biff- Coach Lawrence "Biff" Jones—led to serious and hilarious encounters with Jones, a former star and coach at West Point, who was then a captain in the army.

In his handling of the LSU football matter, Long pretty much disclosed his modus operandi in politics and every other endeavor he undertook.

Ordinarily, the selection of a coach would have been the job of the university president, at the time Dr. James Monroe Smith. But Long took over and, through his influence as senator and de facto governor, won the army's approval to let Jones coach LSU. One of the conditions Jones laid down was that Long had to stay away from the team during games. He did let Long sit at the end of the bench. Long's aggressive personality surfaced in LSU's attempt to win a Rose Bowl bid in 1933 and 1934. At the start of the 1934 season, Long predicted LSU would set a local attendance record, as its stadium had just been enlarged.

When he learned that the season's first game, with SMU, was not a sellout because of the scheduled appearance of the Ringling Brothers and Barnum and Bailey circus on the same day, Long flew into action. The Kingfish vowed that no circus was going to compete with the Tigers. With the compulsory animal dipping law passed in 1930 to control the tick problem in mind, he telephoned John Ringling North, owner of the circus, and asked him if the Baton Rouge date could be rescheduled. No way, explained North, because of its overall fixed schedule. Okay, said Long, but Louisiana's dip law meant that animals brought across state lines would have to be dipped and then quarantined for three weeks. Suddenly, North complied with Long's request and on short notice had the circus diverted to New Orleans for the Saturday showing while LSU played SMU.

The Louisiana senator made another bold move the same year in sending practically the entire LSU student body to Nashville, where LSU, riding the crest of a winning streak, defeated Vanderbilt 29–0. And only a Huey Long could have pulled off the caper he masterminded.

Dr. James Monroe Smith, the university president, threw cold water on the plan when he learned that the fare for each student for the round trip to Nashville would be $19, so high that not many students would be able to afford it. "You worry too much about expenses," Long exclaimed. "I'll take care of that." He called the traffic manager of the Illinois Central Railroad, the principal line to Nashville, and said, "That's too much; I'll give you six dollars per person." He then called the president of the IC and informed the IC head that the railroad owned many bridges in Louisiana valued at more than they were assessed, and that possibly the tax commission would take note of it.

Threatened with higher assessments, the railroad capitulated, and some 4,000 students made the trip. Students who did not have the money were offered loans of seven dollars, six for the fare and a dollar for food.

The rail cars, painted brightly for the trip, proclaimed on their sides, "Hurray for Huey." It was indeed a spectacle. Long was pushing for a Rose Bowl bid for his Tigers, but two upsets blurred the picture. In their last home game of the season, Oregon had run up a 13–0 lead by halftime. Coach Jones reasoned he could win the game by changing strategy. Long appeared at the dressing room door and demanded to talk to the team. Jones refused to let him in, sensing that if the Kingfish gave a pep talk and the Tigers won, he would claim credit. Long, rebuffed, paused at the door and yelled to the coach, "All right, but you better win this one."

Jones fired back, "I don't have to win this one; win, lose, or draw, I'm going to resign at the end of this game." Biff diagrammed new plays for the second half, and LSU pulled off a 14–13 victory. He called Long's bluff and resisted pleas to stay on.

The LSU Tigers failed to get a Rose Bowl bid, but Long's efforts in luring Jones to Louisiana paid off handsomely. Jones's record while at LSU, from 1932 to 1934, was twenty wins, five ties, and six losses over three seasons.

Long's antics were not over, however. Next, he perpetrated a gag by having an LSU backfield star, Abe Mickal, "elected" to a vacant state senatorial seat. Senator J.Y. Sanders Jr. of the Sixth Congressional District had resigned as a state senator after winning a seat in Congress. Long's forces called a mass meeting in the campus Greek Theater, and the crowd "elected" Mickal to the vacancy. The crowd declared him to be the new senator from East Baton Rouge and then dispersed, chuckling that Long had pulled off another good gag. The stunt got national publicity and ended in an embarrassment for Long. Although the move was conceived as a burlesque gig, newspaper correspondents conveyed the impression it was legitimate, which was impossible because Mickal was a citizen of Mississippi. This is the stunt that set off the dismissal of seven students who claimed censorship after the university announced it had put the student newspaper, the *Reveille*, under a faculty adviser. The controversy raised freedom of the press issues touched on earlier in this account.

Mickal did not attempt to take over the senatorial seat, but the caper focused widespread attention on LSU and Huey Long.

In the midst of such "extra-curricular" antics, Long did not neglect his legislative program. In early September 1935, he directed his handpicked successor as governor, O. K. Allen, to call a special session of the legislature. On Sunday night, September 8, he was at the capitol to check on the progress of his legislation. He was accompanied by Supreme Court Justice Fournet, who described in a December 14, 1983, interview with this writer the scene as Huey Long was shot.

"I saw a man with a black pistol shoot Huey," said Fournet, "right next to me. I saw the gun in his hand. I raised my [left] arm and struck him on the arm." Fournet said his action prevented Long from being shot a second time.

"The moment the shooting was over, Huey made a little noise that sounded like 'whoop'—that was when he was hit, I guess," said Fournet. "Huey ran down the stairs to the basement," continued Fournet, who at that point explained Huey had sent Jimmy O'Connor to the basement to get him some cigars.

"O'Connor saw Huey and asked, 'Have you been hurt?' Huey directed O'Connor to take him to the nearby Our Lady of the Lake Sanitarium. They put Huey into a car and rushed him to the hospital."

By this time, after nine o'clock, pandemonium had set in at the scene of the shooting, and the hospital was thrown into chaos also.

Murphy Roden, a Long bodyguard, was near Long. "He grabbed the man and his gun at the same time," said Fournet. "Roden and the man scuffled and a shot from the man's gun broke the watch on Roden's wrist. Roden then shot the man."

Roden and other state policemen, according to press reports, emptied their pistols in a fusillade of bullets into Long's attacker, described as a thin man in a white suit whom no one could identify immediately. Some thirty minutes later, the coroner, Dr. Thomas Bird, removed the man's wallet and found him to be Dr. Carl Austin Weiss of Baton Rouge.

Weiss was a twenty-nine-year-old ear, nose, and throat specialist and son-in-law of Judge Benjamin Pavy. Pavy resided in the district that included St. Landry and Evangeline Parishes and had been a thorn in the side of Long forces there. Bill No. 1 before the special session proposed to place Pavy's stronghold, St. Landry, in a district where the Long forces could unseat him, Fournet said.

"Huey had ordered the special session," said Fournet, "to gerrymander Judge Pavy." Political observers reasoned that Weiss had shot Long because of the situation, and the theory was generally accepted that Weiss was the attacker. But some people believed that Weiss shot Long for another reason, because Long said in front of several people that if Judge Pavy fought the gerrymander, he would "wave the tarbrush," accusing Pavy of having Negro blood, a charge made fifteen years earlier that Long threatened to revive.

In furtherance of this theory, its supporters charged Weiss shot Long to stop him from smearing Judge Pavy with the accusation, because then it would carry to Weiss's wife and child. While this does not sound like a realistic motive now, at that time Negro blood was a stigma for a white, and a person could be classified as a Negro if he had 1/32 Negro blood. Weiss feared his child could be classified as a Negro if birth records were changed.

When Long arrived at the hospital, he asked that two New Orleans specialists be summoned to attend him. The doctors ran into automobile trouble and were delayed. Meanwhile, Dr. Arthur Vidrine, dean of Long's newly founded Louisiana State University Medical School, who happened to be in Baton Rouge at the time, decided that an operation was necessary because his condition was worsening—Vidrine said Long was bleeding internally. Long agreed to the operation, according to Fournet. "Afterwards," recalled Fournet, "Vidrine said the operation was nothing, meaning it was routine. Vidrine said a bullet had perforated an intestine in two places and told Huey, "You'll be all right in a few days."

But Vidrine failed to probe the bullet, said Fournet, and Long was found to be bleeding in the right kidney. He lingered in the hospital until Tuesday, September 10, when he died. "He bled to death," said Fournet. From press comments and interviews at the time, it was clear that this was a most public operation. Politicians and friends lined the walls of the operating room, providing a circuslike atmosphere.

In a forum at the Tulane School of Medicine on September 21, 1984, Dr. Frank J. Loria, a recent medical graduate when Long was operated on and in attendance at the operation, said he bled to death. But Dr. Edgar Hull, who later headed the LSU Medical School at Shreveport and who also was present at the operation, disputed Dr. Loria. Hull defended Vidrine, saying that Long had died not because of medical incompetence but because at that time drugs to control infection were not available. Hull said Long was suffering from fulminating peritonitis. He did not bleed to death, said Hull.

An autopsy might have put to rest any doubt as to the course of the bullet and as to how badly Long had bled, but the family would not authorize one.

As he lay in bed in Our Lady of the Lake Sanitarium, Long insiders suddenly thought it would be wise to find out the location of the box containing cash accumulated from the paycheck deducts of state employees, a secret fund used by the Long organization at election times. Originally it had been kept by Seymour Weiss (no relation to Dr. Weiss) at the Roosevelt Hotel in New Orleans, which Weiss operated. But Long had moved the box to Washington, Fournet said Long had confided, and it was believed he had moved it a second time.

Weiss whispered a question to Long as to the box's location, and Long responded that he had moved it to the Roosevelt Hotel in New York, according to Fournet, who said that he noted that Weiss then left for New Orleans and New York. Presumably he got the box, said Fournet, and then returned to Baton Rouge for Long's funeral, although what actually happened to the box has never been discovered.

In the face of rumors the prized box contained a million dollars, Fournet said it was his understanding it contained twice that figure. Apparently no one knew for sure at the time, and only a few insiders ever learned of the disposition of the funds.

Huey Long was buried on September 12 in a public ceremony in the sunken garden in front of the thirty-four-story state capitol he had built. His tomb attracts thousands of visitors annually.

—W.G.C.

"Cyr Denounces Hotel Man, Long." *New Orleans States.* 1 Feb. 1932.

Deutsch, Hermann B. *The Huey Long Murder Case.* Garden City, NY: Doubleday, 1963.

Fournet, John B. Interview with Walter G. Cowan under the auspices of the Historic New Orleans Collection, 1985.

Hair, William Ivy. *The Kingfish and His Realm: The Life and Times of Huey P. Long.* Baton Rouge: Louisiana State University Press, 1991.

"Impeachment Charges Held over Till Afternoon to Protest Highway Bids." *New Orleans Item*, 26 March 1929.

Long, Huey P. *Every Man a King.* New Orleans: National Book Co., 1933.

———. *My First Days in the White House.* Harrisburg, PA: The Telegraph Press, 1935.

"LSU Dismisses Cutrer, McGuire, Leaders in Fight upon Censorship." *Times-Picayune.* 6 Dec. 1934.

Morgan, Cecil. Interview with Betty Carter under the auspices of the Historic New Orleans Collection, 1985.

"Smith Stands Pat on 'Gag' Rule for Reveille." *Times-Picayune.* 29 Nov. 1934.

Williams, T. Harry. *Huey Long.* New York: Alfred A. Knopf, 1969.

Alvin O. King

1932

"The more I try to get out of politics, the more I get into it," Alvin Olin King said on January 25, 1932, when he was sworn in as governor. King had already decided not to seek reelection to the state senate in 1932, nor to any political office in the future, when he found himself succeeding to the lieutenant governorship and then the governorship. He served as governor until May 16, 1932, when Oscar K. Allen took office.

King was born in Leoti, Kansas, on June 21, 1890. His family moved to Lake Charles when he was only several months old. His father worked as a rice farmer but moved into a series of successful business ventures in rice milling, lumber, and wholesale grocery sales.

King graduated from Lake Charles High School, attended business school, and obtained a law degree from Tulane University in 1915. After opening a law office in Lake Charles, he was appointed city attorney and was elected to the state senate in 1924 and reelected in 1928.

He was an independent in the Senate, and after Huey Long took office, King supported him in some instances and opposed him in others. He did not support the round robin that enabled Long to escape conviction by the Senate. Lieutenant Governor Paul N. Cyr, the president

Alvin O. King, October 7, 1952. Courtesy of the *Times-Picayune*.

of the Senate, had broken with Long and joined the antis, and they now sought the office of president pro tempore of the Senate, vacant because its holder had resigned to take a judgeship. While King was not identified as a Longite, Long's supporters backed him for president pro tem, and he won cross-factional support for the post in 1930.

Huey Long was elected to the U.S. Senate in 1930, but delayed taking his seat, as he did not want Cyr to take the governor's chair, however briefly. Cyr, a dentist known as the "Wild Bull of Jeanerette," contended that Long had vacated the governor's office when he sent his certificate of election to the U.S. Senate's secretary. Cyr filed suit to have Long declared a senator, but instead of waiting for the suit to be heard, he made the mistake of taking the oath of office as governor before a justice of the peace.

Long placed state guards at the capitol and the mansion to forestall a takeover by Cyr, who set up his temporary capitol at a hotel in Baton Rouge, from which he issued bombastic proclamations. What had started as a serious constitutional crisis, however, turned into a farce, with jokesters throughout the state having themselves sworn in as governor.

In an adroit move Long turned the tables on Cyr, announcing that the latter had vacated the office of lieutenant governor when he took the oath as governor. Long called King to Baton Rouge to be sworn in as lieutenant governor on October 14, 1931, and then filed a countersuit against Cyr, which was consolidated with Cyr's suit against him. Long argued his own case in court, maintaining that under the U.S. Constitution only the Senate could determine the qualifications of its members. He said that since he had not gone to Washington to be sworn in as a senator, he was still the governor, and only the legislature could remove the governor. The court held for Long and dismissed Cyr's suit in a decision that the Louisiana Supreme Court upheld.

Cyr refused to give up, took the oath as governor again, and denounced both Long and King in proclamations issued from his Heidelberg Hotel suite. Long persuaded the owners of the hotel to evict Cyr, and he moved to another hotel where he tried to continue his fight. By this time no one paid any further attention to him and his antics.

After the "Complete the Work" ticket of O. K. Allen for governor and John B. Fournet for lieutenant governor swept the January 1932 election, Long prepared to finally take his Senate seat. The "Huey P. Long Special" took him to the nation's capital with several railroad cars of friends and supporters. As soon as he took the oath as senator on January 25, 1932, an open telephone line to the executive mansion in Baton Rouge notified King, who was then sworn in as governor.

Betty M. Field, who wrote extensively on the relations between Louisiana and the New Deal, said that after all of the controversy, "King's demeanor had a calming effect on Louisiana, and members of both political factions readily accepted him as chief executive." He served until Allen's inauguration on May 16, 1932. Having chosen to end his political career, King returned to his law practice and business interests in Lake Charles and served as president of the state bar association. One of his law partners was Sam H. Jones, an anti-Long who became governor in 1940. King died in Lake Charles on January 21, 1958, twenty-six years after he took the oath as governor.

—J.B.McG.

Conrad, Glenn R. *A Dictionary of Louisiana Biography*. New Orleans: Louisiana Historical Association, 1988.

Davis, Edwin Adams. *Louisiana: A Narrative History*. Baton Rouge: Claitor's Publishing Division, 1971.

Dufour, Charles L. *Ten Flags in the Wind: The Story of Louisiana*. New York: Harper & Row, 1967.

Field, Betty M. "Alvin Olin King, Governor, 1932." *The Louisiana Governors: From Iberville to Edwards*. Joseph G. Dawson III, ed. Baton Rouge: Louisiana State University Press, 1990.

Hair, William Ivy. *The Kingfish and His Realm: The Life and Times of Huey P. Long*. Baton Rouge: Louisiana State University Press, 1991.

Sindler, Allan P. *Huey Long's Louisiana: State Politics, 1920–1952*. Baltimore: Johns Hopkins Press, 1971.

Wall, Bennett H., ed. *Louisiana: A History*. Wheeling, IL: Harlan Davidson, 1997.

Williams, T. Harry. *Huey Long*. New York: Alfred A. Knopf, 1969.

Oscar K. Allen

1932–1936

"Oscar was sitting in his office and a leaf blew in through the open window and landed on his desk," Earl Long said. "He thought Huey must have sent it, so he signed it."

No governor was more aptly named than "O.K." Allen. The image of him made indelible in histories is that of the "pliant front man" for Huey Long, the Kingfish's "puppet governor" and "stooge," the "rubber-stamp" whose signature made all of Long's "power grabs" law and under whose administration Long's dictatorial control of Louisiana was perfected. Anything Long wanted, people said, was "O.K." with Allen.

It is a mistake, which most Louisiana historians have made, to portray Allen as a stumblebum, an incompetent lackey, and a dullard. He came up the hard way, made something of himself, won election to several public offices, and was truly devoted to Huey Long, whose political career he helped launch. Allen genuinely believed that he was privileged to serve as the trusted subordinate of a great man and, despite the abuse that he endured at Long's hands, never deviated from that view, and referred to his governorship as the Long-Allen administration.

Oscar Kelly Allen was born near Winnfield on August 8, 1882, in a

Oscar K. Allen, January 29, 1936. Courtesy of the *Times-Picayune*.

log cabin on the farm of a family in poor circumstances. He attended public schools and took business school courses, as well as a brief stint at Trinity University in Texas. Allen taught school in Winn Parish when he was barely older than some of his students, and he operated a small sawmill.

Allen was elected assessor of Winn Parish in 1916, and while still holding that office, was appointed secretary to the police jury in 1924. He became a close friend of Huey Long, who was ten years younger. When Long, in his first campaign for railroad commissioner, was desperate for funds and appealed to Allen for help, Allen went to the bank, borrowed $500, and gave it to him.

Long and Allen were partners in several wildcat oil ventures, and their political and personal relationship was one of the strongest ties Long had to anyone. When Huey made an unsuccessful race for governor in 1924, Allen was his district campaign manager. Allen was elected to the state senate in 1928, when Long won the governorship, and was an ally in the senate when Long staved off conviction of charges of impeachment. Allen signed the "round robin" that defeated Long's removal, and helped obtain other signatures on it.

Long was elected United States senator in 1930 in what he termed a referendum on his program for Louisiana, which included a bond issue for paved roads. Allen resigned as senator to accept Long's appointment as chairman of the state highway commission, where he oversaw an ambitious program of road and bridge construction to "take Louisiana out of the mud."

Long picked Allen to head the "Complete the work of Huey Long" ticket in the 1932 state election. With Speaker of the House John B. Fournet as his running mate for lieutenant governor, and Huey Long carrying the campaign to crossroads throughout the state, Allen won a resounding victory. He got 214,699 votes to 110,048 for public service commissioner Dudley J. LeBlanc and 53,756 for reform candidate George Seth Guion.

Long rewarded Allen's longtime loyalty with the governorship. The new state capitol, which Earl Long derided as "Huey's silo," was dedicated for Allen's inauguration on May 16, 1932. Allen was governor in name only, due to his "unswerving loyalty" to Long; there was never any doubt as to who was in charge. Historian Allen Sindler wrote, "With Allen as his puppet in the executive mansion, Long set out on the distinct, but related, tasks of solidifying his personal power and effectuating his class program."

William Ivy Hair wrote that "O.K. Allen, silver-haired and soft-spoken, possessed a dignified appearance but a weak will. Anti-Longites sneered at him as a dimwit, which he was not, and as putty in the hands of the Kingfish, which he was." Long was confident that Allen would follow orders and that he could continue to run the state through Allen while he was in Washington. T. Harry Williams described Allen thusly: "Mild and modest in manner, he impressed people at first acquaintance, though not always thereafter. Actually, he lacked many of the qualities that even the most ordinary politician has to have. He did not have the knack of remembering people, their names, and associations. His clumsiness in dealing with people became, in fact, proverbial in Louisiana."

Dr. Williams added, "His greatest shortcoming was a weakness of character, an amiability and desire to oblige that made him susceptible to the influence of stronger personalities." Long kept him in line by "dominating Allen himself. He bullied and abused the governor, often in the presence of others." With frequent trips back to Baton Rouge, and daily contact with his leaders, Long kept close watch on matters at home. He ruled the legislative sessions, explaining bills in one-sentence descriptions in committees, ramming them through in record time, and prowling the aisles of the House and Senate chambers or sitting on the dais to pass them. In meetings Long would tell Allen to shut up when the governor ventured an opinion, and Allen was reduced to asking Long to please stop cursing him in public.

While Long "browbeat poor Allen" and made him a "figurehead governor," in private they remained close associates, and Allen made excuses for Long's behavior. With the real power remaining in the hands of the Kingfish, the Allen administration enacted the homestead exemption on property taxes, repealed the poll tax, and levied the first state income tax. A massive program of public works included bridges, highways, hospitals, and expansion of Louisiana State University.

When Huey went to war against the Old Regular machine in New Orleans in the 1934 city election, Allen proclaimed martial law in the city and sent troops in to seize the voter registration office. National guardsmen in the registration office and city volunteers in City Hall faced each other across a narrow street, but an armed clash was averted when the Old Regular, T. Semmes Walmsley, defeated Long's candidate for mayor. Long responded by having a compliant legislature strip the city of many of its powers and reduce its taxes, to "starve" Walmsley into submission.

"From August, 1934, through September, 1935, seven special sessions of the Legislature enacted measures which, in their combined effect, reduced the citizens of Louisiana to political vassalage to the Kingfish and his faction," Allan P. Sindler wrote. Allen was a willing accomplice to Long in placing control of every level of government in the state in the governor's hands. A State Printing Board had to approve the official journals of local governments; approval by a state board was required for every public school teacher in the state; if a city council or parish police jury opposed the state administration or its candidates, a subservient legislature added additional members to the governing body, the governor appointed them, and a new Longite majority was created. A State Bureau of Criminal Identification was created, the governor named its agents, and a retinue of BCI and state police bodyguards surrounded Long, whose fear of assassination grew with each grab for power he made.

The state capitol was an armed camp when a special session began on September 8, 1935. Long was ensconced in an apartment created for him on the twenty-fourth floor, while rumors abounded that an attempt would be made on his life, and security at the capitol was tightened. Among the items in the call for the special session was a bill to redraw the boundaries of a judicial district; the gerrymander was intended to rid the Kingfish of an anti-Long district court judge, B. H. Pavy. Another bill provided for the registration of sawed-off shotguns and submachine guns, so the administration would know if opponents held such weapons.

Long appeared on the floor of the House that evening and lounged at the dais with Speaker Allen J. Ellender. When the House adjourned he headed for Allen's office. Walking in briskly, he shouted orders for all of the administration legislators to be there for a caucus in the morning, and turned back into the hallway. He was accosted there by Dr. Carl Austin Weiss, Judge Pavy's son-in-law, who shot Long once before being gunned down by a hail of bullets from the bodyguards. Governor Allen, rushing to the door after hearing the first shots, turned around as the enraged bodyguards emptied their weapons at the prostrate Weiss. Allen locked the door and shouted, "Give me a gun. If there's going to be any more shooting, I want in on it."

Huey Long died at Our Lady of the Lake Sanitorium on September 10, 1935. Allen, overcome with grief, said that Long's last thoughts were of the students at LSU. Allen had the legislature authorize Long's burial in the sunken garden in front of the capitol, and he was one of the pallbearers in the imposing funeral ceremonies. He issued a lengthy statement extolling Long's virtues and accomplishments, and recalled their friendship and collaboration over the years.

Allen put up with humiliation because he thought Long was the greatest man Louisiana had ever produced. He was proud to serve as the Kingfish's loyal lieutenant in the Long-Allen administrations. Long not only made him governor; he made him rich.

Long had moved his November 1936 U.S. Senate election to January, to coincide with the governor's election, so that he would already be reelected and have a free hand with his plans for the presidential election. With his death, there were two elections for his seat, one for the remaining months of his term, the "short" term, and one for the new six-year term, the "long" term. Allen was elected to the "short" term and Ellender to the "long" term. Allen intended to take the Senate seat for several months when his term as governor ended in May, but he died suddenly of a hemorrhage at the mansion on January 28, 1936. Although not as large as Long's, Allen had a "massive funeral on the same state capitol grounds where Huey was buried," after which a special train carried his body to Winnfield for burial there.

—J.B.McG.

Boulard, Garry. *Huey Long Invades New Orleans: The Siege of a City 1934–1936.* Gretna, LA: Pelican, 1998.

Davis, Edwin Adams. *Louisiana: A Narrative History*. Baton Rouge: Claitor's Publishing Division, 1971.

Dufour, Charles L. *Ten Flags in the Wind: The Story of Louisiana*. New York: Harper & Row, 1967.

Field, Betty M. "Oscar K. Allen, Governor, 1932–1936." *The Louisiana Governors: From Iberville to Edwards*. Joseph G. Dawson III, ed. Baton Rouge: Louisiana State University Press, 1990.

Haas, Edward F., ed. *The Louisiana Purchase Bicentennial Series in Louisiana History. Vol. VIII: The Age of the Longs: Louisiana, 1928–1960*. Lafayette: Center for Louisiana Studies, University of Louisiana at Lafayette, 2001.

Hair, William Ivy. *The Kingfish and His Realm: The Life and Times of Huey P. Long*. Baton Rouge: Louisiana State University Press, 1991.

Kane, Harnett. *Louisiana Hayride: The American Rehearsal for Dictatorship, 1928–1940*. Gretna, LA: Pelican, 1971.

Martin, Thomas. *Dynasty: The Longs of Louisiana*. New York: G.P. Putnam's Sons, 1960.

McGuire, Jack B. *Uncle Earl Deserved Better*. New Orleans: Good Reading Books, 1995.

Sindler, Allan P. *Huey Long's Louisiana: State Politics, 1920–1952*. Baltimore: Johns Hopkins Press, 1971.

Wall, Bennett H., ed. *Louisiana: A History*. Wheeling, IL: Harlan Davidson, 1997.

Williams, T. Harry. *Huey Long*. New York: Alfred A. Knopf, 1969.

James A. Noe

1936

James A. Noe, in forming the Win-or-Lose Corporation to deal in oil lease interests, had the good fortune to create an enterprise that always won and never lost. The fact that his partners included Governor O. K. Allen and Senator Huey Long, and that the oil properties in question were leases on state lands that Allen awarded to Noe, who then gave them to Win-or-Lose, which transferred them to major oil companies in return for royalties, may have had something to do with their success.

Noe was the first blood donor to Huey Long as the Kingfish lay wounded in Our Lady of the Lake Sanatorium in Baton Rouge. When Long died, Noe believed that the Kingfish would have named him his political heir as the state administration candidate for governor in 1936. The machine's failure to anoint him set in motion the seeds of its own destruction at Noe's hands.

James Albert Noe was born near West Point, Kentucky, on December 21, 1890. He served in the infantry in France in World War I and moved to Monroe, Louisiana, following his discharge, where he enjoyed success in the independent oil business. He amassed a fortune in a wide

James A. Noe, 1968. Courtesy of the *Times-Picayune*.

range of enterprises, and later owned radio stations in Monroe and New Orleans and a television station in Monroe.

Huey Long selected Noe to run against an incumbent anti-Long state senator in the 1932 election. Noe soon emerged as a floor leader for the Allen administration, which was dominated by Long; he was elected president pro tempore of the senate in 1935, and after Lieutenant Governor John B. Fournet took a seat on the state Supreme Court, Noe became the acting lieutenant governor.

Noe chartered the Win-or-Lose Corporation in 1934, with himself as president, Seymour Weiss, treasurer of the Long machine as vice president, and Earle J. Christenberry Jr., Long's secretary, as secretary-treasurer. Shares were transferred to Governor Allen, and thirty-one of the one hundred shares were transferred from Noe to Huey Long. This formed the basis of the Long family fortune that has amounted to many millions of dollars in holdings and income.

Noe wanted to continue Long's program after his death, including Share-Our-Wealth and opposition to the Roosevelt administration, while the organization's leaders now wanted peace with Washington and were prepared to terminate Share-Our-Wealth and embrace the New Deal. Noe claimed that Long had planned to designate him as Allen's successor, but when Governor Allen and Mayor Maestri announced that Judge Richard W. Leche had been Long's choice and would be the candidate, Noe backpedaled and said that Long had indeed tapped Leche, but with Noe for his running mate for lieutenant governor. In Noe's scenario, Leche was to run for a seat on the state supreme court in 1938, allowing Noe to become governor. The organization disregarded Noe and put Earl K. Long on the ticket for the second spot.

Nursing his disappointment at having his claims to the succession fail to be recognized by other members of the Long organization, Noe sought reelection to the Senate in 1936 and won. With Allen's sudden death on January 28, 1936, he became governor, serving until Leche was inaugurated on May 12, 1936.

Governor Allen had been elected to complete the remaining months of Huey Long's U.S. Senate term, and with his death, Noe appointed Mrs. Rose Long, Huey's widow, to the seat. When Russell Long was elected senator in 1948, he became the only person in U.S. history to follow both his father and his mother to the Senate.

From the outset, Noe was a foe of the Leche administration. He was prepared to continue Long's legacy through the Share-Our-Wealth organization, which Leche disbanded. Noe's vindictiveness against the machine insiders who had shoved him aside found fruit when he employed investigators of his own to look into corruption in the state government. He became a clearinghouse for information, gathering a total of 980 affidavits covering forced payroll deductions for the organization's "deduct fund," and misuse of state property, equipment, and materials. Noe provided information to the newspapers and to the "Washington Merry-Go-Round" column of Drew Pearson and Robert Allen, which focused attention on political dealings in Louisiana. The infamous Louisiana Scandals of 1939–40 broke wide open when he passed on to the New Orleans *States* a tip he received that window frames and other building materials from LSU were being delivered to the construction site of a home being built by a friend of Leche. The front-page story with photographs of the truck was the first of many exposés of corruption and favoritism. Photographer Wilfred L. d'Aquin and writer Meigs O. Frost lay in the bushes for hours awaiting arrival of the evidence.

Governor Leche resigned on June 26, 1939, pleading ill health, and turned his office over to Lieutenant Governor Earl K. Long. Long sought a full term in the 1940 election, but Noe challenged him as the "true Huey Long candidate." Noe berated Earl Long for testifying against his brother at a U.S. Senate hearing into election fraud, and he ridiculed Earl Long's claim that he was not part of the inner workings of the Leche administration and had not been aware of what was happening. Earl Long, Noe said, was either part of the scandals or, if he knew nothing, was too stupid to be governor.

With the traditional Long vote split, reform candidate Sam H. Jones of Lake Charles went into a runoff with Earl Long. The vote was Long, 226,385; Jones, 154,936; Noe, 116,654; and Jimmy Morrison, 48,243.

Facing an uphill battle, Jones opened negotiations with Noe for his support in the runoff. Jones's managers agreed to pay Noe's campaign debt of $100,000 and give him a full 50 percent share of state jobs. Jones and Noe brought their organizations together in a massive rally in New Orleans. Jones won the runoff 51.8 to 48.2 percent, defeating Long by only 19,000 votes. Allan P. Sindler wrote that "the Jones-Noe friendship was at best an alliance of convenience made for material considerations." While Jones maintained that he had not compromised his reform principles, he did not hesitate to follow up his arrangement with Noe by negotiating a deal with Mayor Maestri and the Old Regulars in New Orleans. The city organization supported Jones's candidates for Congress in New Orleans in return for the good government organization's support of their incumbent judges for reelection. Compromises were also made with Maestri to secure support of Old Regular legislators for the Jones program.

Under the Jones-Noe patronage arrangement, state jobs in New Orleans were awarded through the Jones and Noe ward leaders and through their respective parish leaders for the rest of the state. By the end of 1940 the agreement was falling apart, with an angry Noe expressing disappointment at the distribution of jobs. Noe said that they had "an understanding that my people would get 50 per cent of the jobs." A new patronage committee was established by Jones, but Noe said that Jones was reneging on the promise of equal distribution. Some of Noe's leaders went over to the Jones camp, and with his own organization collapsing as his lack of influence became evident, Noe said that the Jones administration was "nothing more than dictatorship dressed up in silk stockings."

In reneging on his patronage deal with Noe, Jones probably thought that his group had put too much stock in Noe's claim that he could "deliver" his following in the runoff. In his study of state politics, Allan P. Sindler concluded that "Noe had no personal following to deliver. There was nothing in his brief political career as state senator and acting governor which would account for the large country parish organization of over 100,000 voters imputed to his personal leadership." Instead, Sindler averred, Noe "was the voice of those Longites outraged by the Long organization betrayal of Huey and consequently hostile to Earl's candidacy," and in the runoff, like Noe they went for Jones. Sindler said that "Noe, in 1940, by asking his supporters to vote in the second primary for the candidate most of them were going to support anyway, merely created the illusion of a following both personal and deliverable."

In the primary Jones attacked Earl Long but left Noe alone, and did not try to put the issue as a Long versus anti-Long fight. "My pappy was for Huey," Jones told rural audiences, and he promised to continue the liberal program Huey had instituted. "I am not running against a dead man," Jones said. "I am running against a live gang of thieves who betrayed him just as they have betrayed you." With the corruption of the Scandals foremost, many Huey Long devotees were comfortable with the Jones appeal and responded positively to it.

One commentator said that Noe's "dedication to reform was based on obtaining revenge on the Longites for thwarting his political ambitions." After his break with Jones, he planned another run for governor in 1944 but was soon preoccupied with his own defense in a criminal matter. Noe and Seymour Weiss were charged with tax fraud for failing to report their Win-or-Lose profits. The government alleged that they had each evaded $32,000 in income and excess profits taxes on their 1935 distribution from the corporation. Weiss pleaded guilty in return for a lesser sentence and went to federal prison. Noe went to trial and was acquitted. He testified that when he signed the corporation's tax return, he was not aware of its content, as he had not prepared it, and he had not intended to evade taxes. He argued that absent willful intent to defraud, he should go free, and that was the verdict.

Following his acquittal, Noe announced for governor, but did not run. Returning to the good graces of the Longites, he supported the ticket of Lewis Morgan and Earl Long in 1944, in the election won by Jimmie Davis and his running mate. Noe considered a race in 1948, but in 1946 he was indicted for jury tampering in the income tax trial of an associate. He was not convicted, but withdrew from politics to concentrate on his business interests. In 1959, Governor Earl K. Long persuaded his old rival to reenter politics as a candidate for governor on a Noe-Long ticket, with Earl himself the candidate for lieutenant governor. Noe was sixty-eight and had been out of politics for almost twenty years, but Long said that he was glad to run on a slate led by his "old friend." Echoing the LSU football team, their slogan was "The Noe Team is the Go Team."

Earl Long had sought to circumvent the state constitution's ban on consecutive terms by saying that if he resigned as governor before the election, then he would not be his own immediate successor, but would follow after his lieutenant governor, who would become the acting governor. He gave up on that idea, however, and asked Noe to head his ticket. This led to charges by their opponents that Noe was merely a stalking horse for Long, and if they were elected, Noe would resign soon after the inauguration to let Long succeed him. Noe said that he would put up a $100,000 performance bond to guarantee that he would serve his full term.

Noe finished a dismal fourth, behind New Orleans mayor deLesseps S. "Chep" Morrison, former governor Jimmie Davis, and state senator Willie Rainach, leader of the segregation forces in the legislature. Although Earl Long ran third for lieutenant governor, he finished with 60,000 more votes than Noe. Noe endorsed Morrison in the runoff, while Long supported the winner, Davis.

Some observers said that Long wanted Noe to head the ticket because he expected Noe to finance the campaign, which was probably accurate. Noe withdrew from politics after this race, but was active in business affairs, and he and his family were generous supporters of civic projects and charitable endeavors in Monroe and New Orleans. He died in Houston on October 18, 1976.

—J.B.McG.

Conrad, Glenn R. *A Dictionary of Louisiana Biography*. New Orleans: Louisiana Historical Association, 1988.

Davis, Edwin Adams. *Louisiana: A Narrative History*. Baton Rouge: Claitor's Publishing Division, 1971.

Dufour, Charles L. *Ten Flags in the Wind: The Story of Louisiana*. New York: Harper & Row, 1967.

Field, Betty M. "James A. Noe, Governor, 1936." *The Louisiana Governors: From Iberville to Edwards*. Joseph G. Dawson III, ed. Baton Rouge: Louisiana State University Press, 1990.

Haas, Edward F., ed. *The Louisiana Purchase Bicentennial Series in Louisiana History. Vol. VIII: The Age of the Longs: Louisiana, 1928–1960*. Lafayette: Center for Louisiana Studies, University of Louisiana at Lafayette, 2001.

Hair, William Ivy. *The Kingfish and His Realm: The Life and Times of Huey P. Long*. Baton Rouge: Louisiana State University Press, 1991.

Kane, Harnett T. *Louisiana Hayride: The American Rehearsal for Dictatorship, 1928–1940*. Gretna, LA: Pelican, 1971.

Martin, Thomas. *Dynasty: The Longs of Louisiana*. New York: G.P. Putnam's Sons, 1960.

McGuire, Jack B. *Uncle Earl Deserved Better*. New Orleans: Good Reading Books, 1995.

Sanson, Jerry Purvis. *Louisiana During World War II: Politics and Society, 1939–1954*. Baton Rouge: Louisiana State University Press, 1999.

Sindler, Allan P. *Huey Long's Louisiana State Politics, 1920–1952*. Baltimore: Johns Hopkins Press, 1971.

Wall, Bennett H., ed. *Louisiana: A History*. Wheeling, IL: Harlan Davidson, 1997.

Williams, T. Harry. *Huey Long*. New York: Alfred A. Knopf, 1969.

Richard W. Leche

1936–1939

The death of Huey P. Long from an assassin's bullet threw the line of succession to the governor's office in 1936 into great confusion as four Long loyalists claimed anointment by the Kingfish himself. Considering the political climate at the time, it was a cinch that whoever was seen as Long's choice would sail to victory.

The quartet included James A. Noe, state senate president pro tem; John B. Fournet, who had been elected to the state supreme court while serving as lieutenant governor under Governor O. K. Allen; Wade O. Martin Sr., public service commissioner; and Allen J. Ellender, speaker of the House of Representatives. Fournet said that Long told him he would head the Long ticket in 1936; Noe, Martin, and Ellender also claimed Long had told each one he would get the nod.

Long's henchmen came up with a compromise candidate, however: Richard W. Leche, a New Orleans Court of Appeals judge whom Long had arranged to put in Governor Allen's executive office as a watchdog on Allen's activities until his subsequent appointment to a vacancy on the bench.

Leche was selected as the candidate by Long's political cronies, Robert S.

Richard W. Leche, September 21, 1941. Courtesy of the *Times-Picayune*.

Maestri, the state conservation commissioner; Seymour Weiss, treasurer of the Long organization and keeper of the "deduct" box in which the group maintained ready cash exacted from the paychecks of state employees; and other Long leaders. To give the ticket the stamp of Longism, the conferees chose Huey's brother, Earl K. Long, as their candidate for lieutenant governor.

Leche, with his jovial, outgoing manner, was a natural candidate as he carried Long's mantle through the campaign, defeating the anti-Long candidate, Cleveland Dear, by a vote of 362,502 to 176,150.

Sweet victory turned sour some three years later, however, when Leche became involved in the now infamous Louisiana Scandals and wound up going to federal prison. He served four years of a ten-year sentence for his part in defrauding the state highway department of $31,000 in the purchase of trucks for the department. He was the first American governor of Louisiana to be sentenced to prison.

Leche, born on May 15, 1898, in New Orleans, went to Fortier High School and Tulane University, but left his studies to enlist in the army. After being discharged he received a law degree from Loyola University and became active in city politics. He sought election to the state senate in 1928 but lost. It was in that race that Huey Long noticed him and later made Leche his campaign manager in New Orleans during his successful race for the United States Senate.

Long mounted a fierce campaign against the administration of Franklin D. Roosevelt after being elected to the Senate. As a result, he shunned federal public works projects for Louisiana and actually had the legislature pass laws to keep the federal agencies from operating in the state, despite the fact that the Great Depression had fallen hard on Louisiana. Under Long the Works Progress Administration and other federal projects were unwelcome.

Historian Mark T. Carleton wrote that Leche's administration built roads, bridges, and schools and added to the state's medical facilities. When Charity Hospital in New Orleans was torn down for replacement with a twenty-two-story gleaming white building, Governor Leche led the groundbreaking ceremonies by jumping into the massive tractor crane on the spot, hailing the start of work and showing his exuberance for the project.

Leche took a forward-looking business stance by establishing the Department of Commerce and Industry and inaugurating a ten-year property tax exemption program for new or expanded businesses. He enacted the state's first old age pension, provided tenure and a retirement system for teachers, and raised their pay. Because Leche had become governor after Long had the legislature pass "dictator" laws in seven special sessions of the legislature in 1934 and 1935, he wielded great power, but records show he did not use it to reward friends or punish enemies.

The Internal Revenue Service had begun an investigation of Long's tax returns prior to his assassination, and several leading figures in the Long organization, including Seymour Weiss and Abraham L. Shushan, president of the Orleans Levee Board, had been indicted for tax evasion. Roosevelt's administration in Washington was determined to use the Department of Justice to destroy the Long machine.

Long insiders saw his passing as an opportunity to make peace with the national administration, and Leche, encouraged by Maestri and Weiss, extended the olive branch. Long's war on Washington was terminated, and the Reverend Gerald L. K. Smith, the Share-Our-Wealth organizer who claimed six million members and who planned to carry on the fight against Roosevelt, was expelled from the Long organization and sent packing from the state.

In the 1936 session of the legislature, Leche had Long's anti-Roosevelt laws repealed. A cynical Long had banned the WPA and Public Works Administration because he expected the patronage to go to several anti-Long congressmen. The Leche administration now welcomed the federal programs and pledged its cooperation.

With a new era of good feeling between Baton Rouge and Washington, the Justice Department dismissed its criminal tax evasion cases against organization leaders, although it collected back taxes and penalties in civil cases. To demonstrate its regard for the president, who stopped at the Texas Centennial Grounds in Dallas on his way to a fishing trip in the Gulf of Mexico, the Leche administration convened the Louisiana legislature for a special session there to pay tribute to FDR. Hundreds of state politicians went to Texas on a special train, accompanied by the LSU band. This may be the only instance in which the legislature of one state met in another state. At the 1936 Democratic National Convention, the Louisiana delegation, led by Seymour Weiss as its national committeeman, seconded Roosevelt's nomination. Leche received the federal patronage, and WPA and PWA funds flowed into Louisiana.

An accommodation was born between state and federal administrations, in which FDR obtained the loyalty of the Long organization and administration, and the Share-Our-Wealth movement ended. The indictments were dismissed and further investigations were not pursued. Louisiana was brought back into the Roosevelt administration's fold, the arrangement becoming known as the "Second Louisiana Purchase."

Leche ended Huey Long's war on New Orleans as well as the war against Washington. Long had determined to destroy the political influence of the city machine except as an adjunct of his own; he had Governor Allen send the National Guard into New Orleans in 1934, to intimidate opponents of his candidates in the city election. After the Old Regular candidate, T. Semmes Walmsley, was elected mayor, Allen named Long special counsel to investigate vice in the city. At Long's direction the legislature stripped the mayor of important powers of his office, including control of the police department, and reduced the city's tax revenues, to force the Regulars to come to terms. After Long was killed, peace overtures were made; the Leche forces agreed to restore the city's tax revenues and powers, but only if Walmsley resigned as mayor. The Old Regular ward leaders abandoned Walmsley, several members of the commission council who in turn succeeded to the mayoralty resigned, and Maestri was named to the council, moving into the line of succession. Once Maestri became mayor the legislature added two years to his initial term of office, so he did not have to face voters until 1942. In the new era of political peace, the anti-Longs supported the arrangement that made Maestri mayor.

It was said that Long wanted the nation, while his heirs wanted only Louisiana, and that while Long wanted to share the nation's wealth with the people, his heirs sought only to share the state's wealth among themselves. Long was reported to have said that, "If those fellows ever try to use the powers I've given them, without me to hold them down, they'll all land in the penitentiary." His prophecy came true.

Leche was not overly ambitious and would have been happy to remain in an undemanding judgeship, but he yielded to Maestri's insistence that he had been anointed by the Kingfish as Allen's successor. In 1938, when two new federal district court judgeships were created for Louisiana, Leche sought one, which would have given him the appointment for life, allowing Earl Long to succeed him for the remaining part of his term and run for a full one in 1940. An FBI investigation of Leche's fitness, however, turned up damaging charges of corruption in the state administration.

Noe, using his own investigators, collected some 980 affidavits of alleged wrongdoing, and fed his information to the newspapers. Beginning in 1938, the New Orleans *Times-Picayune* and its afternoon daily, the *States*, published exposés of deductions from state employees' salaries for political contributions, forced subscriptions to the *American Progress*, the Longite newspaper, and other misdeeds. Not much attention was paid to these stories until June 1939, when the *States*, tipped off by Noe, published photos of an LSU truck delivering window frames to a home being built for one of Governor Leche's friends. The resulting outcry triggered the investigations that became known as the Louisiana Scandals of 1939–40, which saw 250 indictments, three suicides, and a claim that $100 million of state funds had been plundered.

James Monroe Smith, president of LSU, forged Governor Allen's signature to $500,000 of university bonds, which he deposited as collateral to speculate in grain futures. When word of his activities leaked, he met with Leche to ask the governor to approve the "loan" of the bonds to him. Leche refused. Dr. Smith fled to Canada but was apprehended and extradited to stand trial. He was sentenced to prison. With rumors of corruption abounding, an embattled Leche, after meeting with Mayor Maestri and Earl Long, resigned as governor on June 26, 1939, citing ill health.

The national and state administrations had been close allies before the onset of the scandals. The attorney general of the United States, Frank Murphy, received an honorary degree from LSU at the 1939 commencement at which Leche presided. They were joined on the platform by another special guest, FBI director J. Edgar Hoover. The president, on a visit to New Orleans, was feted at a luncheon at Antoine's Restaurant with Governor Leche, Mayor Maestri, and city and state dignitaries. Leche, in early 1939, called for a third term for FDR. As the extent of graft, fraud, and corruption became known, however, the Roosevelt administration disowned the heirs of Huey Long and organized federal prosecutions. After their brush with the IRS in 1936, state politicians routinely paid federal taxes on their political deals, so that avenue was not open to prosecution by the Justice Department. Mail fraud statutes were available, however, and since checks were then routinely cleared between banks by mail, many of the prosecutions were made for mail fraud.

Leche at his trial denied receiving any money from the truck sale, but under questioning by Assistant U.S. Attorney General O. John Rogge, the special prosecutor sent from Washington, he conceded that he had become a wealthy man during his three years in office. He acknowledged that he made $67,000 in an oil deal with Weiss and that his own $75,000 St. Tammany Parish home cost him personally only $10,000. He also admitted that he had accumulated about $450,000 in his three years as governor on a $7,500 salary. His income tax returns showed an increase from $14,000 in 1934 to $282,000 in 1938.

Leche insisted that most of his money came from oil and gas commissions that were legal and that he made a "windfall" profit from the sale of the *American Progress*, a Long organization newspaper. Leche paid $38,000 for the paper when he became governor in 1936 and sold it in 1938 for $187,500. He also received $36,000 in dividends. He bought the *Progress* from the Long organization and sold it back in an arrangement that Maestri facilitated, with the purchase price supposedly paid from the "deduct fund." Leche said the paper was worth much more when he sold it because the circulation had been increased to 100,000 and the advertising revenue had multiplied. Critics said that state employees were forced to sell subscriptions and that companies doing business with the state saw the wisdom of advertising. The paper failed soon after Leche was sent to prison.

Leche's sentence was viewed in some quarters as unusually harsh. Allen P. Sindler, in *Huey Long's Louisiana*, wrote that "Many Louisianians believed that the sentence was too severe, particularly since Leche's codefendants were only fined. It should be noted, however, that the federal government did not press other cases pending against Leche."

Leche was paroled in 1945 as an exemplary prisoner who had taught classes to other inmates. Among the many letters sent in behalf of his parole and early release were a large number from anti-Longs and others who believed that he had been convicted in an atmosphere of "partisan politics."

President Truman gave Leche a full pardon that restored him to citizenship. The former governor returned to his home community and resumed the practice of law.

Leche also operated a tourist attraction called Bayou Gardens at a home in Lacombe, which is now the headquarters of the Big Branch National Wildlife Refuge. He remained interested in politics but stayed in the background. He showed up in Earl Long's hotel suite to celebrate Long's first primary victory for governor in 1956.

Leche died in New Orleans on February 22, 1965. Carleton wrote that "an embittered Leche protested his innocence to the end, charging that others made him a scapegoat."

Despite all of the allegations of scandal with which Leche's name is indelibly linked, the actual offense on which Leche was convicted was based on the accusation of a single individual who was granted immunity for his own role in the alleged transaction. Exhaustive investigations by various federal and state prosecutors, grand juries, and the Crime Commission established by the reform administration of Governor Jones produced no further evidence of wrongdoing.

Sindler, in discussing the "magnitude of official malfeasance under the Leche Administration," wrote that "The seeds of Huey Long thus bore bitter fruit in the scandals of Dick Leche. The heirs of the Kingfish, inheriting his power and class support, solidified factional control by making peace with federal and state opposition, and then proceeded to conduct the affairs of government as a plunderbund. Yet the scandals were, in reality, not a betrayal of Huey but a natural and logical fulfillment of the mass acceptance of amoral politics induced by the Kingdom of the Kingfish."

—J.B.McG./W.G.C.

Carleton, Mark T. "Richard Webster Leche, Governor, 1936–1939." *The Louisiana Governors: From Iberville to Edwards*. Joseph G. Dawson III, ed. Baton Rouge: Louisiana State University Press, 1990.

Davis, Edwin Adams. *Louisiana: A Narrative History*. Baton Rouge: Claitor's Publishing Division, 1971.

Dufour, Charles L. *Ten Flags in the Wind: The Story of Louisiana*. New York: Harper & Row, 1967.

Haas, Edward F., ed. *The Louisiana Purchase Bicentennial Series in Louisiana History. Vol. VIII: The Age of the Longs: Louisiana, 1928–1960*. Lafayette: Center for Louisiana Studies, University of Louisiana at Lafayette, 2001.

Hair, William Ivy. *The Kingfish and His Realm: The Life and Times of Huey P. Long*. Baton Rouge: Louisiana State University Press, 1991.

Kane, Harnett T. *Louisiana Hayride: The American Rehearsal for Dictatorship, 1928–1940*. Gretna, LA: Pelican, 1971.

McGuire, Jack B. *Uncle Earl Deserved Better*. New Orleans: Good Reading Books, 1995.

Sanson, Jerry Purvis. *Louisiana during World War II: Politics and Society, 1939–1945*. Baton Rouge: Louisiana State University Press, 1999.

Sindler, Allan P. *Huey Long's Louisiana: State Politics, 1920–1952*. Baltimore: Johns Hopkins Press, 1971.

Wall, Bennett H., ed. *Louisiana: A History*. Wheeling, IL: Harlan Davidson, 1997.

Williams, T. Harry. *Huey Long*. New York: Alfred A. Knopf, 1969.

Earl K. Long

1939–1940; 1948–1952; 1956–1960

In a broadcast to the people of Louisiana, Governor Earl K. Long assured them that he was doing well, was sound in mind, and looked forward to touring the state soon. What was unusual about the statement was that his attorney had tape-recorded it during a visit with him at which they discussed strategy for obtaining his release from the Southeast Louisiana State Hospital, a mental institution where he was confined under court order. It was the second time within less than thirty days that he had been legally committed, first in a clinic in Texas to which he had been flown against his will, and then in the hospital he had built in Mandeville. He obtained his release on June 26, 1959, in a manner that his brother, Huey Pierce Long, the Kingfish, would have applauded, by dismissing the officials responsible for holding him and appointing replacements who set him free.

Earl Kemp Long was born near Winnfield on August 26, 1895, the eighth of nine children. Despite Huey's later claims that they lived in poverty and had no shoes growing up, the Longs were middle-class by the standards of their area, and all of the children went to school. Three boys,

Earl K. Long, June 27, 1956. Courtesy of the *Times-Picayune*.

Julius, Huey, and Earl became attorneys; George became a dentist; and several sisters were teachers.

Earl Long grew up loving life on the family's 300-acre farm, gladly performing the chores Huey tried to escape. Earl attended school in Winnfield but dropped out to take to the road as a traveling salesman. When Huey ran for railroad commissioner in 1918, Earl covered the district for him, nailing up posters and nailing down votes. Huey won, and in 1924 was a candidate for governor. He failed to make the runoff, but finished a strong third and positioned himself for the 1928 race, which he won. Earl was active in both campaigns and was a close adviser and confidante.

Earl did not receive a college degree, but took law courses at Loyola University in New Orleans and passed a bar examination in 1926. Huey appointed him attorney for the state inheritance tax collector for Orleans Parish, a lucrative position, but Earl's ambitions brought them into conflict. Huey was elected to the U.S. Senate in 1930, but delayed taking the seat until he could install a friendly successor. Earl believed Huey should support him for governor in 1932, but Huey refused; Earl then asked to go on the Longite ticket as its candidate for lieutenant governor, but Huey again turned him down. Huey explained in his autobiography that it would have been a mistake to have more than one Long in high office, but his real concern was that he knew he could not control Earl and wanted a loyal puppet in the governor's office. Earl ran for lieutenant governor anyway, with the support of Julius and other family members, and allied himself with the anti-Long ticket headed by George S. Guion. Huey and Earl crossed paths several times during the campaign and attacked each other. On one occasion, Earl challenged Huey to a fight.

The "Complete the Work of Huey P. Long" slate won a smashing victory. Earl was given a job as an attorney for the Home Owner's Loan Corporation by the Roosevelt administration, which was directing patronage to Huey's opponents. Earl continued to nurse his wounds, and when a Senate subcommittee came to New Orleans to investigate vote fraud in the election of Huey's candidate, John H. Overton, to the Senate in 1932, testified to ballot stuffing by the Long organization in prior elections and said a utility company lobbyist had given Huey $10,000 for the 1928 campaign. "Liar Earl Long!" Huey, acting as counsel for Overton, shouted at him. Earl said that he opposed building the new state capitol because he knew "there was going to be graft in the cement and architects and other things."

Despite the bad blood between the brothers, they needed each other. Earl knew he would have no political future without Huey, and Huey valued Earl's political skills. Huey sought a reconciliation in 1934, and Earl was an adviser to him during the series of special sessions of the legislature in 1934 and 1935 that consolidated Huey's control over every aspect of government. In the jockeying for position by administration leaders after Huey's death, Earl emerged as the candidate for lieutenant governor on a ticket headed by Judge Richard W. Leche, a compromise choice. The Leche-Long ticket won in a landslide during a campaign in which Huey's martyrdom was the only issue. They assailed their opposition, led by Congressman Cleveland Dear, as the "Assassination Ticket."

After his break with Huey, Earl was never trusted by many of his brother's intimates, and he was kept out of their inner circle. He continued to build his own network of political contacts, however, and when Leche resigned as the Louisiana Scandals of 1939–40 unfolded, Earl Long became governor, taking the oath for the first time on June 26, 1939. "It's a terrible thing when a man shows up crooked," he said, "but when Jesus Christ was on Earth he picked twelve men, and one of them was a son-of-a-gun."

Long ran for a full term in the 1940 primary. He was opposed by James A. Noe, a Huey Long stalwart who served briefly as governor when O. K. Allen died in office; Sam H. Jones, a Lake Charles attorney who led anti-Long reform forces; and James H. Morrison, attorney for the strawberry farmers of Hammond. Earl denied any involvement in the scandals, saying, "They'd indicted me if I'd spit on the sidewalk." Jimmy Noe, who claimed he had Huey's blessing to run in 1936, exacted his revenge on those who had denied him the succession by helping newspapers expose the scandals and then running for governor as "the true Huey Long candidate." Sam Jones noted that his "pappy was for Huey," and promised good government, honesty, and efficiency.

Jones stumped the state and attacked Earl for testifying against Huey. "He betrayed his own brother," Jones said. "How can you trust him not to betray you?" Morrison's campaign featured a "Convicts' Parade" on Canal Street in New Orleans, a Mardi Gras extravaganza of floats satirizing the scandals, with Earl Long in prison stripes. Morrison carried around a trained monkey that he called Earl Long. When the monkey ran away, Morrison said "He went nuts from being called Earl Long." Earl said he fled because "Morrison was too cheap to pay him, even though he was working for peanuts." Jones denounced Earl as a "draft-dodger" in World War I. Earl responded that Jones got no closer to the front lines than Texas and said "his mammy had to bring him cake every day." Jones, Earl sneered, was "High Hat Sam Jones, the High-Kicking, High-Falutin' Snide Sam."

In the January 16, 1940, primary, Long led with 226,385 votes to Jones's 154,936. Noe polled 88,832 and Morrison 41,558. Long had received 40 percent of the vote to 28 percent for Jones, but he was in trouble in the runoff. Jones obtained Noe's endorsement by promising him a 50 percent share of the state patronage, and they combined forces. Jones won a narrow victory in the February 20, 1940 runoff: 284,437 (51.8 percent) to 265,403 (48.2 percent).

While most observers thought Earl Long was through, they failed to recognize just how close he had come to victory, despite all of the bad baggage of the scandals that he carried. He spent the next four years in a continuing campaign, attending the legislative sessions and building his network of supporters when not attending to his Pea Patch Farm in Winnfield or an apartment building in New Orleans.

Long announced for governor in the 1944 election, but ran for lieutenant governor on a ticket headed by former Congressman Lewis Morgan of Covington after New Orleans Mayor Robert S. Maestri refused to support Earl for the top spot. Maestri, Huey's principal financial backer, had served as commissioner of conservation before becoming mayor. Devoted to Huey's memory, he did not fully trust Earl. Public Service Commissioner James H. "Jimmie" Davis, composer of "You Are My Sunshine," ran, as did Jimmy Morrison, now a congressman. Davis ran ahead of Morgan in the primary, but Long outdistanced his running mate. With Davis favored to win, Long sought to persuade Morgan to withdraw, as under state law if there was no runoff for governor, the top finishers would be elected to other offices, and Long would become lieutenant governor again. Morgan stayed in the race, which Davis won. Long ran ahead of Morgan again and narrowly lost for lieutenant governor.

The people were bored by eight years of reform rule as the 1948 state election approached. Earl Long declared early, dismissing the Jones-Davis administrations as "do-nothing" and pledging a broad program of benefits, including an increase to $50 in old-age pensions, free hot school lunches, a $5,000 homestead exemption, $2400 minimum salaries for schoolteachers, a one-time veterans' bonus, public improvements in roads and institutions, and a trade school in every parish. Sam Jones ran again, with the support of Governor Davis and the reform mayor of New Orleans, deLesseps S. "Chep" Morrison, who ousted Maestri in 1946. Jones sought to rekindle the reform crusade of 1940, but the scandals were no longer an issue, and Jones's platitudes and "cold fish" personality could not compete with Long's promises and stump performances. Jimmy Morrison ran again, with the support of the Old Regulars in New Orleans, although former mayor Maestri and several other leaders left the caucus to back Long, and Judge Robert F. Kennon of Minden, proclaiming himself the only true reform candidate, headed an all-veterans ticket.

In the January 20, 1948, primary, Long led Jones 267,253 to 147,329.

Kennon finished a strong third with 127,569, and Morrison had 101,754. With about 41 percent of the vote, Long was in the same position as in 1940's first primary, but this time Jones was the one in trouble. Earl enlisted the support of Huey's widow, Rose, and their son, Russell B. Long, and consolidated his support from rural parish courthouse officeholders.

In the runoff he carried his entire state ticket and a majority of both houses of the legislature into office with him. In the February 24, 1948, runoff, he defeated Jones by 432,528 to 223,971, receiving 66 percent of the vote. "Happy days are here again," he proclaimed. "The Longs are back in the saddle. We'll improve on everything Huey did." The inauguration was held in the LSU stadium, with a crowd of thousands that consumed hot dogs, buttermilk, and soft drinks. Long had sent out a postcard inviting everyone in the state to come and, observing the crowd, he said, "It looks like they all did."

In his first legislative session he pushed through $200 million of new and increased taxes. The total amount of state taxes increased by 50 percent before he was through. He repealed civil service and mounted an assault on New Orleans reminiscent of Huey's fight with Mayor Walmsley, in which he reduced the city's sales tax and enlarged the commission council so that a member would be elected from each of the municipal districts from which assessors were elected. With the Old Regulars holding most of those posts, Earl expected to elect an anti-Morrison majority on the council in 1950. He delivered on his pledges for increased old-age pensions, hospitals, highways, trade schools, the veterans' bonus, and teacher pay raises, and he equalized the pay of black teachers with that of whites. Blacks had heretofore been paid less.

Long's increases in taxes on cigarettes, wine, beer, liquor, and gasoline were especially unpopular, and his efforts to politicize the port board in New Orleans and the LSU Board of Supervisors through constitutional amendments drew fire. He even passed a tax on slot machines, which were illegal.

Although Long won the runoff with a two-to-one majority, his popularity nosedived, and a special election for the U.S. Senate became a referendum on his administration that he almost lost. Senator John H. Overton had died with two years remaining in his term, so a special election was set for August 31, 1948. Russell Long, serving as his Uncle Earl's executive counsel, was opposed for the seat by Judge Kennon, buoyed by the name recognition he garnered in his run for governor.

Russell Long won by fewer than 11,000 votes, 264,143 to 253,668. Kennon, with Mayor Morrison's support, carried New Orleans by over 25,000 votes. All of the governor's constitutional amendments went down to defeat. Chastened, Earl Long mended his ways and supported a home rule charter for New Orleans. Russell Long was overwhelmingly elected to a full term in 1950, although the governor's proposal for a $140 million bond issue for highways was defeated. In New Orleans, Mayor Morrison won a resounding reelection and carried most of his council ticket with him.

A party loyalist, Long supported Truman's election in 1948 despite the president's unpopularity in Louisiana. Dixiecrat forces in the state won a Democratic State Central Committee vote to award the rooster, traditional emblem of the state party, to the Thurmond-Wright electors. Long called a special session of the legislature to place Truman electors on the ballot, but the Dixiecrats carried the state.

Long floated the idea of holding a constitutional convention to modernize the 1921 document that had been amended countless times, but had to abandon the proposal when it was criticized on the grounds that he would control a large number of delegates and would use it to extend his term or to remove the ban on consecutive terms. He considered running for lieutenant governor, but when reaction was lukewarm from his own group, he fielded a ticket headed by Judge Carlos G. Spaht of Baton Rouge for governor and State Representative John J. McKeithen of Columbia for lieutenant governor. Lieutenant Governor William J. Dodd, elected on Long's ticket in 1948, had expected to head the Long slate in the 1952 election, but the governor declined to support him. Long thought Dodd had tried to "take over" in 1950 while he recovered from a severe heart attack at his Pea Patch Farm in Winnfield, and the two men feuded thereafter. Lucille Mae Grace, the register of the state land office, sought to become the state's first woman governor, while State Senator Dudley J. LeBlanc, the patent-medicine man of Hadacol fame, pledged to bring new industries and jobs. The reform forces split between Judge Kennon, making his third statewide race after losing for governor and senator in 1948, and Congressman T. Hale Boggs of New Orleans. Russell Long broke with his uncle to join Mayor Morrison in supporting Boggs. An Alexandria cattleman, James M. McLemore, ran on a states' rights program. Cliff Liles, an employee of the legislature, and New Orleans druggist Kermit Parker, the first black since Reconstruction to seek state office, were also candidates.

Spaht led in the primary with 173,987 votes to 163,434 for Kennon, who edged Boggs out to go into the runoff. Spaht never shook the tag that he was "Earl's boy," and despite claims by some historians that Long wanted Spaht to lose, to lay the groundwork for his own comeback after four years of dull reform rule, Long raised money and stumped for him. Kennon won the second primary easily, 482,302 to 302,743.

Describing Long as "every inch a masterful spoils politician," Allen P.

Sindler wrote that "Earl Long's administration from 1948 to 1952 taught the voters to appreciate good government in a manner more dramatic than could a dozen Jones-Davis administrations. The uglier manifestations of Longism reappeared, including a controlled Legislature, a war against New Orleans, and tendencies toward dictatorial power. Most shocking of all, taxes kept pace with expanding benefits, which undermined Longism's persuasive propaganda that its liberalism was somehow free of charge."

Long, however, had learned his lessons well. There was "no hint" of scandal in his administration, and he was no "second Kingfish." Sindler wrote that "Earl outstripped the Kingfish only in the magnitude of state taxation and expenditure. Huey's younger brother never scaled the dizzy heights of adulation and dictatorship that the Kingfish did."

The Kennon administration gave the state "civics textbook government," with an independent legislature and a reform program. Civil service was reinstated and then protected in the constitution. Other constitutional amendments also won passage.

When he announced for governor in the January 1956 primary, Earl Long said that no matter how many candidates ran, "There will be no second primary." The 1956 campaign was a replay of 1948, with promises of higher old-age pensions, more and better roads, pay increases for schoolteachers, and other benefits. His principal opponent was deLesseps S. Morrison, elected to a third term as mayor of New Orleans in 1954.

Other candidates included outgoing Governor Robert F. Kennon's superintendent of state police, Francis C. Grevemberg; the chairman of the state highway commission, Fred Preaus; and James McLemore.

Long knew that television was not kind to him. "It makes me look like a monkey climbing a stick," he said. He made only two formal broadcasts with his ticket and crisscrossed the state, making over 300 stump speeches in a grueling campaign. Thomas Martin, in *Dynasty: The Longs of Louisiana*, described him: "There you would find him, in any score of backwoods parishes in the heat of an election campaign, standing on the platform or the rear of a truck. The steaming Louisiana sun would heat up and Earl would get hot with it. Hands jammed into hip pockets, coat off, sleeves rolled to the elbows, the galluses showing, he would roar his message with a gravel-tinged voice that took on a tremulous falsetto when he became excited." Railing against his opponents, he shouted, "Vote for a man who looks like you, thinks like you, talks like you, and smells like you on Saturday night."

True to his word, Long won an astounding first primary victory with 51.4 percent of the vote, leading his closest opponent, Morrison, by 421,681 to 191,576. "Huey never done that," he noted as he basked in his victory. Preaus got 95,955, Grevemberg 62,309, and McLemore 48,188. The Kennon legislature had strictly limited inaugural costs, so Long was sworn in on a platform in front of the capitol. It was an impressive show, with Governor Earl K. Long, Democratic National Committeewoman Mrs. Earl K. Long, U.S. Senator Russell B. Long, and Congressman George S. Long.

In the 1956 session of the legislature, Long showed his disdain for Kennon's "blue ribbon boards" by having the legislature address out of office those who did not accept his invitation to resign. He engaged in a feud with longtime secretary of state Wade O. Martin Jr., triggered by Long's desire that his father, Wade O. Martin Sr., retire from the public service commission so that a Long ally could seek the seat. The younger Martin and Long wrestled over the microphone at a committee hearing on bills Long introduced to separate the ex-officio functions of insurance commissioner and custodian of voting machines from the secretary of state and make both of them elective offices. Long won his battles with the Martins; the father retired and Long's candidate took the seat, and the son's powers were reduced. Calling Martin "the king of the bow-tie boys," Earl bragged that "we trimmed Little Wade's sails," but the raw exercise of gubernatorial power appeared unseemly to many. The governor became a familiar figure at committee meetings and on the floor of both chambers, reminding longtime observers of the Kingfish "cracking the whip" on legislators. When it was suggested to Long that he was "buying" legislators' votes like "a sack of potatoes," as Huey had boasted, he laughed, "No, I only rent 'em; it's cheaper that way."

The Longs had always brought their supporters together on the basis of class, the have-nots against the haves, with their program fueled by "welfare state" benefits. The Supreme Court's 1954 *Brown v. Board of Education* decision was slow in implementation, despite the intent that desegregation be accomplished "with all deliberate speed"; but after the 1956 state election, race came to the forefront as an issue, with Senator William Rainach and Representative John Garrett leading the agenda of the White Citizens' Councils in the legislature. Long saw that civil rights for blacks could be the wedge issue that would split his following, with poor whites more concerned with keeping the Negro down instead of raising the level of the lower economic class. In Long's 1948–52 administration, black registration increased from 7,000 to over 109,000 as he encouraged registrars of voters to put blacks on the rolls. He was a segregationist; no white Louisiana politician could afford not to be one. Even Mayor Morrison, viewed as a liberal, bragged that he had "been sued more times by the NAACP than any other public official in the state."

Long's political future was put on the line when the White Citizens' Councils undertook purges of blacks from the voting rolls, challenging their registrations and having them stricken for the most minor reasons, such as failing to sign their names as they appeared on the form, or not dotting an "i" or crossing a "t." In Washington Parish alone, Citizens' Council challengers succeeded in striking 1,377 of the 1,500 registered blacks from the rolls. They even went to Winnfield and purged Long's cook, Sadie. The removal of blacks, who had voted for him in record numbers, threatened Long's base, and he was caught between defending their right to vote and alienating rural whites opposed to integration and civil rights. In the end, Long opted to fight a battle to preserve black voting rights.

In the May 1959 session of the legislature, Long sought to halt the purges of blacks by introducing bills that grandfathered in voters who had been on the rolls for a number of years. A House committee ruled these bills were not germane, as the legislature then alternated regular and fiscal sessions, and 1959 was a fiscal one. Long then had his floor leaders in both houses propose his registration bills as amendments to another bill, on the grounds that operations of registrars' offices involved fiscal matters. The stage was set for a confrontation between the governor and the extreme segregationists.

At a Senate committee hearing on June 19, 1959, taunted by Rainach, who said Long was turning his back on the white people of Louisiana, Long told him, "After this is all over, you can go home with your mind at peace and go out on the porch, look at the moon, and talk with your God. And when you do, you'll know that Negroes are human, too! There's no longer any slavery! But this is not a Nigger bill. I'm as much for segregation as you are. Some of our finest, oldest citizens now stand disqualified. There are poor old men and poor old women who have been told they are too ignorant to vote."

Things went downhill from there. Long was convinced that he was the only politician who could guide Louisiana through the integration crisis, and he feared that if older blacks were scratched from the rolls, illiterate rural whites who had supported him in the past would be next. The Longs had never resorted to race-baiting and appeals to Southern tradition, but instead addressed economic and social issues.

Long had not been sleeping well and had started smoking and drinking again. He was mixing pills to calm him down with pills to keep him alert. His wife, Blanche, wanted him to slow down and take a rest, but he refused. He sought diversion by spending several evenings at striptease clubs on Bourbon Street in New Orleans, and was seen in the company of an exotic dancer, Blaze Starr.

In an appearance before a House committee on May 26, 1959, in support of his registration bills, Long lost control. He berated legislators for over an hour, exchanging insults with several and lapsing into profanity. His floor leaders finally persuaded him to leave the podium, and he agreed to appear before a joint session the next day to apologize. On May 27, 1959, he began his speech with the text that had been prepared for him, but he quickly discarded it and went into another tirade until they led him from the podium.

Long's leaders, concerned about their own fortunes in the coming primary, refused to go further with the registration bills, which had become a race issue.

It was obvious that the governor was suffering a breakdown. He was determined to embark on a weekend stumping tour to take his case to the people. His wife feared for his health and was afraid the effort would kill him. Russell Long was afraid that the governor would cause further embarrassment, and he and Mrs. Long both felt he had suffered a breakdown that affected his mental health as well as his physical well-being. They consulted with other family members and asked State Hospitals Department director Jesse H. Bankston to send attendants from Southeast Louisiana Hospital in Mandeville to the mansion.

The governor was given a sedative by a cousin, Dr. Arthur Long, and confined to his bedroom by the hospital attendants. After weighing alternatives, and Bankston's recommendations, the family decided the only way that he could receive needed rest and care would be to take him out of the state, to the Harris Clinic, a mental health care facility at John Sealy Hospital in Galveston, Texas, where he could not exercise his powers as governor. Long was strapped to a gurney, taken against his will to the airport, and flown to Galveston. Dr. Titus Harris, director of the clinic, had been led to believe Long was coming as a willing patient, and was surprised by his protests that he had been "kidnapped" when he arrived.

The hospital, which indicated that his condition was improving and he was responding well to treatment, said it could not continue to hold him against his will unless he was legally committed. Mrs. Long signed the papers, and he was ordered held for a sanity hearing on June 16, 1959. Long filed a habeas corpus petition, and the hearing on it was set for June 15. The sanity hearing was then postponed for a week. Long told Blanche and Russell that he would file federal charges of kidnapping against them for taking him across a state line; they got him to agree to treatment, and he promised to go to Ochsner Foundation Hospital in suburban New Orleans if they would dismiss the commitment proceedings.

The deal was cut, and Long flew home. He entered Ochsner and went through tests, but at breakfast the next morning told Blanche he was going to the Pea Patch Farm to recuperate. She reminded him of his promise, and he said he had kept it. He went to Ochsner but had not said how long he would stay. Long had to go through Baton Rouge to get to

Winnfield, and Blanche Long feared what he might do if he stopped at the capitol and sought to punish those responsible for his hospitalization as well as allies who had failed to come to his side. She called the East Baton Rouge Parish Coroner, Dr. Chester Williams, and asked him to prepare papers to commit Earl to a state institution. She left ahead of her husband to sign the commitment request, and after she did so, sheriff's deputies pulled the governor's state police car over and one of them took the wheel. They let Earl think they were escorting him to the mansion, but instead drove to the basement of the courthouse, where Dr. Williams and a psychiatrist, Dr. Sparkman Wyatt, waited to examine him, as there had to be a medical diagnosis if he were to be committed by a judge.

Long refused to get out of the car. The doctors sat on the curb and talked to him. After this questionable example of curbstone psychiatry, the doctors said Long was suffering from paranoid schizophrenia, a common diagnosis until further examination. The commitment order was signed by District Judge Fred S. LeBlanc, defeated for reelection as attorney general by Long's candidate in 1956. "It was the happiest day of LeBlanc's life when he signed that paper," Long said.

Sheriff's deputies dragged Long kicking and screaming from the state police car to put him in a sheriff's car. Several punches landed on him. He was taken to Southeast Louisiana State Hospital, where he was greeted by Dr. Charles Belcher, who introduced himself as the acting superintendent. "The hell you are," Long told him. "You were Dr. Belcher."

Long demanded access to an attorney and contacted Joe Arthur Sims of Hammond, who had been his candidate for attorney general on the Spaht ticket in 1952, when LeBlanc won. Sims filed for a writ of habeas corpus, and a hearing was set before District Judge Robert D. Jones in Covington on June 26, 1959. In a visit from Sims to map legal strategy, Long taped a message to be given to radio stations, in which he said, "I feel certain that I'll be a free man Friday."

On June 25, 1959, Long filed for separation from Blanche, to remove her legal right as next-of-kin to commit him again. Acting through Sims, he called a meeting of the State Hospitals Board immediately prior to the court hearing. Lieutenant Governor Lether Frazar, who had remained steadfast in his loyalty, and several of Long's legislative allies asked Bankston to order Long's release, or failing that, to resign. Bankston declined.

The habeas corpus hearing was limited to determining whether Long was being legally held. It was not a sanity hearing, as most writers have stated. Had Long presented his case, he would have contended that he was the duly qualified governor, that the constitution had no provision allowing removal or suspension from office for illness, and the only way he could be legally removed was through impeachment. That was unnecessary, however. Sims advised the court that the Hospitals Board had dismissed Bankston; his successor, Dr. Charles Rosenblum had dismissed Dr. Belcher, and the new acting superintendent, Dr. Jesse McClendon, had pronounced Long sane and ordered his release. The state had no cause to hold Long, and the court dismissed the proceedings.

Long set up headquarters at the Pine Manor Motel in Covington, fired the superintendent of state police for failing to protect him, and called a panel of doctors to his side, to assure the people that he was all right.

After resting at the motel and visiting the farm in Winnfield, Long embarked on a western excursion. He flew to Dallas, but was so aggravated by reporters and cameramen, and their flashbulbs popping in his face, that he cut eye and nose slits in a pillowcase and pulled it over his head. The resulting pictures made many think that he must truly be "crazy," and he recognized that he had "just given them what they wanted" by thinking they would not take his picture if they could not see him. Disembarking in Fort Worth, he was met by his limousine and driver, and went on an excursion that took him through several states and briefly into Mexico. Several writers have called the western trip "bizarre," without realizing that the governor was making a tour of racetracks. Along the way, he sent crates of cantaloupes to friends.

Long returned refreshed and ready for battle. He called a special session of the legislature for August 10, 1959, but when it convened his own leaders moved to adjourn immediately. Long strode into the Senate chamber as members were leaving, but instead of launching another tirade, he was subdued. He apologized for losing his temper in May and said, "If I was crazy then, I have always been crazy. So you might say now that you have an opportunity to see a crazy governor."

Long toyed with the idea of trying to circumvent the constitution's limit to one term by suggesting that if he ran for governor but resigned before the election, then Lieutenant Governor Frazar would become governor, and he would be a candidate to succeed Frazar. He soon gave that up, and instead fielded a ticket headed by former governor Noe for governor and himself for lieutenant governor. Some observers said he persuaded Noe to come out of a twenty-year retirement from politics to head the Noe-Long ticket because Earl needed a wealthy man to finance the campaign.

Mayor Chep Morrison and former governor Davis were the favorites in the December 1959 primary. State Senator Willie Rainach ran as the candidate of white supremacy. Bill Dodd also ran, saying that those who truly loved Earl Long should vote for Dodd. He suggested that if the Noe-Long team won, Noe would resign midway in his term to let Long become governor again. Noe offered to put up a $100,000 cash bond that he would serve his full term.

Long stumped the state, flailing his enemies, from "Big Bad Bill" Dodd to "Della Soups" Morrison. Davis, he said, "Didn't do nothin' before and he won't do nothin' if you elect him again." He had nothing against Davis, Long said, "He just loves money more than a hog loves slop." Proclaiming his and Noe's support for segregation, he said that should not be an issue because all of the candidates were for it. The difference was, he said, "That Jimmy Noe and I are reasonable men. We believe in segregation, but we don't want to bring on a race war like Little Willie Rainach. All Rainach wants to do is boil all the poor old colored people in oil. Well, I've got news for Willie Rainach; he has no more chance to be governor than I do to become Pope of Rome, and I'm not a Catholic."

Morrison took a big lead in the first primary, with 278,956 votes to Davis's 213,551. Rainach trailed with 143,045, followed by Noe at 97,654 and Dodd at 85,436. Long ran third for lieutenant governor, behind Mayor George Bowden of Alexandria, on the Morrison ticket, and State Representative C. C. "Taddy" Aycock, Davis's running mate. Long received 60,000 more votes than Noe. The election marked the first time since Huey's 1928 victory that a Long candidate failed to make the runoff. Davis waged a racist campaign in the runoff and defeated Morrison.

Written off again as a has-been, with his health failing, Long announced for the Eighth District seat in Congress held by Harold McSween, who had won it after George S. Long died in office in 1958. A former House floor leader, State Representative Ben Holt, entered the fray in what turned out to be a knock-down, drag-out campaign. "I'm the last of the Red-Hot Papas," Long said. "I invented rock 'em, sock 'em politics." His circulars listing his stumping schedule said, "Nothing will be said to offend anyone. None of my opponents' names will be mentioned in this campaign until they have started in on me."

McSween and Holt attacked Long for what they claimed was the "ridicule and embarrassment" he had brought the state. McSween ran ads with pictures of Long arriving in Fort Worth with the pillowcase over his head. Both criticized him for his socializing with Blaze Starr. "They say I'm runnin' stripteasers," Long thundered. "What the hell, I mean what the devil, would I do if I caught one? Sixty-four years of age and I just had one of the worst operations a man can have."

Long said that Holt had betrayed him, "after all I done for him," and that McSween "needed a lickin'."

McSween ran first in the primary, with 29,747 votes to Long's 26,010 and 10,221 for Holt. Long pulled out all the stops in the runoff, making six or eight stump talks a day, carrying a hillbilly band with him that alternated country and gospel music, with a young singer, Jay Chevalier, belting out "The Ballad of Earl K. Long." Raffle tickets were handed out for drawings for whole hams, sides of bacon, and sacks of flour. Cakes and loaves of bread were given away to all the women, from station wagons that had been filled the night before from "day-olds" at an Alexandria bakery.

Most of Long's friends thought the odds were against him. McSween failed to take the campaign seriously enough when Long announced because he had learned through the medical grapevine that Long's doctor, his sister's husband, had told him that his heart could not stand the stress of a campaign. "I didn't expect him to live until the first primary," McSween said. Holt endorsed McSween in the runoff, and McSween and Long went at each other with no stones unthrown. They almost came to blows when they showed up in the same town. "He's a high hat," Long sneered. "He can talk, sing, smoke, and tell a lie out of one side of his mouth all at the same time. He wears four hundred dollar suits and a high collar. Put one of those suits on Uncle Earl, and it wouldn't go on, it'd be like puttin' socks on a rooster."

Long emptied a safe deposit box of cash, raised what he could from old friends, sold a piece of property he owned at Hot Wells, while pushing himself unmercifully on the stump. In one memorable talk, he said, "I don't know if I talked a week, I could tell you good people more than you already know about me. Please go vote! Vote for me! You won't be sorry. I won't get the swell head. I been governor and I been lieutenant governor, I been a salesman, a lawyer, a farmer, a stock raiser, I picked cotton and I can remember when I put a watermelon in the bag to make my hundred pounds. I been a little bit of everything. I been up and I been down, and I got the same size head, I wear the same size hat that I always wore. And when my little ol' head gets to swellin' to where I think I'm better than you fine people that made me, then I hope she pops. I—hope—she—pops!"

Several days before the runoff, a cousin told Long he was campaigning so hard, the strain was going to kill him. "That's all right," he said. "I'll die happy." He told another person that he would rather win the election and die than lose it and live. He was stumping when he was seized by intense pain; finishing his talk, he went to his suite in the Bentley Hotel in Alexandria. His doctor told him he had suffered a heart attack and must go to the hospital immediately. He refused and put out a story that he had eaten some "overripe pork" at a roadside barbecue stand and had severe indigestion. On Friday, August 26, 1960, the day before the election, and his sixty-fifth birthday, Long had another heart attack, but refused to leave his hotel room until the polls closed and the returns were in. He was afraid that if word got out, people would think he was dying and not bother to vote.

"I'm going to stay here 'til they get finished counting those votes," he told aides. "Only death will get me out." He won, 38,800 to 34,302, told reporters at the door of his room that "I showed that sapsucker that I've still got snap in my suspenders," and was taken to the hospital in an ambulance. He appeared to rally for several days and said he looked forward to going to Washington, although no one doubted that he had his sights set on Baton Rouge again in four years. On September 5, 1960, he died. He was laid in state in the capitol, and 25,000 people passed by his bier to pay their respects. On September 8, twenty-five years to the day after Huey was shot, Earl Long was buried in Winnfield.

During a long career, Earl Long made a remarkable series of political comebacks in 1948, 1956, and 1960, after anti-Long editors and political pundits held premature burial services for him each time. One of the secrets of his success was his common touch; people may have loved Huey, but he did not like to be touched. Those who loved Earl wanted to hug him. He was, he told them, "just a country boy from over in Winn Parish."

Long regarded the hot school lunches, the old age pension, and establishment of Louisiana State University in New Orleans as his greatest accomplishments. In stump speeches he recalled his own school days, when children of poor families went behind the schoolhouse to "eat an old cold biscuit and cold greens. Those biscuits were so hard, you could knock a mule out with one." He said he was proud to have given "a good hot meal and cold, sweet milk for kids," many of whom received their only full, balanced meal of the day at school.

He established LSUNO, now the University of New Orleans, over the opposition of the New Orleans business community, the city government, and the influential LSU Alumni Association. Mayor Morrison favored a small commuter college only, and the alumni wanted assurances that there would be no dormitories, as they did not want to see a large campus that would compete for resources with the flagship in Baton Rouge. When a 178-acre Naval Air Station on the Lakefront was transferred to the Orleans Levee Board, Long's site selection committee asked for it. Louis J. Roussel, an important campaign contributor and supporter, was chairman of the levee board, and he announced that the tract would be developed by the board, with building lots sold for luxury homes. When Long sent word that he wanted the site for the campus, Roussel snapped, "If that's what the governor wants, tell him to get a new board."

Long did exactly that. He replaced four holdovers from the Kennon administration, had the new members he appointed remove Roussel as chairman, and the university got a campus. It is important to realize that in championing the New Orleans campus, he did so over the opposition of a majority of the LSU board of supervisors. The *Times-Picayune* opposed it as a "land grab." The New Orleans chapter of the LSU Alumni Association adopted a resolution declaring LSUNO graduates ineligible for membership.

When LSUNO opened its doors on an integrated basis in 1958, it did so without fanfare or any trouble after the governor made clear that he would not tolerate any disturbances.

Many errors and myths surround Earl Long's career, perpetrated by Hollywood and a small group of Louisiana historians. Thirty years after his collapse in the Legislature, he was the subject of a movie starring Paul Newman and a biography by Morgan Peoples and Michael Kurtz.

The movie, *Blaze*, is good entertainment but bad history. It placed Blaze Starr at the center of events in which she had no part, credited her with engineering his release from the Mandeville hospital and persuading him to run for Congress, and had him dying in her arms. Movie promotions billed it as a steamy love affair that tore the state apart. Blanche Long broke years of silence on the subject of Blaze Starr by saying that Earl's relationship with her was "merely an insignificant extra-marital affair that didn't amount to anything."

Kurtz and Peoples, in their biography, made numerous errors in names, dates, and the sequence of events. They used amateur psychiatry and dubious material in the FBI file on Long, obtained under the Freedom of Information Act, to claim that he suffered from bipolar disorder all his life and had received kickbacks from organized crime. Their contention that he was "crazy" was based on several textbooks and a review of their manuscript by a psychiatrist who was still in undergraduate school when Long died.

The doctors who spent several days with Long following his release from Southeast Louisiana State Hospital included the chairman of the Department of Psychiatry and Psychology at the Tulane University School of Medicine and the chairman of the Department of Psychology at the LSU Medical School. Their conclusion was that the governor had suffered a nervous breakdown caused by overwork and a series of strokes, "sufficiently small so as to produce no obvious or dramatic effect such as muscular incapacity, but severe enough to precipitate serious physical illness."

The doctors concluded:

> In the presence of such physical illness, it is not uncommon to have accompanying emotional symptoms. Frequently such symptoms appear as an exaggeration of an individual's usual mode of behavior.

> As is generally known, Governor Long has always tended to be unusually active, and when faced with a stressful situation, he has responded by increasing his activities. Increased stress or overactivity superimposed upon a damaged nervous system which is not completely healed can cause an overloading. This tendency in behavior coupled with even a mild stroke resulted in a marked physical debilitation. Over-compensation in turn tended to make the governor accelerate his activities to an even greater degree. In lay terminology, eliminating the additional complication of a stroke, this is commonly recognized as a nervous breakdown from overwork.

The medical panel said that Long's recovery from a serious heart attack in 1950 was "indicative of his recuperative powers," but they said his heart was still weakened and suffering from that event and that it could fail under a strain. "At present the governor is rational with no intellectual impairment," the doctors said. Long, sitting on a sofa next to them at a press conference at the motel said, "That means I'm not crazy."

The FBI file reports on Earl Long were a collection of memorandums forwarding information from anonymous informants and regular "crime surveys." While much credence was placed by Kurtz and Peoples on reports to J. Edgar Hoover by B. E. Sackett, a special agent in the New Orleans bureau office, regarding rumors of graft and corruption, the same source breathlessly reported that Leche had resigned as part of a plot by administration insiders to make Long governor so that he would "make a fool of himself" and they would not have to support him for a full term. Sackett reported that Long was "about the dumbest white man I have ever talked to" and said he had "very little intelligence" and "not very much common sense." Sackett had no understanding of the factional nature of state politics when he wired Hoover that Long had been named to head the "party's slate" in the 1940 primary, and that since the Long organization was the "official Democratic Party" in the state, this guaranteed his election. Other reports in following years were of a piece with that. In 1959, one bureau office wired Hoover that Teamster thugs were going to kidnap Governor Long and hold him prisoner until he signed pardons for union members imprisoned in Angola State Penitentiary. On the day that report was sent to Washington, Earl K. Long was under commitment at Southeast Louisiana Hospital.

Long's death marked the end of an era in Louisiana politics. He was a candidate for governor or lieutenant governor in every election but one from 1932 to 1959. He lost for lieutenant governor in 1932, 1944, and 1959, and won in 1936. He lost for governor in 1940, but won in 1948 and 1956. In his final race, for Congress in 1960, he sought redemption, determined to go out a winner, knowing that the strain of the campaign could kill him.

At the end, he was a politician of a past era. Unsurpassed as a stump speaker of the old school and person-to-person buttonholer, his techniques were inadequate for the new era of television. His harangues, the shrieking, high-pitched, rasping voice, his verbal assaults on opponents, and purposely sloppy dress—pants baggy, suspenders snapping—were all devices of a bygone time. He could not make the transformation to the "cool" medium of television. The downfall of 1959 began in 1956, when television for the first time began reporting the doings of the legislature. It was only after his election in 1956 that television's full-dress coverage gave many citizens their first close-up view of their governor in action. Many did not like what they saw. The freewheeling attacks on his enemies and his ranting performances, while colorful and entertaining on the stump, were not well received in many living rooms. For the first time many citizens saw confirmed on their television screens what the newspapers had reported all along.

Uncle Earl's profane presentations, liberally lacing his outbursts with damns and hells, and his anger when he did not get his way, were captured by television. The camera, while honestly objective, seems to emphasize the worst qualities of its subjects, and in that sense Earl Long was surely one of the most dramatic and publicized victims of the television camera's eye. When he battled for black voting rights in the 1959 session of the legislature, he had everything going against him, not only poor health and public opinion, but history as well.

He was in many respects a better politician than Huey. He was the best personal contact campaigner Louisiana ever produced, a rousing, rough-and-tumble Last of the Red-Hot Papas. That he was able to win his "last hurrah" in a hard-fought contest on his old home ground was both a tribute to him, after the ordeal of 1959, and, in the closeness of the contest, an indication of just how much the times had changed.

—J.B.McG.

Dodd, William J. *Peapatch Politics: The Earl Long Era in Louisiana Politics, by Earl's Lieutenant Governor, William J. Dodd.* Baton Rouge: Claitor's Publishing Company, 1991.

Jeansonne, Glen S. *Race, Religion, and Politics: The Louisiana Gubernatorial Elections of 1959–60.* Lafayette: USL History Series, University of Southwestern Louisiana, 1977.

Kurtz, Michael, ed. *The Louisiana Purchase Bicentennial Series in Louisiana History. Vol. IX: Louisiana Since the Longs: 1960 to Century's End.* Lafayette: Center for Louisiana Studies, University of Southwestern Louisiana, 1998.

Kurtz, Michael and Morgan Peoples. *Earl K. Long: The Saga of Uncle Earl and Louisiana Politics*. Baton Rouge: Louisiana State University Press, 1990.

Liebling, A. J. *The Earl of Louisiana*. New York: Simon and Schuster, 1961.

Litton, G. Dupre. *The Wizard of Winnfield*. New York: Carlton Press, 1982.

Long, Blanche R. "His Wife's Story of the Commitment." *Life* (vol. XLVI), 15 June 1959.

Long, Huey P. *Every Man a King*. New Orleans: National Book Company, 1933.

Martin, Thomas. *Dynasty: The Longs of Louisiana*. New York, G.P. Putnam's Sons, 1960.

McCaughan, Richard B. *Socks on a Rooster: Louisiana's Earl K. Long*. Baton Rouge: Claitor's Book Store, 1967.

McGuire, Jack B. *Uncle Earl Deserved Better*. New Orleans: Good Reading Books, 1995.

Optowsky, Stan. *The Longs of Louisiana*. New York: E.P. Dutton, 1960.

Peoples, Morgan. "Earl Kemp Long, The Man from Pea Patch Farm." *Louisiana History* vol. XVII, no. 4 (Fall 1976).

Sindler, Allan P. *Huey Long's Louisiana: State Politics, 1920–1952*. Baltimore: Johns Hopkins Press, 1971.

Wall, Bennett H., ed. *Louisiana: A History*. Wheeling, IL: Harlan Davidson, 1997.

Williams, T. Harry. *Huey Long*. New York: Alfred A. Knopf, 1969.

Sam Houston Jones

1940–1944

Sam Houston Jones, born July 15, 1897, in a log cabin in the piney woods near Merryville, was maturing as an attorney when Huey P. Long won the governorship in 1928, and from that perspective experienced firsthand Long's manipulation of the legislature and flaunting of the law to serve his own purposes while creating a virtual dictatorship.

Young Sam, thus endowed with the heritage of pioneering America, won admittance to the bar in 1922 by studying under an attorney in DeRidder, where his family moved when his father became clerk of court in Beauregard Parish. While serving as an assistant district attorney for nine years, Jones had a front row seat as the Louisiana Scandals unfolded after Huey's assassination in 1935. He developed interest in state politics to the point that, when remnants of the powerful Long machine were being convicted in vigorous prosecutions for violations of state and federal laws, he was ready to take on the political chieftains. Urged by Preston Foster, son of a former governor, and a group of southwest Louisiana businessmen, Sam threw his hat into a crowded race for governor in 1939.

A polished but not dynamic speaker, Jones had won a scholarship to

Sam Houston Jones, May 14, 1940. Courtesy of the *Times-Picayune*.

Louisiana State University in an oratorical contest in his college days. He augmented the meager scholarship funds by waiting tables. When World War I broke out he joined the army.

Without sufficient funds to return to LSU after the war, Sam became a deputy in his father's office, and after getting his law practice credentials, he served as city judge in DeRidder, then joined a law firm. At twenty-one he was the youngest delegate to the 1921 constitutional convention. His later service as Louisiana commander of the American Legion gave him a network of contacts throughout the state.

In a bitter, hard-fought campaign in the winter of 1939–40, Jones won the governorship, defeating Huey's brother Earl K. Long, who as lieutenant governor had succeeded to the post following the resignation of Richard W. Leche. The vote was 284,437 for Jones and 265,403 for Long.

Jones was hailed locally and nationally as the man who dismantled the heretofore invincible political machine built by Huey Long. After campaigning on a pledge of honesty and reform of the state government, Jones swung into action when the legislature convened in Baton Rouge, the state capital. He accomplished a lot in that session, revising the election laws to eliminate fraud at the polls, setting up a constitutional amendment to eliminate the poll tax, abolishing the state sales tax, revising the voter registration law, establishing civil service for state employees, eliminating deducts from state workers' payrolls, passing a public records act, providing voting machines in the cities, and—the jewel of the package—reducing the cost of automobile license plates from $15 to $3 annually.

Jones was an effective campaigner but did not possess the natural, country-style wit of Earl Long, who dubbed him "sweet-smelling Sam, the guy who pumps perfume under his arms," or "High Hat Sam, the High Society Kid," and many more such epithets. But Jones bore down heavily on the scandals which had grabbed the headlines of the state's newspapers for several years. Stump speeches were still in vogue, but each candidate relied heavily on radio; television had not yet come to Louisiana.

A citizens' revolt developed in the wake of the scandals. State law enforcement agencies would do nothing to prosecute the guilty, bringing appeals to the Franklin D. Roosevelt administration to intercede and clean up the continuing scandals. The appeals to federal authorities paid off in 1939 when Attorney General Frank Murphy dispatched a crusading assistant attorney general to New Orleans with instructions to eliminate corruption in state government. Suddenly, the anti-Long faction had a powerful ally.

O. John Rogge (rhymes with foggy), newly appointed head of the criminal division of the Justice Department, arrived in Louisiana with a zealousness to do the job. Graduated Phi Beta Kappa from the University of Illinois at nineteen and Harvard Law School at twenty-one, he exhibited a voracious appetite to fight white-collar crime. It was the perfect setting for him, as a feeling of indignation had swept the state.

In short order, Rogge empaneled grand juries that indicted a string of prominent persons. These included:

- Dr. James Monroe Smith, president of Louisiana State University; Seymour Weiss, the man who handled the deducts from state employees in setting up a political fund; and three others for fraudulent handling of the purchase of a hotel to be used for state purposes. All were convicted and sent to federal prison.
- Abraham L. Shushan, president of the Orleans Levee Board, and four others in a bond-refunding scheme, in which the interest refunds realized found their way into the pockets of the defendants. One defendant committed suicide during the trial and the others landed in federal prison.
- Governor Richard W. Leche for defrauding the state in the purchase of trucks for the highway department. He also went to federal prison, and served two-and-a-half years before being paroled.

There was federal action against others, too, including William G. Rankin, state conservation commissioner who regulated the flow of oil from state-owned lands. Rankin spent a year in federal prison for his part in buying a "gift" yacht for the governor with state funds. And Dr. Smith additionally was convicted of embezzling $500,000 from LSU.

Rogge, by this time a commanding figure in the state, laid the groundwork for Sam Jones to mount a fierce campaign for governor. The road for the prosecutor was not without blocks, however, and it took a genius to arrange the necessary detours. For instance, in the Bienville Hotel deal, in which the state paid $575,000 for the property, the defendants later billed the state $75,000 for the furnishings, which were included in the original purchase. Rogge had hoped to prosecute those involved under the income tax evasion laws, but found each had been careful to pay his taxes.

Rogge began holding daily briefings on his plans, holding forth most mornings in a patio at the Pontchartrain Hotel. He confided to reporters, including this writer, his plans. "I'm going at them through the mail fraud statute of the 1850s," said Rogge. "That statute is so strong that if you even cause someone else to use the mails fraudulently, you can be held just as guilty as the main perpetrator."

The tactic was a winner. Rogge won convictions of the group involved in the hotel deal, proving they had used the mails illegally, as checks involved in their transactions had been sent, received, and cleared by mail. The furniture in the hotel was included in the original deal, Rogge proved, and the perpetrators of the scheme wanted an extra $75,000 to divvy up among themselves.

When a defense attorney complained that the mail fraud statute was enacted to cover minor postal cases, Rogge responded: “Major criminals should not commit minor crimes.”

Rogge spent only eight months in Louisiana, trying cases in New Orleans and Alexandria, but he left impressions that lasted for years.

As for Jones, he led a successful administration in bringing about reforms, reducing 170 state departments to twenty; cutting the size of the New Orleans Dock Board, a state agency that had become an employee deadhead roost, from some 3200 to 900 employees; cutting the tax collector’s payroll staff from 742 to 395; and making comparable reductions in several other agencies. He fulfilled almost all of his campaign pledges but was without a job four years after being elected because the state constitution did not permit successive terms.

Despite his many successes Jones could not overcome the bitter opposition of the district attorney of Plaquemines and St. Bernard Parishes, Leander H. Perez, who became his major nemesis, and that fight developed into a classic Louisiana political battle. While Jones was governor, the sheriff in Plaquemines Parish died. Under the law at that time, the governor was empowered to appoint a successor. However, Perez, a longtime supporter of the Longs, did not want a Jones man, and he blocked the appointee from taking office. Jones called out the National Guard to enforce his order, but Perez blocked the only highway leading to the courthouse in Pointe a la Hache, the parish seat, which lies between the highway and the Mississippi River. After blocking the highway, he took the parish records and boarded a ferry, anchoring it in the middle of the river. A court battle as to who was the legitimate sheriff dragged on until another election took place. The Jones and Perez candidates fought it out at the polls, and the Perez man won.

Jones sought the office again in 1948, but this time it was a different story. His successor in office, Jimmie Davis, paid little attention to keeping up the political infrastructure that helped put Jones over in 1940, with the result that Jones’s base of 1944 had faded and the indignation factor had subsided.

Earl Long swept to victory this time, receiving 432,528 votes to Jones’s 223,971. Although he won heavily, Long never was able to restore the virtual dictatorship enjoyed by brother Huey.

After his 1948 defeat, Jones returned to the practice of law in Lake Charles. He was widely acclaimed for his role in breaking the Long faction's hold on Louisiana government, but did not seek office again, though he was widely sought as a speaker before public interest groups. He was one of the founders of the Public Affairs Research Council of Louisiana, a good government watchdog agency. Jones died in Lake Charles in 1978.

As to Rogge's life after his Louisiana service, he returned to Washington and took up a fight against Nazi influence in the United States. He believed Nazism was more of a threat than Communism and gathered evidence against pro-Nazis in the United States. He ran afoul of Justice Department regulations in disclosing what he claimed were ties between pro-Nazis and U.S. congressmen, and was fired by Attorney General Tom Clark. He died of cancer in 1977.

—W.G.C.

Lake Charles American Press. Files on coverage of Sam Jones during his campaign.

New Orleans Item. Coverage during the period of the Louisiana Scandals trials during 1938–39.

New Orleans States. Coverage during period of Louisiana Scandals. Trial coverage and interview of O. John Rogge by Walter G. Cowan.

Jimmie H. Davis

1944–1948; 1960–1964

The only song played more often, recorded more frequently, and translated into more languages than Jimmie Davis's "You Are My Sunshine" is "Happy Birthday," but the latter song did not elect a governor, as "Sunshine" did.

"How you going to run against that clown?" Earl Long said. "All he does is sing that song and say sweet things." Uncle Earl was not the only politician who found it frustrating to oppose Jimmie Davis, whose stump speech consisted of a few words about how much he loved Louisiana, a promise to serve her well, and an appeal to "peace and harmony" from factional strife, followed by a thirty-minute songfest with the Jimmie Davis Band.

James Houston Davis was born near Beech Springs, a hamlet no longer marked on a map, one of eleven children of an impoverished sharecropper family. The date of his birth was not noted, but he knew it was at the turn of the century, probably 1899 or 1900, so he adopted September 11, 1899, as his birth date. Home was a two-room cabin, and he recalled that "there were never enough beds, so I slept on the floor. I didn't sleep in

Jimmie H. Davis, November 8, 1960. Courtesy of the *Times-Picayune*.

a bed until I was eight or nine. The only good thing was you always had company." He remembered that his presents one Christmas were a dead blackbird and a hog bladder. He said they ate the blackbird and inflated the bladder to make a ball.

Davis was determined to get an education. He picked cotton in the fields, worked odd jobs, and graduated from the tiny Beech Springs High School in 1920. He worked his way through Louisiana College, a Baptist institution in Pineville, by playing his guitar and singing on street corners in Alexandria for nickels. With degree in hand, he went home to Beech Springs, where he taught school and coached basketball until he saved enough money to enroll at Louisiana State University. He earned a master's degree in education and joined the faculty at Dodd College, a Baptist girls' school in Shreveport.

Davis continued to sing and write songs, and he appeared on KWKH radio for five dollars per week. He gained local popularity and came to the attention of Decca Records, which signed him to a contract. His reputation in country music was established with his song, "Nobody's Darling But Mine."

Davis found music to be a wonderful part-time job, but he needed full-time employment to pay his bills and support his wife, Alvern Adams, a schoolteacher whom he married in 1936. He had played music to gather crowds for a judge seeking reelection; the judge won, appointed him clerk of the criminal court in Shreveport, and became his mentor. Davis toured in Louisiana and Texas with a band he formed while holding down the clerk's job. The judge prodded him to seek office, and he ran for and won the post of public safety commissioner for Shreveport in 1938. One observer said that in his first race for elective office, "Davis fully realized the value of entertainment in politics, and his campaigns thereafter stressed his music over his political programs."

In 1940 Davis released his signature song, "You Are My Sunshine." He later said that "Sunshine" became his meal ticket. Millions of copies were sold over the years, and 350 other artists have recorded the song.

This was the era of the "singing cowboy" in the movies, and with his newfound fame, Davis acted in a half-dozen B-grade films he called "horse operas." While he was enjoying his music and the movies, Alvern thought that his future lay in politics, and she urged him to run for the Third District seat on the Public Service Commission in 1942.

"He sang his way to major public office," defeating two Longites, with Alvern mindful that Huey Long went directly from that seat to the governor's chair.

There were eight candidates for governor in 1944. Earl Long announced for governor, but New Orleans Mayor Maestri refused to support him, so he took second place on a ticket headed by former Congressman Lewis H. Morgan of St. Tammany Parish. Other candidates were Mayor Sam Caldwell of Shreveport, Dudley J. LeBlanc, Congressman James H. Morrison of Hammond, and State Senator Ernest Clements, the conservation commissioner under Governor Leche who said he was the "true" Huey Long candidate.

Outgoing reform governor Sam Jones said it was against his principles to endorse a successor, as that smacked of the machine politics that had preceded his election, but he made a series of statewide radio addresses in which he stressed the importance of retaining the reforms and improvements he had made. After considering several alternatives, Jones urged Davis to enter the race, an effort in which he was joined by Julius Long, the estranged brother of Huey and Earl, and Prescott Foster, son of former Governor Murphy J. Foster and father of governor-to-be Mike Foster.

Davis agreed to run but made it clear that he did not want Jones's public support, which he said the governor offered. Jones insisted that he had agreed to back Davis behind the scenes but would not give a public endorsement. Jones thought Davis was a lightweight, not a good candidate but a good campaigner.

Davis said that he did not want to run in 1944 because his records were selling well, "but in politics sometimes you do things that your friends want you to do." While it was clear that Davis was carrying the "good-government" banner, he declined to be labeled, explaining that he "didn't care if they were Long or anti-Long."

Historian Allan Sindler wrote that Davis offered "Peace and Harmony" from factional fighting and "preached soft words even unto the Longites." Davis said his song, "Live and Let Live," would be his policy as governor, because "I'm not mad at anybody."

Earl Long ridiculed Davis as a "banjo-picking song-and-dance man," but the people came out in droves to hear him sing. Opponents attacked him for recording a number of risqué songs early in his career. Earl Long rasped that "He sings 'Nearer My God to Thee' in a Baptist church in North Louisiana on Sunday morning, and then he goes to a honky-tonk in South Louisiana to play 'Bed Bug Blues' Sunday night." When Jimmy Noe, supporting the Morgan-Long slate, assailed Davis's "indecent" songs about "red-hot women" and played one at a stump speech, instead of being embarrassed, Noe's listeners danced to the tune.

Davis led Morgan 167,434 to 131,682 in the primary. The also-rans were Jimmy Morrison, 76,081; Dudley LeBlanc, 40,392; Sam Caldwell, 29,990; and Ernest Clements, 20,404. Earl Long, seeking to be lieutenant governor, ran ahead of Morgan by 63,000 votes, leading Emile Verret, the

Davis candidate for lieutenant governor 194,225 to 128,232. The law then provided that if a candidate for governor won in the primary, or if one of the two runoff candidates for governor withdrew, then there would be no second primary, and the leading candidates for lesser offices would be named the nominees. Earl Long did not believe Morgan could win, so he tried to persuade Maestri to withdraw Old Regular support and force Morgan to drop out of the race. Long could then claim the lieutenant governorship. Maestri declined, and Davis won the February 29, 1944, runoff by a vote of 251,228 to 217,915. Long lost to Verret by only 11,000 votes.

Governor Jones proclaimed Davis's election "a great victory for clean government," but it was apparent from the returns that he won with cross-factional support. While Jones said that Davis's win marked "the first time in forty years that an independent governor has been succeeded by an independent governor," the intense bi-factional politics cooled during Davis's term. "I never take stock in anybody's politics but my own," Davis said.

Wartime conditions and shortages of labor and materials prevented an extensive construction program, but the Davis administration had a number of solid accomplishments. He balanced the budget, built surpluses, increased teacher salaries, provided additional support for education as well as mental health facilities, established the state retirement system, and restored the tax exemptions for new industries that were curtailed in 1941. He created the Department of Wildlife and Fisheries, separating it from the Conservation Commission, and instituted the first driver's license program. Sindler wrote:

> the campaign and administration of Jimmie Davis was a strange interlude in the intense bi-factionalism of Louisiana politics which perhaps satisfied a populace weary of global war and local political bitterness. An era of peace and harmony settled upon the state, with the governor happily presiding over the distribution of ever-increasing state revenues in a manner calculated neither to enlarge reform prestige nor to arouse factional animosities.

Another writer said that Davis had only "a mild commitment to the Jones reform program." While there were notable successes, Davis was criticized for a lack of executive and legislative leadership and for absenteeism. Davis saw no reason to discontinue his music or film activities; the band was put on the state payroll. Davis went to Hollywood for several movies, including 1947's *Louisiana*, in which he starred as himself. One account said, "he was out of the state for more than three hundred days during his term."

Davis's reform credentials were polished when he joined Sam Jones and other good-government types in supporting deLesseps S. "Chep" Morrison's upset victory for mayor of New Orleans in 1946. It was the first time that reform forces held both the governorship and the mayoralty since John M. Parker and Andrew McShane in 1920. Davis, however, was never accepted by some of the reformers who had supported him in 1944. Sindler wrote that they "never became reconciled to the notion of 'Singing Jimmie Davis' as the flag-bearer of good government."

Jones ran for governor again in 1948 against Earl Long, Jimmy Morrison, and Judge Robert F. Kennon. Jones had narrowly beaten Long in 1940, and Davis had needed support of some Longites to defeat Morgan in 1944, but Jones mistakenly sought to recreate his reform crusade of 1940. In his study of state politics, Sindler wrote that, "the Scandals no longer fed the flames of an increased morality, and the reforms so dear to the heart of Jones appeared to many voters to have less value than the welfare-state pledges of Earl Long." He concluded, "Good government, as defined by the actions of Sam Jones and Jimmie Davis, had failed to win the allegiance of a majority of voters."

Long won an overwhelming victory in the runoff, defeating Jones by a margin of two-to-one. While Jones had made it a point of principle not to endorse Davis as his successor in 1944, he had no compunction in asking for Davis's endorsement in 1948. Some Jones people blamed Davis for failing to maintain the Jones organization and for letting the factional animosities diminish. Long got away with attacking Jones and Davis as "do-nothing" governors despite their accomplishments.

Addressing the question of whether the Davis administration was "the lull that caused the storm" of Earl Long's triumphant return, Sindler said that "reform forces tended to blame Jimmie Davis for the decline in popularity of the good-government movement," and added that "there seemed to be considerable evidence for that judgment." While Sindler felt that Davis's leadership was "woefully inept," he noted:

> There were elements of strength in the Davis performance never clearly realized by the reformers and completely obscured by Sam Jones's campaign in 1948. For all his tendencies toward indecision, fiscal circumstances made Davis anything but a 'do nothing' governor. That mistaken verdict was stamped in the minds of a majority of Louisiana voters by the ineptitude of anti-Long campaigning in 1948, together with the personal unpopularity of Jones, rather than by the actions of the Davis administration itself.

Davis left office on a wave of popular approval. He led a songfest at a joint session of the legislature. Saying that he had no regrets about anything, he sang "It Makes No Difference Now."

Davis toured with his band, had radio shows, and operated a nightclub in Palm Springs, California, after leaving the governorship, but he kept a keen eye on state politics. He considered a race for governor in 1956, but felt that Earl Long would again be unbeatable. He bided his time until the 1959 primary election, in which the field included Mayor Chep Morrison of New Orleans; State Auditor William J. Dodd, a Longite who served as lieutenant governor under Long from 1948 to 1952; former governor Noe, with Earl Long as his running mate for lieutenant governor; and State Senator William Rainach, the leader of segregation forces in the legislature.

In the first primary, in which all candidates were on record in support of segregation, Morrison led Davis 278,956 to 213,551. Rainach had 143,045; Noe, 97,654; and Dodd, 85,436. In the runoff, Davis secured the support of Rainach by promising to establish a State Sovereignty Commission with Rainach as chairman. Davis abandoned his peace and harmony line and said that a "sinister element" had been injected into the race, a "bloc vote" by blacks for Morrison. The runoff campaign characterized Morrison as "soft" on segregation. Davis won 487,681 to 414,110 for Morrison.

The second Davis administration was marred by "charges of racial obstructionism, cronyism, and fiscal irresponsibility." Davis had not been comfortable with the racist appeal of his runoff campaign, and after taking office, he "seemed to be embarrassed by, and reluctant to accept, his role of anti-integration leader, but he fulfilled most of his commitments," observed Floyd M. Clay in an essay about Davis.

The federal court in New Orleans ordered desegregation of the public schools beginning with the 1960 school term. A state court enjoined the Orleans Parish School Board from obeying the federal order. In August 1960 the legislature authorized Davis to take over the city's public schools. The federal district court then struck down that act as unconstitutional, restored the authority of the school board, and enjoined the governor from interfering.

To forestall integration Davis called five special sessions within four months. Forty-seven bills to preserve segregation were passed and signed into law by Davis, but every one of any consequence was struck down by the federal court. In some instances U.S. district court judge J. Skelly Wright followed the legislature's proceedings on television and wrote his orders striking down the state actions even before the acts were published.

Davis signed into law legislative acts that stripped the school board of its authority to operate the schools, denied all state funding to integrated schools, and replaced the duly elected school board with a legislative committee. The state "denied accreditation to all racially integrated schools and deprived the students of the right to graduate, receive academic credit, and attend state colleges and universities." The state fought a losing battle; two schools were integrated on a token basis under protection of U.S. marshals, and while resistance continued, it was to no avail. Calmer heads prevailed, and Louisiana did not go through the massive resistance in other states that saw federal troops deployed to enforce court orders.

In later years Davis claimed he had guided the state through the integration crisis. "Everybody ran on the segregation ticket," he explained. "You couldn't be elected without it. When desegregation came we did it without having anybody killed. We didn't even have a fist fight." Davis was a decent man who did not want to do a single thing to harm anyone, but he was a product of his times, and in doing everything he could to preserve segregation, he genuinely thought he was doing his duty to represent the wishes of a majority of the state's people.

His reputation was damaged by the way he handled the integration crisis, and he appeared to give in to Rainach and the extremists. He did have some notable accomplishments in his second term, which included creation of the Legislative Budget Committee and the Legislative Auditor's Office. Critics thought a new million-dollar governor's mansion was an extravagance and ridiculed the Sunshine Bridge built over the Mississippi River at Donaldsonville, saying all it did was connect two sugar cane fields. The Sunshine Bridge, however, became a spur to the growth of industry in the area, and the Toledo Bend Reservoir, which Davis built in North Louisiana, became a catalyst for development there and a prime recreational area.

Scandals rocked the second administration as well. Cronies of the governor chartered the Baker State Bank, and millions of dollars of state funds were deposited in it at no interest. The adverse publicity prompted Davis to propose legislation requiring that idle state funds be placed in interest-bearing accounts; he signed the act into law and later claimed investment of state funds as one of the great accomplishments of his administration. With all of the charges of cronyism on everything from the Baker Bank to the contract to build the mansion, Davis turned around and proposed the first state Code of Ethics, and took credit for its adoption. Criticized for buying a new Cadillac limousine in 1961 rather than keeping Earl Long's 1959 model, Davis rode his horse, Sunshine, up the steps of the capitol, through the Memorial Hall, and into the governor's office. He deadpanned that he wanted to show Sunshine where he worked, but he let it be known that if people did not want him to have a proper official car, he could always go to and from the capitol on horseback.

Davis left a surplus to his successor, John McKeithen, whose election he supported behind the scenes, and turned the direction of his singing career from country music to gospel music in following years. His wife Alvern died in 1968, and he later married Anna Gordon Carter, a member of the Chuck Wagon Gang.

In 1971 Davis sought a political comeback, but failed to make the runoff. He said in later years that not winning was the best thing that had happened to him. He was pushed into the race by friends, and probably ran so that Anna might be the state's first lady, as Alvern had been. He was a proud man, very sensitive to the criticism of his second administration, and he wanted to restore his tarnished image.

Recovering from a severe heart attack in 1987, he said he had no plans for retirement but would just keep going. "When the birds stop singing and the fish stop swimming, I'll keep quiet," he said. "But as long as the public keeps buyin' I'll keep tryin'." His friends built the Jimmie Davis Tabernacle in Jonesboro, near his birthplace, and the Jimmie Davis Homecoming was held there annually on the first Sunday in October.

For years Davis would appear at each year's session of the legislature with his band, to sing and share his homespun wisdom, and he was still making over one hundred appearances a year when he was ninety-five. At a birthday dinner attended by a thousand people, he got up from a wheelchair, locked leg braces into place, and stood up for forty-five minutes. He entertained for forty minutes at his ninety-ninth birthday in 1998, and managed four songs at his one hundredth birthday dinner in 1999, taking the stage with the aid of a walker. In his later years, his vigor was remarkable, and his rich, deep baritone voice lost little strength, but seemed to grow in its emotional depth as he sang of "going home" to the "city on a hill."

One opponent said that it was "just impossible to stay mad" at Jimmie Davis. His warmth and good humor were infectious, and with the exception of the school integration crisis, he avoided controversy. When he was campaigning in 1959, a farmer in the audience asked his stance on a proposed livestock law requiring that cattle be fenced so they didn't wander onto highways. Davis turned to the band, asked for an A-chord, and sang, "Don't Fence Me In." When he was criticized for singing on the campaign trail instead of discussing substantive issues, he said, "If Ted Williams visited a ball park, wouldn't people expect him to take a swing at a ball?"

During his first term as governor Davis recorded "There's a New Moon Over My Shoulder," and it was No. 1 on the *Billboard* country music chart for a week in 1945. In his second term he recorded "Where the Old Red River Flows," and it was a Top 20 country hit. The Peermusic website noted that "Politicians have dabbled in music and musicians have flirted with politics, but it's rare for one person to climb to the top in both fields," as Davis did.

Davis died on November 5, 2001, at 101 years of age. When he was asked how he wished to be remembered, he said, "as someone who scattered a little sunshine along his path."

—J.B.McG.

Clay, Floyd M. "Jimmie Davis, Governor, 1944–1948, 1960–1964." *The Louisiana Governors: From Iberville to Edwards*. Joseph G. Dawson III, ed. Baton Rouge: Louisiana State University Press, 1990.

Davis, Edwin Adams. *Louisiana: A Narrative History*. Baton Rouge: Claitor's Publishing Division, 1971.

Davis, Jimmie. "Country Music Is Part of the People." *Louisiana Heritage* (Summer 1969).

Dufour, Charles L. *Ten Flags in the Wind: The Story of Louisiana*. New York: Harper & Row, 1967.

Gentry, Robert, and Patricia Martinez, eds. *Jimmie Davis 100th Birthday Souvenir History-Picture Book*. Many, LA: Sweet Dreams, 2000.

Gill, Kenny. *Jimmie Davis: More Than Sunshine*. Many, LA: Sweet Dreams, 2000.

"Jimmie Davis." www.peermusic.com.

McGuire, Jack B. Collection, Jimmie Davis File. Various newspaper articles and publications concerning the musical and political career of Jimmie Davis, Special Collections Division, Tulane University Library.

Sanson, Jerry Purvis. *Louisiana During World War II: Politics and Society, 1939–1945*. Baton Rouge: Louisiana State University Press, 1999.

Sindler, Allan P. *Huey Long's Louisiana: State Politics, 1920–1952*. Baltimore: Johns Hopkins Press, 1971.

Wall, Bennett H., ed. *Louisiana: A History*. Wheeling, IL: Harlan Davidson, 1997.

Weill, Gus. *You Are My Sunshine: The Jimmie Davis Story*. Gretna, LA: Pelican, 1987.

Robert F. Kennon

1952–1956

It was former governor Robert F. Kennon's misfortune when he sought a second term in 1963 that his flyers attacking President John F. Kennedy and pledging to oppose the Kennedy administration's civil rights and other "liberal" programs, were put in the mail on November 21, 1963, and arrived in voters' homes the day after the president was assassinated in Dallas. In the aftermath of the martyrdom of the young president, Kennedy's positions that were anathema to a majority of Louisiana citizens were forgotten, and Kennon's campaign collapsed in the bad timing of his criticism.

Bob Kennon was "America's Youngest Mayor" in 1926 when he was elected to that office in Minden at age twenty-three. It was the beginning of a distinguished political career that saw him ranked as one of the triumvirate of Louisiana's great reform governors—John M. Parker, Sam. H. Jones, and Robert Floyd Kennon.

Kennon was born in Minden on August 12, 1902. He received undergraduate and law degrees from LSU and returned to Minden to practice. He served a single term as mayor and several years later was elected district attorney for the Twenty-Sixth Judicial District Court, comprised

Robert F. Kennon, February 20, 1952. Courtesy of the *Times-Picayune*.

of Webster and Boissier Parishes. He earned an excellent record as a prosecutor and in 1940 was elected to the state Second Circuit Court of Appeal.

Following service as a staff officer in the European Theater of Operations in World War II, he was discharged as a lieutenant colonel and returned to the bench. Governor Davis appointed him an associate justice of the Louisiana Supreme Court, to complete an unexpired term of two years. He took leave from the Court of Appeal to serve in that post, after which he resumed his seat on the Court of Appeal.

Kennon ran for governor in the 1948 primary, heading an "all G.I. Ticket." While Governor Sam Jones, having sat out a term, ran again, Kennon claimed to be the only true anti-Long "reform" candidate. He reminded voters of Jones's accommodations with Mayor Maestri and the Old Regulars, and his agreement, later broken, to split state patronage with Jimmy Noe in return for Noe's support in his 1940 runoff victory over Earl Long.

Jones had the support of Governor Jimmie Davis and New Orleans mayor deLesseps S. "Chep" Morrison. Earl K. Long, seeking his first full term, denounced the Jones-Davis administrations as "do-nothing" and promised an extensive program of benefits. He criticized Kennon for not resigning his judgeship to run for governor. Congressman James H. "Jimmy" Morrison of Hammond had the support of the Old Regulars in New Orleans.

Kennon's campaign divided anti-Long forces. He attacked all of his opponents as "machine politicians" and said that Jones was "a wolf in sheep's clothing." Kennon pledged to end industrial tax exemptions, abolish the state property tax, and reform state budget procedures. One observer noted, "His attacks on Jones, coming from the same side of the factional fence, probably helped to persuade many voters that Jones's professions of virtue were more claimed than real."

Kennon began the campaign as an obscure candidate, but gained strength as it progressed. In the January 20 first primary, the totals were Long, 267,253; Jones, 147,329; Kennon, 127,569; and Morrison, 101,754.

Political observers thought Kennon ran a surprisingly strong race in finishing only 20,000 votes behind Jones. He did well in rural parishes and in Lake Charles and Shreveport. Kennon earned Jones's undying enmity by declining to endorse him in the runoff. Jimmy Morrison and the Old Regulars jumped on the Long bandwagon, which overwhelmed Jones 432,528 to 233,971 in the February 24 runoff.

Taking office with a large legislative majority, Long rammed through substantial tax increases to pay for the old-age pensions, hot school lunches, veterans' bonuses, and increased spending on schools, highways, and institutions he had promised. Reminded that he had also promised not to increase taxes, Long said, "How the hell did people expect us to pay for these things?" Long had the subservient legislature repeal civil service, reduce the sales tax of the city of New Orleans in a move reminiscent of Huey's effort to drive Mayor Walmsley from office, and pass constitutional amendments that anti-Longs denounced as "power grabs" to take control of the Dock Board in New Orleans and the LSU Board of Supervisors. Within three months of taking office his popularity had plummeted, and a special election for the U.S. Senate became a referendum on his record. Senator John H. Overton had died with two years remaining in his term. Governor Long appointed a wealthy backer, William C. Feazel, to the seat until an election could be held, in which Russell Long would run. He could not appoint his nephew, who was Huey's son, because Russell was not yet thirty, the minimum age to serve in the Senate; however, if Russell won the special election, while still twenty-nine, he would be thirty by the time he took the oath.

Russell, who was serving as his Uncle Earl's executive counsel, had problems distancing himself from the tax increases, which hit working people with higher levies on cigarettes, beer, liquor, and gasoline. Kennon, with his strong performance in the state election in January, entered the August 31, 1948, primary and united anti-Long forces behind his candidacy. Russell Long won a very narrow victory, 264,143 to 253,668. In New Orleans, where Mayor Morrison supported him, Kennon outpolled Long 78,071 to 52,329.

It took three days to count all of the votes, with the lead going back and forth, and Kennon was convinced that he was "counted out" in a number of Long-dominated rural parishes. In the November election Governor Long's constitutional amendments were defeated, and a chastened Long pursued a new policy of conciliation in which he supported home rule for New Orleans. It paid off in the 1950 election in which Russell Long won overwhelming election to a full term.

With two statewide races behind him, Kennon bided his time for the 1952 gubernatorial primary. He maintained his contacts throughout the state and made an informal agreement with Mayor Morrison by which Morrison would support him in 1952 and he would return the favor in 1956.

The wily Earl Long had to cancel his plans for a constitutional convention to revise the 1921 document when it appeared that he would select a large number of the delegates and would use the rewrite to extend his term of office. Long then considered running for lieutenant governor on a ticket he would field, but the old rumors from 1944, that he would utilize this scheme for a back-door return to the governorship through resignation of the governor in mid-term, discouraged him.

Lieutenant Governor William J. "Bill" Dodd, a Longite who ran with Earl in 1948, thought he had a legitimate claim to leadership of the Long ticket. Earl, however, became disenchanted with Dodd's behavior when Long had a heart attack in 1950. Long claimed that "Big Bad Bill" tried to take over while Long was recuperating at his farm in Winnfield. Others said that "Uncle Earl" was already plotting a race in 1956 and did not trust having Dodd in the governor's chair.

Dodd ran as the "true" Long candidate, while Earl endorsed a ticket headed by Judge Carlos G. Spaht of Baton Rouge for governor and State Representative John J. McKeithen for lieutenant governor. James M. McLemore, an Alexandria cattleman, ran on a states' rights platform; State Senator Dudley J. Leblanc, promoter of the patent medicine Hadacol, said he would use his talents to attract new industry; Lucille Mae Grace, register of the State Land Office, thought a woman governor would make a difference; and New Orleans druggist Kermit Parker was the first black candidate.

Kennon ran as an independent reform candidate. Mayor Morrison had to renege on his commitment to support Kennon when Congressman T. Hale Boggs of New Orleans declared for governor. Boggs and Morrison had been law partners before the war, and Boggs's wife Corinne Claiborne "Lindy" Boggs was Morrison's first cousin. Morrison was upset when Boggs picked State Senator C. E. "Cap" Barham of Ruston as his running mate. Barham had supported Earl Long's assault on New Orleans in the 1948 session of the legislature, and his selection was influenced by William C. Feazel, a major contributor to the Boggs campaign, and Senator Russell B. Long, who broke with his uncle to support Boggs. Boggs also had support from former Governor Jones and Congressman Jimmy Morrison. Some of Mayor Morrison's contributors and political allies in New Orleans, who had backed Boggs in his races for Congress, declined to participate in his alliance with Russell Long and went for Kennon. The *Times-Picayune*, recoiling at the support of Long and Feazel, and the selection of Barham for lieutenant governor, could not bring itself to endorse Boggs, and instead backed McLemore. It was a curious stance on the paper's part, but was explainable by the hostility the paper bore Kennon for splitting the anti-Long vote in the 1948 gubernatorial election.

Some writers contend that Earl Long wanted Spaht to lose. The voters were bored by the reform administrations of Jones and Davis and returned Long to office in 1948, and he fully expected that after another experiment with "good government" under Kennon or Boggs they would bring him back again. Long, however, raised money for Spaht and stumped the state for him. Allan Sindler, in his study of state politics, wrote that "while Earl's selection of an able judge without known Longite standing or statewide recognition reflected his awareness of the intensity of anti-Longism in the state, the vigorous campaign he conducted on Spaht's behalf denied the latter any independent standing," so much so that he could not escape the tag of "Earl's boy."

Long assailed Kennon in the campaign, calling him "Jug Ears." A handsome man, Kennon did have unusually large ears. Earl said that they were so big, he could hear an election coming four years away, and that "His hearing's so good, he can stand in the courthouse in Opelousas and hear a dollar bill drop in Ville Platte."

Kennon, a keen observer said, "spent most of his campaign attacking state Longism and spelling out his pledges of tax reductions and good government reforms in greater detail than other candidates." Kennon said Louisiana was famous for three things—Mardi Gras, black coffee, and corrupt politics, and he was going to change the politics. He and Dodd both claimed that Spaht and Boggs were a Longite "double-entry," with Earl in one camp and Russell in the other, and that Earl Long would be satisfied by the election of either.

In the January 15, 1952, primary, Spaht led with 173,987 votes, followed by Kennon with 163,434, Boggs with 142,542, McLemore with 116,405, Dodd with 90,925, and LeBlanc with 62,906. All of the losing candidates, along with Mayor Morrison and Congressman Jimmy Morrison, supported Kennon in the runoff. He won with 376,232 to Spaht's 242,518, and then defeated a Republican by a margin of 123,000 to 5,000 in the general election. Kennon carried his runoff ticket in with him. Almost half of the House and Senate incumbents seeking reelection were defeated, and a majority of the members of the Kennon legislature were freshmen.

Kennon's "civics book" administration reduced the governor's powers and achieved a solid reform record. He restored civil service by statute and then enshrined it in the constitution. The Departments of Highways, Institutions, and Welfare were placed under "blue ribbon" citizen boards. Voting machines, heretofore required by law only in New Orleans, Baton Rouge, and Shreveport, were made mandatory in every precinct. Kennon, firm in his belief that the Long parish organizations had counted him out in the 1948 Senate race, said that the machines would assure honest elections. Earl Long said, "Give me all five poll commissioners and I'll make them machines play 'Home, Sweet Home.'"

Kennon's admirers hailed his "businesslike administration," as well as the state's "healthy business climate" and "improved national image." He had a truly independent legislature, which he encouraged, "handled troublesome political problems with patience and tact, and was moderate in spite of pressures for an increased program of governmental spending."

The legislature passed and Kennon signed a "right-to-work" law, which allowed employees at unionized plants to keep their jobs without compulsory union membership and payment of dues.

All thirty-four constitutional amendments sponsored by the Kennon administration were passed by large majorities in the November 1952 election. While he regarded the strong state civil service system as one of his greatest accomplishments, Kennon also made needed reforms at the Louisiana State Penitentiary at Angola, bringing in a professional administrator to reorganize and reform the prison, and reduced the gasoline tax by two cents. The legislature passed the first open meetings law, to require that decisions by governing bodies take place in public sessions, and the Legislative Council was established to provide professional counsel to members of the legislature. Teachers' pay was increased and a broad-based effort was made to attract new businesses and industries. A bond issue provided funds for highways, and the Lake Pontchartrain Causeway was made possible through creation of the Greater New Orleans Expressway Commission, a Jefferson and St. Tammany Parishes agency that was authorized to issue its own bonds. A new bridge over the Mississippi River in New Orleans was also authorized.

The Kennon administration, a historian said, "took giant strides in the field of good government." While most of his reforms were well received, Kennon earned the enmity of sheriffs and local officials by sending the state police on gambling raids. Francis C. Grevemberg, Kennon's superintendent of state police, received enormous publicity for personally leading raids and wielding a sledgehammer to destroy dice tables and slot machines. There had long been an understanding, honored by Jones, Davis, and Long, that the state police would patrol the highways and assist local law enforcement agencies when called upon, but that sheriffs would handle gambling in their jurisdictions and determine the nature and extent of enforcement regarding vice. Many voters, particularly in easygoing South Louisiana, saw nothing wrong with a little gambling, and were aggravated by Kennon's tough stance.

Some supporters claimed that Kennon had failed to keep campaign promises regarding jobs, and that once he took office, he did not maintain close ties with local officials who had helped elect him. One writer commented that Kennon "did not keep harmony within his faction nor retain the organization which had elected him."

Kennon went to the 1952 Democratic national convention as titular head of the party in Louisiana, where he refused to sign the "loyalty oath" demanded of Southerners, pledging them to support the nominees in the November election. The Louisiana delegation supported Senator Richard B. Russell of Georgia on all three roll calls, but joined in making the nomination of Governor Adlai E. Stevenson of Illinois unanimous. A conservative, Kennon was opposed to the liberalism of the Truman administration, including the president's support for a Fair Employment Practices Commission and the administration's position on Tidelands oil revenues, which the president insisted belonged to all of the states. When the Republican nominee, General Dwight D. Eisenhower, pledged to support Louisiana's position that a substantial part of the revenues belonged exclusively to the state, Kennon endorsed him. Stevenson carried the state 345,027 to 306,925, but the new Congress enacted the Eisenhower administration's Submerged Lands Act, which gave Louisiana hundreds of millions of dollars in revenues in the following years.

In 1954, the Supreme Court ruled, in *Brown v. Board of Education of Topeka, Kansas*, that segregation of the races in public schools violated the equal protection clause of the Fourteenth Amendment. The court threw out the "separate but equal" doctrine enunciated in *Plessy v. Ferguson* in 1896, and in 1955 the court followed up its ruling with an order that desegregation commence "with all deliberate speed."

Kennon, an avowed segregationist, denounced the court's decision and urged the president not to enforce it. The legislature established a Joint Legislative Committee on Segregation to champion the state's resistance to integration, and Louisiana joined other Southern states in preparing to defend its "way of life."

As seems to be the fate of reform governors, Kennon's popularity waned by the end of his tenure. Political pundits said in 1952 that his election was a repudiation of Earl Long, but it was cut short when Long won a smashing first primary victory in 1956. One chronicle said, "A maverick to the end of his administration, Kennon retired in 1956 spurned by professional politicians and rejected by the voters but with an impressive record of political reform and fiscal responsibility." The Public Affairs Research Council, while applauding good government reforms, said that the Kennon years were "the heyday of large bonuses received by the state for leasing its oil-rich lands. Money poured into the treasury at a reckless pace and was spent even more recklessly." While PAR believed that oil-lease "windfalls" should go into a "rainy-day" fund, Kennon left a surplus of over $61 million to Long.

Earl Long spent the four years between his administrations on a continuous campaign and was the odds-on favorite in 1956. Mayor Morrison made the first of three unsuccessful races for governor, and James

McLemore ran again as a champion of segregation, which all candidates supported. After resigning as head of the state police, Grevemberg ran as well but was disappointed by Kennon's failure to support him. Mayor Morrison sought Kennon's backing but, despite a good working relationship during the past four years, Kennon had not forgiven the mayor for reneging on their agreement for the 1952 election. Kennon endorsed Frederick T. Preaus, a Farmerville auto dealer, who was chairman of the blue-ribbon Louisiana Highway Commission. Earl Long had belittled him with the comment that if you wanted to buy one car, Preaus would be a good man to go to, but if you needed two cars, you should go elsewhere because it would be too big a deal for Preaus to handle.

Kennon practiced law in Baton Rouge, and his politics became more conservative. He supported Eisenhower again in 1956, when the president carried Louisiana, and Nixon in 1960, when Kennedy won the state. With the scandal-plagued second administration of Jimmie Davis drawing to a close, Kennon entered the December 1963 primary, which featured former New Orleans mayor Morrison, Public Service Commissioner John J. McKeithen, State Superintendent of Education Shelby M. Jackson, and Congressman Gillis Long of the Eighth District, a distant cousin of Huey and Earl.

Margaret Dixon wrote in the Baton Rouge *Morning Advocate* that "the main issue seemed to be who could hate Mr. Kennedy the most." With the president and his brother, Attorney General Robert F. Kennedy, reviled in the South for their support of civil rights and the use of federal marshals and troops to enforce integration, Kennon based his campaign on outspoken opposition to the Kennedys. Kennon said that Morrison, Long, and McKeithen were "the Kennedy triple entry," pointing to Morrison's appointment as U.S. ambassador to the Organization of American States, Long's support of Kennedy bills in the House of Representatives, and McKeithen's leadership in the 1960 Kennedy-Johnson campaign in north Louisiana. Kennon appeared to be the leading contender against Morrison, who was conceded a runoff spot, until Kennon's attacks on President John F. Kennedy and his administration backfired in the outpouring of grief following the president's murder and funeral. Morrison led with 299,702 votes, followed by McKeithen with 157,304; Long with 137,788; and Kennon with 127,870. McKeithen came from behind to win the runoff by 70,000 votes.

Kennon continued the practice of law until illness forced him to enter a retirement home in Baton Rouge, where he died on January 11, 1988. He became a physical fitness buff in his later years, and at seventy-five was proud of the fact that he was the same weight as when he played center for the LSU football team fifty-five years earlier.

A *Times-Picayune* editorial on his passing called him "one of the state's pivotal modern governors." The newspaper said that "he changed budgetary procedures and controlled spending so well that he was able to increase money for social programs while reducing taxes and even producing surpluses."

Earl Long had claimed that Kennon was a "high-hat" and that his blood was "75 percent champagne and 25 percent talcum powder," but Charles Hargroder, a newsman who served as his executive assistant, wrote that most people were not familiar with Kennon's gentle manner, compassion, modesty, and concern for others. Hargroder said, "He was colorful, he was resolute, he was loyal, and he was honest." Bob Kennon would have been satisfied with that obituary.

—J.B.McG.

Carter, Doris Dorcas. *Robert Floyd Kennon: Reform Governor*. Lafayette: Center for Louisiana Studies, University of Southwestern Louisiana, 1998.

Davis, Edwin Adams. *Louisiana: A Narrative History*. Baton Rouge: Claitor's Publishing Division, 1971.

Dufour, Charles L. *Ten Flags in the Wind: The Story of Louisiana*. New York: Harper & Row, 1967.

Kurtz, Michael L. "Robert F. Kennon, Governor, 1952–1956." *The Louisiana Governors: From Iberville to Edwards*. Joseph G. Dawson III, ed. Baton Rouge: Louisiana State University Press, 1990.

Sindler, Allan P. *Huey Long's Louisiana: State Politics, 1920–1952*. Baltimore: Johns Hopkins Press, 1971.

Times-Picayune. 17 and 19 January 1988.

Wall, Bennett H., ed. *Louisiana: A History*. Wheeling, IL: Harlan Davidson, 1997.

John J. McKeithen

1964–1972

Louisianians needed a strong voice of moderation in the mid-1960s in the face of federal desegregation and the disrupting civil rights movement. They got it in 1964 with election of Governor John J. McKeithen, who quickly showed an enthusiasm for change that surprised even his critics.

Right away, "Big John," as he was familiarly known, decided he would need more time than the law limiting a governor to a single term would permit. So he hit the ground running almost as soon as the polls closed, lining up support of newspaper publishers, editors, and television officials before passing a constitutional amendment to effect the change to permit two consecutive terms.

Ironically, McKeithen did not fit the role of moderation he later adopted after defeating New Orleans mayor deLesseps S. Morrison, coming as he did from a north Louisiana segregationist background. Once elected, he showed a willingness to work with differing political, religious, and business factions. It was ironic, also, that his accomplishments in his first term were followed by disappointment in the second.

McKeithen was widely praised as the best first-term chief executive

John J. McKeithen, July 16, 1970. Courtesy of the *Times-Picayune*. Photo by H. J. Patterson.

Louisiana had experienced in modern times, the high points being quieting racial crises in Bogalusa and Baton Rouge, passing the state's first strong code of ethics, and reorganizing state offices, as recommended by a commission led by the former governor, Sam Jones, who broke the back of the virtual dictatorship established by Huey Long, and launching a drive for new industry, expanding the state civil service system, raising teacher pay, and increasing support of higher education.

The second term, for which McKeithen defeated a Ku Klux Klan–backed candidate—Sixth District Congressman John R. Rarick, an ultraconservative—in steamroller fashion, was disappointing because he faced a fiscal crisis and charges of ties to racketeering figures.

McKeithen was quick to grab the ball and run with it when he proposed building the Louisiana Superdome, the brainchild of New Orleans mayor Victor H. Schiro and sports enthusiast David Dixon, who foresaw the possibilities in having a giant indoor stadium which could accommodate professional football, the Sugar Bowl, and many related activities. It became the jewel of his governorship.

Segregation was the underlying issue in the 1964 governor's race. A native of north Louisiana, McKeithen was paired against New Orleans mayor Morrison in the Democratic runoff election. Although the candidates did not campaign on the race issue openly, its effect was felt because of population divisions between north and south Louisiana. In the aftermath of a bitter campaign, one of McKeithen's first acts as governor was to appoint his opponent to head an economic development office to search for new industry. The move ended in tragedy, however, as Morrison was killed in an air crash soon after the election, on a pleasure trip to Mexico.

Supporters of McKeithen pointed to his appointments of two African Americans to judgeships in New Orleans as examples of the new statesmanship that was emerging in Southern politics. The two were Ernest N. "Dutch" Morial, named to the Orleans Parish Juvenile Court, and Israel Augustine, named to the Criminal District Court of Orleans Parish. The appointments represented the first blacks chosen for judgeships since the days of Reconstruction after the Civil War.

McKeithen found himself facing a serious racial crisis shortly after winning the governorship. The national civil rights campaign of the 1960s had focused on protests by African Americans in the Bogalusa and Baton Rouge areas. They were threatening to march from Bogalusa to the state capital to air their grievances, and McKeithen defended their right to do so. He called out the national guard to protect them as they marched from Hammond to Baton Rouge.

"The Guard did not have one live round of ammunition, just fixed bayonets on rifles," McKeithen revealed after the march, which was peaceful. Because of McKeithen, Louisiana "never had a Selma," observed John E. Martzell, executive director of the Louisiana Commission on Human Relations, referring to an ugly outbreak of violence in the Alabama civil rights protest. Martzell credits a speech McKeithen made before an AFL-CIO convention in 1966 as "turning around" the state's climate in race relations by urging blacks and whites to find common ground in handling race problems.

The project that caught his eye, however, was the plan to build a domed stadium in New Orleans, which had won a National Football League franchise and had to play in the open-air Tulane stadium, where rain was a frequent threat.

McKeithen literally picked up the ball and ran for a score in the drive for the stadium. This was a classic effort of cooperation by public officials. New Orleans mayor Victor Schiro had appointed sports enthusiast David Dixon chairman of the Mayor's Sports Advisory Committee and charged it with the task of obtaining that franchise and building an all-weather, enclosed stadium, one much like the Houston Astrodome.

When it became clear the city of New Orleans would exhaust its bonding capacity to build such a stadium, then estimated to cost $35 million, Schiro and Dixon visited McKeithen seeking state support for the project. Thus, the Louisiana Stadium and Exposition District was created with McKeithen as its chairman, Schiro its vice chairman, and Dixon as its chief promoter.

Schiro's term as mayor ended in 1970. Mayor Moon Landrieu, who succeeded Schiro, inherited his role and teamed with McKeithen. Meanwhile, opposition to the project by State Senator John Schwegmann caused protracted delays, which in turn increased projected costs to $160 million. Bankers were not in a mood to buy the bonds to finance the proposed stadium until the governor arranged a feasibility study, which endorsed it.

McKeithen later found himself in a swirl of controversy concerning the building of a levee with state dollars at Churchill Farms, which encompasses some 6,000 acres of land in Jefferson Parish, land that was mostly under water. Former governor Jimmie Davis, in one of his last acts as governor in 1964, signed a contract authorizing the state and a regional flood control agency to share $1 million in construction costs for a levee designed to protect the fringe of low-lying Churchill Farms. The contract called for payment by the state of $500,000, half of the original cost of the tract owned by Carlos Marcello, described by *Life* magazine as a powerful mob chieftain. Governor McKeithen, it was claimed, authorized issuance of a check in 1967, saying that he was bound to honor Governor

Davis's commitment, even though the drainage would benefit no one but Marcello. The levee and a drainage station ostensibly were built to enable construction of highways in the area and make the land usable.

The *Life* story did not surface until April 10, 1970, and when it did, McKeithen denied that his administration had issued such a check. There was no official inquiry since the whole deal had been consummated within the law.

In early 1970 McKeithen authorized spending $130,000 to carry the "South's message" on desegregation to the rest of the nation through full-page advertisements in prominent nationally circulated and respected newspapers. He claimed the South, although often criticized, fostered better race relations than other parts of the country. He also had flirted with the idea of being chosen as Hubert Humphrey's vice presidential running mate in 1968.

McKeithen's successes lay in his personal charm as well as in his ability. An open, raucous man with a booming voice and large hands, he was a hit at stump-speaking and on television. Unlike other old-line politicians of that era, he seemed to be devoid of bitterness toward his foes and he showed compassion to blacks in his treatment of them and some of the appointments he made.

Born in Grayson, Louisiana, on May 28, 1918, he attended college in High Point, North Carolina, for two years and then earned a law degree at Louisiana State University in 1938. Following World War II he practiced in Columbia, Louisiana, and was elected to the state House of Representatives in 1948, becoming a legislative leader for Governor Earl K. Long. He ran for lieutenant governor in 1952 but lost. He was elected to the Public Service Commission in 1954 and ran for governor in 1963–64. He lost a race for the U.S. Senate in 1972. Following his terms as governor, McKeithen practiced law in Baton Rouge, and in 1983 he was named a member of the LSU Board of Supervisors. He died on June 4, 1999.

On the way to the governorship, Big John developed a signature phrase that became a trademark of his campaign. Tired after a hard day's campaigning, he did a television ad in which he omitted the "l" in help.

A staff member noticed the gaffe and urged him to do the spot over. McKeithen said, "No, leave it in."

So, "Won't you hep me" it remained. It turned out to be a master stroke, undoubtedly "hepping" him into the governor's chair.

—W.G.C.

"Carlos Marcello: King Thug of Louisiana." *Life*. 8 September 1967.
Chandler, David. *Life* 10 April 1970.

Kelso, Iris. "Governors Were Vastly Different." Interview with Gus Weill. *Times-Picayune*. 1 May 1983.
Smith, Sandy. "Treen: A Governor and a D.A.: An Offer of Resignation." *Life*. 29 September 1967.
States-Item. News stories about Governor McKeithen.
Times-Picayune. Library files.

Edwin W. Edwards

1972–1980; 1984–1988: 1992–1996

Power tends to corrupt and absolute power corrupts absolutely.

—Lord Acton to a correspondent, 1887

When the Louisiana legislature authorized a specified number of casino and riverboat gambling licenses in 1991, it was natural that Governor Edwin Edwards, given his love of rolling the dice, would become involved in seeing who got the licenses. During his four terms in office he built himself into a position of power, and power had become a commodity to market. It was the perfect setting in which to apply the axiom enunciated by Lord Acton a hundred years earlier.

A jury in Federal District Court in Baton Rouge on May 9, 2000, found Edwards and four others, including his son Stephen, guilty of racketeering, mail and wire fraud, conspiracy, and money laundering. Edwards, at that time ex-governor, was convicted of extorting nearly $8 million from

Edwin W. Edwards, April 24, 2000. Courtesy of the *Times-Picayune.* Photo by G. Andrew Boyd.

companies that applied for the licenses during his final term in office, ending in 1996, and also after his retirement.

Edwards was found guilty on seventeen counts. Four others, including the governor's son Stephen, were judged to be guilty on a varying number of counts. Corruption was absolute. Witnesses against the two Edwardses and Andrew Martin, a former aide to the governor, had testified they made large payoffs to the defendants.

The big payoffs were made in deals by applicants for licenses in Kenner, Lake Charles, and an as-yet-to-be-selected site. Eddie DeBartolo Jr., former owner of the San Francisco 49ers, testified he gave Edwards $400,000 for his help in rigging the award of the state's last riverboat license; other defendants testified that they gave payoffs in the amounts of $1.5 million to Edwards and his associates for the Kenner casino, and $550,000 for the Edwards group's help in getting the Lake Charles casino. Other payoffs ran the total to $8 million.

Besides the revelations of the payoffs, there was excitement at the trial when Judge Frank Polozola, a tough-minded jurist, removed Juror No. 68 because he refused to deliberate. (Jurors were identified only by number.) His removal brought furious objections from the defense, which appealed the ruling but lost.

The former governor was sentenced by Judge Polozola to ten years in federal prison; his son got seven years. The former governor was jailed at the federal prison in Fort Worth, Texas, for two years, then moved to the prison camp in Oakdale, Louisiana. Stephen moved from a prison in Beaumont, Texas, to one in Pollock, Louisiana. Their cases were appealed to the United States Supreme Court, which upheld the verdicts. Under federal guidelines, Edwin Edwards would serve at least eight and a half years, and Stephen seven years.

The convictions hit Louisiana like a bombshell falling from the sky. Not since the assassination of Huey Long had the state been so stunned. The convictions vie with the Louisiana Scandals of the 1930s as the foremost era of corruption in Louisiana politics. Veteran court observers credited two factors as contributing to the convictions of the Edwardses: the gag order Judge Polozola slapped on the former governor, known for his charm in swaying opinions, and the change of venue for the trial, which was moved from New Orleans to Baton Rouge, where prosecutors got a more favorable jury pool. In Baton Rouge, it was explained, potential jurors were less likely to be African American or poor people who were solid Edwards supporters. There was only one African American on the jury that returned the guilty verdicts.

Trial of the Edwardses was seen by oldtime political observers as a throwback to Louisiana's legendary corruption that became a style of doing business with the state through the centuries. Without shame at the time, Edwin and Stephen Edwards bargained away gambling boat licenses for casinos in extortions that lasted for years before federal prosecutors broke up the practice.

The governor's mansion in Baton Rouge, the ultimate Southern stately residence of the sitting chief executive of the state, was turned into a seamy headquarters for negotiations for the licenses amid Thursday night poker games in which the governor's friends paid $10,000 each to sit at the table. Some players would lose purposely, it was said, as a way of gaining favor with the governor. Cash flowed freely through Thursday nights during the games. The FBI produced tapes that told of the deals. The governor kept stacks of $100 bills in a mansion safe and used the money to pay for construction work on a $1.2 million home he built during his last term. One contractor was paid $60,000 in cash from the stockpile, a tape showed. On an April 1997 raid, federal agents found $480,000 in cash inside the homes of Edwin and Stephen Edwards, according to testimony at the trial.

The governor, referring to his conviction, said, "I'm sure this will be an important part of whatever history remembers of me—whatever is written about me. But I hope also that everyone will realize there is much more to me than this. No matter how serious it is what I have done or alleged to have done, it is not a reflection on the people of this state. That is a reflection on me, not the people of Louisiana. Whatever happened, happened because I did what I was found guilty of and it does not involve a single citizen of Louisiana."

Edwin Edwards, a French-speaking Cajun, had a meteoric rise to the governorship, which he won in 1972, and during his sixteen years in office he weathered other indictments. He fought off federal charges in 1985 and 1986 of brokering the sale of state hospital and nursing home licenses. The 1985 case ended in a hung jury, and the 1986 trial ended in an acquittal. Showman that he is, the governor showed up for the second trial in a horse-drawn carriage, saying the mode of transportation matched the pace of the prosecution. Edwards was no stranger to the federal courts even before the guilty verdict in 2000.

Born near Marksville, Louisiana, on August 7, 1927, the son of Agnes Brouillette and Clarence W. Edwards, Edwin Washington Edwards graduated from Marksville High School in 1944 and from Louisiana State University Law School in 1949. He was a member of the Crowley City Council from 1954 to 1962, when he was elected to the state senate. In 1965 he was elected to Congress, and in 1972 entered a crowded race for governor.

He ran ahead of the pack, defeating J. Bennett Johnston in the runoff and a Republican, David Treen, in the general election.

Early on as governor, Edwards established his hold on the state political machinery. He called a constitutional convention in 1973, which delivered an updated document to replace the constitution of 1921. The legislature adopted it, and voters ratified it. The state's election process was changed to provide an open primary where candidates of all parties would run at the same time. The winners then would meet in the general election, reducing the number of times voters would cast ballots from three to two. Crossover voting became possible for the first time, and Republicans began picking up crossovers from the outset.

The new constitution also provided for equalized property assessments, an increase in homestead exemptions to $75,000, and the creation of two education boards, one for elementary and secondary schools and another for colleges.

When the state later faced a budget crisis, Edwards came up with a new formula for taxing oil revenues, basing the take on value rather than quantity. This helped to remedy the deficit at that time, bringing millions more dollars to the treasury.

Edwards left a legacy of getting things done as he moved through his four terms. He sparked a drive that brought about the construction of the Interstate highway (I-49) that slices almost the entire north-south length of the state, built a new bridge across the Mississippi at Luling, and led the movement that provided a second Mississippi River bridge at downtown New Orleans.

After serving successive terms, Edwards was not eligible to run again until 1984, at which time he knocked Republican David Treen out of office to gain a third term. During the four-year sit-out period Edwards maintained an office near the state capitol and became pretty much a "sub-governor." He served on the Louisiana Supreme Court temporarily in 1980. In 1988 he ran for a fourth term, but because Charles "Buddy" Roemer, a Republican, ran first in the primary, he pulled out of the general election to await a better political climate.

In the four races for governor he won, Edwards beat his opponents handily. He was seen as a governor who could get things done, and fast. The threatened close of the 1984 World's Fair in New Orleans six weeks ahead of schedule because of impending bankruptcy is a good example.

Faced in early September of that year with bankruptcy, fair sponsors realized their only hope to carry operations through November 12, the set closing date, was to appeal to Governor Edwards, after bankers had refused to provide more funds to see the fair through.

Edwards, contacted while making an inspection of possible industrial sites in Shreveport by helicopter, pledged he'd arrive in New Orleans in three hours. Sitting in the chair from which the fair's director, Peter Spurney, worked, he got a good look at the scope of the grounds, people attending various exhibits and generally appearing to enjoy the festival. His assessment was immediate: "We're not going to let this s.o.b. close before its time," he said, giving assurances to the bankers involved that the state would underwrite any losses they might incur. The fair ran its course.

By 1991 the political climate had improved for Edwards, and this turned out to be a different kind of race, because in the general election he faced David Duke, the neo-Nazi state representative who threw fear into the minds of voters as he espoused Hitler-like beliefs. Edwards trounced Duke and resumed the governorship in 1992. In this race, people who formerly had opposed Edwards flocked to him, fearing the consequences if Duke should win. Business leaders, especially, were concerned. The race brought new political alignments. Bumper stickers proclaiming, "Vote for the Crook: It's Important," flooded the state.

Governor Buddy Roemer had appointed a tough newspaper investigative reporter, Bill Lynch, as the state's first inspector general. He and Edwards became immediate enemies because of Lynch's discoveries of fraud in state contracts, frequently accusing Edwards and his administration of mismanagement. When Edwards asked a Shreveport newspaper for its endorsement over Duke, the answer was, "Only if you agree to retain Lynch." Edwards agreed and held to his pledge.

From the outset, Edwards had been a womanizer and partygoer, though he did not drink. He enjoyed appearing at extravaganzas, but most of all, he enjoyed gambling, frequently flying to Las Vegas, where he gambled thousands of dollars a visit. He was investigated by the Internal Revenue Service for his forays, but not indicted. In 1971 he faced a congressional ethics committee probe because he and his then-wife, Elaine, accepted a $20,000 payment from a South Korean government agent. Edwards later divorced Elaine and married twenty-nine-year-old Candace Picou, whom he also divorced while in prison.

After defeating Treen in 1984, Edwards and his coterie of friends and officeholders arranged a trip to Paris, for $10,000 per person, to celebrate and to wipe out a $4 million campaign debt. Marion Edwards, Edwin's brother who handled the campaign finances, said that he raised $17 million for the 1983 campaign, including the take from the Paris trip, more than President Jefferson paid for the entire Louisiana Territory. The crafty Cajun governor and his friends frolicked on the Champs-Elysées amid the bright lights of Paris. They did not suspect at that time that Edwards would return to face justice another day, and this time he would land in federal prison performing menial chores and, as he told friends, writing his memoirs.

The four-time governor announced in April 2005 he would write his memoirs to tell his life story "from my perspective without malice and acrimony, for both friend and foe alike." He said he would devote a chapter to the casino licensing business and his trial. He hired a Baton Rouge writer, Leo Honeycutt, to help.

"I acknowledge some mistakes," said Edwards. "I feel I owe all Louisianians and my own grandchildren an explanation, not excuses. It won't be easy, but I am comforted in knowing that I did do some things right, from rewriting Louisiana's Constitution in 1973 to making sure those who did not have a voice got one when I appointed minorities to key positions for the first time in state history." The book should be published in late 2007 or early 2008, said Edwards, who began serving his ten-year term in October 2002.

The high-flying Edwards, who ruled with the support of powerful voting majorities, thus crashed ignominiously.

—W.G.C.

Baughman, Christopher. "Optimistic and Fatalistic: Edwin Edwards Prepares for Next Stage of Life." *Baton Rouge Sunday Advocate*. 20 October 2002.

Kelso, Iris. "Black Solidarity Wins It for Edwards and Louisiana." Editorial. *Times-Picayune*. 18 November 1991.

Maginnis, John. *The Last Hayride*. Baton Rouge: Gris Gris Press, 1984.

"A New Era Dawns." Editorial. *Times-Picayune*. 20 October 2002.

Ritea, Steve. "Edwards to Write Memoirs from Jail." *Times-Picayune*. 16 April 2005.

"Life behind Bars." *Times-Picayune*. 20 October 2002.

Roig-Franzia, Manuel. "Edwards Case Shines Light on 'Louisiana Way.'" *Times-Picayune*. 14 May 2000.

"Edwards Guilty: Ex-Governor Faces Forfeiture of Millions, Long Jail Term." *Times-Picayune*. 10 May 2000.

David Treen

1980–1984

David Treen, the first Republican governor in more than a century, was a behind-the-scenes operative who studiously handled every detail of the office as though tomorrow depended on it.

Elected in 1980 after Edwin Edwards finished his second consecutive term, Treen served from 1980 to 1984, when Edwards reclaimed the governorship in a landslide. But the vote returns do not really tell the story of Dave Treen. It was a tough time, being turned out of office after one term, and he understood why. Edwards, the flamboyant campaigner and deal-maker, never really gave up the office. He established a law office near the capitol and campaigned to take it back as soon as the state constitution would allow.

Ironically, Edwin Edwards was responsible for Treen's surge to the governorship in 1980. Edwards decided after his 1972 election as governor that the law requiring party primaries was unfair to Democrats. Under that system, Democrats and Republicans held separate primaries, and the winners would face each other in the general election.

The Democratic candidates would have to mount expensive, months-

David Treen, December 12, 1979. Courtesy of the *Times-Picayune*. Photo by Burt Steel.

long campaigns to win the party nomination, and then would have to defeat a Republican challenger nominated by the party leadership.

In 1975 Edwards pushed a unique primary law through the legislature that would permit all candidates to run in an open primary, thus eliminating a party runoff within its own ranks. It had the effect of reducing the number of elections by at least one, possibly two. Republicans opposed the change, but they benefited greatly by its passage. Under the Open Primary Law, as it became known, all candidates would run in the same primary, with the two leaders squaring off against each other in the general election.

In the 1979 open primary for governor, Treen was faced with a field of strong Democrats, including Lieutenant Governor James E. Fitzmorris Jr., Public Service Commissioner Louis J. Lambert, House Speaker E. L. "Bubba" Henry, State Senator Edgar Mouton, and Secretary of State Paul Hardy. Treen ran first, with 297,469 votes, followed by Lambert with 282,708 and Fitzmorris with 280,412. Fitzmorris claimed that there had been election irregularities that favored Lambert, and he endorsed Treen in the general election, as did Henry, Mouton, and Hardy. With their support, Treen defeated Lambert by the narrow margin of 9,557 votes, 690,691 to 681,134. Outgoing governor Edwin Edwards endorsed Lambert, but his support was perfunctory and it was apparent to political insiders that the wily Edwards, already planning a comeback, preferred a Treen victory so that he could run against him in four years.

In 1983 Edwards secured his third term as governor by unseating Treen. Edwards polled the highest vote ever received by a candidate for governor until that time, 1,008,282 to 586,643 for Treen. During the campaign Edwards quipped that Treen was so slow that "it takes him an hour-and-a-half to watch *60 Minutes*," but he respected Treen and ran a gentlemanly race against him. Treen had received only a handful of minority votes in his election, but appointed blacks to positions in his administration and actively sought black votes in his reelection campaign. That proved a futile effort; blacks voted overwhelmingly for Edwards. Treen was modest, genuine, and charming in personal contacts and with small groups but had the misfortune of coming across as cold and aloof on television, while the colorful and charismatic Edwards was masterful in playing to an audience.

Treen did not shy from talking about his defeat, telling Bill Lynch, veteran New Orleans *States-Item* and *Times-Picayune* reporter, "To the great bulk of voters, Edwards is a more interesting person. A number of people believe he is able to get things done and is more effective. I don't think that is true, but I think that perception exists. It comes from style. He's very articulate and glib, which I mean as a compliment."

The record shows that Treen did accomplish a significant number of things. He was probably most proud of his efforts in swinging a deal with the U.S. Department of Justice in settling a desegregation dispute between the state and the federal government, avoiding a federal court battle.

The agreement he forged called for an improved academic program in the state's predominantly black public colleges and universities and an inducement program to lure more black students to other institutions. In the same vein Treen established the Professional Improvement Program, designed to supplement public school salaries of teachers who took special courses. He also established the Louisiana School for Math, Science, and the Arts, a high school for gifted and talented students on the Northwestern State University campus in Natchitoches.

Treen admitted that he lost ground in his legislative program that regulated worker compensation of employees and reduced costs to employers. Union voters turned against him.

Treen worked out a compromise agreement to preserve the wilderness area in the Atachafalaya River Basin, and is credited with establishing the Department of Environmental Quality. He also set up enterprise zones for economically distressed areas of the state.

Treen is especially proud of his efforts in blocking the U.S. Department of Commerce's attempt to kill the 1984 World's Fair in New Orleans. Malcolm Baldridge, the U.S. secretary of commerce, wanted to call off the New Orleans venture in light of a disastrous fair in Knoxville, Tennessee, two years earlier. Treen prevailed, and while the New Orleans fair was not a financial success, it spawned rebirth of New Orleans's latent riverfront area.

Gus Weill, a leading Louisiana public relations veteran who has handled statewide campaigns for several governors, including Treen, said in a May 1, 1983, *Times-Picayune* interview with political reporter Iris Kelso that Treen was the biggest surprise of his clients. "I, like everyone else, thought he was a very cold, Calvinistic, quiet, solemn man . . . when I got to know him I realized he alone of all the others has no ego. None. For example, he'll tell you to call him Dave, and he's not just being polite. . . . He will not let you lie. And lying is a very important part of public relations. By lying, I mean a slight colorization of reality. . . . But he won't buy it."

Treen came to prominence in Louisiana Republican politics when elected to Congress in 1973, serving until March 10, 1980, when he resigned to become governor.

David Conner Treen, born in Baton Rouge July 16, 1928, graduated from Fortier High School in New Orleans and won undergraduate and law degrees from Tulane University. In the 1960 presidential election he was a States Rights party elector for Senator Harry F. Byrd Sr., of Virginia. He moved to the Republican party and ran against Congressman Hale Boggs for the Second District seat three times, in 1962, 1964, and 1968, narrowly losing in the 1968 contest. He was the Republican candidate for governor against Democratic nominee Edwin Edwards in the 1971 general election, receiving 42.8 percent of the vote while carrying 27 parishes.

Treen was placed in the Third Congressional District by a reapportionment plan designed to protect Boggs, and ran for the open seat vacated by Patrick T. Caffery of Lafayette in 1972. He was a leading figure in the Republican party in Louisiana prior to being elected governor, and has remained active in party affairs after serving as governor. A good, decent man, Treen's thoughtful approach to decision-making hurt him in the eyes of legislators and other politicians, and several members of his staff were accused of blocking supporters' access to the governor. His personal integrity was never questioned. While he said there was no quid pro quo involved, his appointments of the four Democrats who endorsed him in the general election victory to high state jobs angered some conservative Republicans. Edwards, viewed by many as the "governor in waiting," exercised considerable influence over the legislature and made things difficult for Treen.

Following Treen's defeat for reelection, President Reagan nominated him for a seat on the Fifth Circuit Court of Appeals, based in New Orleans, but the nomination did not go forward when some Democratic senators objected to it, raising old issues of his involvement with the States Rights party when he appeared on the same ballot as an elector with Leander Perez, the racist political boss of Plaquemines and St. Bernard Parishes.

In 1991 Edwin Edwards, seeking a return to the governor's mansion, went into a general election contest with David Duke, the former Ku Klux Klansman, after incumbent governor Buddy Roemer failed to make the runoff. In the national uproar over Duke's candidacy, with his neo-Nazi and anti-Semitic background, Treen joined other Republicans, including President George H. W. Bush, in supporting Edwards, who received contributions and support from business and other interests that had opposed him in the past.

Treen toyed with running for U.S. Senator or governor in the ensuing years, and in 1999 he sought a political resurrection by running in a special election for the First Congressional District seat held by Robert Livingston, who resigned when his own extramarital affairs were revealed while he was condemning President Bill Clinton and leading his impeachment by the House of Representatives. The eight other candidates included David Duke and State Representative David Vitter. Treen finished first in a bruising primary, but lost to Vitter in the general election by only 1,812 votes, with 61,661 for Vitter and 59,849 for Treen.

Treen resides in Mandeville, a widower since the death of his wife Dodie.

—W.G.C.

DuBos, Clancy. "Our No-Party System." *Gambit Weekly*. 27 May 2003.

Kelso, Iris. "Governors Were Vastly Different." Interview with Gus Weill. *Times Picayune*. 1 May 1983.

Lynch, Bill. "Treen Sums up Highs, Lows of Four Years." *Times-Picayune*. 11 March 1984.

Maginnis, John. *The Last Hayride*. Baton Rouge: Gris Gris Press, 1984.

Mollere, William J. *History of the Department of Environmental Quality*. October 2002. http://www.dep.state.la.us/organization/hisIMhtm. August 10, 2005.

Wardlaw, Jack. "Treen's Legacy." *Times Picayune*. 26 October 1983.

Buddy Roemer

1988–1992

"Often wrong, but never in doubt" was the characterization of Congressman Buddy Roemer by Speaker of the House Thomas "Tip" O'Neill. The speaker, who proclaimed that "All politics is local," joined most of his colleagues in the belief that the freshman congressman was brash, arrogant, and a headline hunter. Roemer, chafing at the idea of being one of 435 members, sought to call attention to himself by challenging his party's leadership and aligning himself with "Boll Weevil" Democrats, conservatives from the South who were as close to Republicans as possible while still remaining Democrats. They provided President Ronald Reagan with strong support on many issues and distanced themselves from national Democrats on policy matters. After several terms Roemer was bored with Congress, and set his sights on the governorship.

Charles Elson Roemer III was born in Bossier City on October 4, 1943, and raised on Scopena Plantation, a few miles from there. The family had a cotton farming and ginning operation, and his father was a behind-the-scenes mover and shaker in state politics. Buddy graduated from Bossier High School, entered Harvard at sixteen, and earned undergraduate and master's degrees in business administration.

Buddy Roemer, September 29, 1987. Courtesy of the *Times-Picayune*.

Charles E. Roemer II invited several of the candidates for governor in 1971 to meet with the family; they came because they knew that his support would include raising a substantial amount in campaign contributions. The family, led by the elder Roemer, decided on Congressman Edwin W. Edwards of Crowley as its candidate.

Edwards, impressed by Buddy Roemer, brought him into the campaign to lead his effort in north Louisiana. After Edwards's election, the elder Roemer took the powerful position of commissioner of administration. He wielded enormous influence because Edwards delegated the day-to-day operation of state government to him and concentrated on the policy and political aspects of governance. Buddy Roemer started a computer company, Innovative Data Systems, and marketed himself as a political consultant and campaign manager, trading on his relationship with the Edwards administration.

Roemer was elected a delegate to the 1973 constitutional convention, and in 1978 he ran for an open seat in congress. He finished third, but two years later won the seat and was reelected without opposition in 1982, 1984, and 1986. His House colleagues, in a *Congressional Quarterly* ranking of members, called him "an unguided missile on the House floor."

Roemer entered the 1987 primary campaign for governor as the longest of long shots, with 1 percent in the polls. Governor Edwin Edwards, who served the maximum two consecutive terms from 1972 to 1980, had been returned to the mansion in 1984 after ousting the Republican incumbent, Dave Treen. Edwards was now seeking what would be a fourth term. Congressman Billy Tauzin of Chackbay ran, and pundits expected him to take a sizable part of the south Louisiana Cajun vote from Edwards. Congressman Bob Livingston of New Orleans bore the Republican party banner, and Secretary of State James H. "Jim" Brown promised good government after Edwards's brushes with the law, in which federal prosecutors charged him with receiving bribes in return for influencing the award of nursing home certificates. Edwards was indicted but not convicted, and rumors of corruption overshadowed the election.

In 1971 Edwards had gone through two bruising Democratic primaries, only to have to face a fresh Republican, Dave Treen, who had no primary opposition, in the general election. Edwards persuaded the legislature to adopt an open primary law through which all contenders, regardless of party affiliation, would run in a primary, with the top two finishers going into a general election. With Livingston the only Republican in the 1987 race, and Edwards, though wounded, working his contacts throughout the state, most political observers predicted a runoff between those two.

Roemer mounted a grassroots campaign, sounding like an evangelist, preaching how he would restore confidence in state government. In the last thirty days before the October 24 primary he ran an extensive television campaign that featured him full-face, looking directly into the camera, saying what he would do. Roemer promised to eliminate "deadheads" and said that he would close the top four floors of the Education building, where Kelly Nix held sway as state superintendent of education. Roemer believed most problems involved how the state spent its money and he pledged to reform state finances and fiscal policy. He called his plan the "Roemer Revolution," and his supporters reveled in the name "Roemeristas."

Roemer performed well in a television debate, and his campaign gained ground as he called on voters to "slay the dragon," Edwin Edwards. Two weeks before the primary all of the state's major daily newspapers endorsed him. Some said that the timing was a coincidence and that papers in New Orleans, Baton Rouge, Lake Charles, Alexandria, Shreveport, and Monroe arrived at their decisions independently; others suspected that the publishers had gotten together to push Roemer into the runoff with Edwards.

"I love Louisiana, but I hate Louisiana politics," Roemer proclaimed in earnest appeals. The irony of Buddy Roemer's campaign was that he ran as an outsider, a revolutionary who would change things dramatically, when he was in fact the consummate political insider. He ran against what he called "the corruption of the Edwards Administration" without seeing any conflict in the fact that his own father, the commissioner of administration, was convicted in an FBI "sting" investigation called "Brilab" that involved kickbacks on state insurance contracts; his codefendant was Mafia boss Carlos Marcello. The convictions were later set aside.

During the first two Edwards administrations, before he went to Congress, Roemer was aggressive in seeking favors from political friends. Tyler Bridges, in *The Rise of David Duke*, wrote that "as a political consultant, Roemer received government contracts and additional favors from Edwards and other public officials he had helped elect."

John Maginnis, whose books on the 1983 and 1995 elections are classics on Louisiana politics, wrote that Roemer "hit the statewide scene in 1987 as the dragonslayer, the maverick, the revolutionary at the palace gates. But he started the journey years before that, as the young political insider who grew up in the very system he now pledged to take apart." Maginnis noted that Roemer had managed Education Superintendent Kelly Nix's campaign; now, "to shrink the state bureaucracy, the revolutionary candidate promised 'to brick up the top three floors of the Education Building.' No wonder. That's where his office used to be."

Edwards, who had won a straight string of over twenty primary, runoff, and general elections, for city councilman in Crowley, state senator, congressman, and governor, now suffered his first defeat at the hands of a onetime protégé, Buddy Roemer. By the final week of the campaign, Roemer moved from fifth to first place, and a bandwagon, fueled by the newspaper endorsements, his television campaign, debate performance, and an outpouring of support from young business and professional people who had previously disdained politics, was under way.

In the October 24 primary Roemer received 33 percent to 28 percent for Edwards. The vote totals were Roemer, 516,128; Edwards, 434,802; Livingston, 287,770; Tauzin, 154,444; and Brown, 138,324. Instead of a heated runoff campaign in which he could decisively defeat Edwards and claim a mandate, Roemer became governor-elect with only a plurality when Edwards declined to contest the general election and withdrew from the race early in the morning after the primary. The jubilant Roemer camp failed to understand what Edwards had done, while Edwards observed that election night would be Roemer's last happy day for the next four years.

Edwards followed his withdrawal by announcing that he wanted to do everything possible to assist with the transition. He would make no major decisions without consulting Roemer, and he appointed Roemer's designee as commissioner of administration for the remaining three months of his term.

Despite the lengthy transition, Roemer failed to organize his administration or rely upon people with experience in state government for his office staff. The whiz kids he brought into the governor's office may have been valued comrades in the revolutionary campaign, but their arrogance and rudeness burned bridges from their first day in the capitol. One staff member delighted in telling other Roemeristas how he had put state Senate president B. B. "Sixty" Rayburn in his place by refusing to put him through to the governor and referring him to a low-level staffer. Legislators were turned off by the long hair and casual dress of the governor's staff members and their failure to return telephone calls or follow up on requests.

Roemer was the worst offender. Legislators found him opinionated, arrogant, and self-righteous. They had always been able to talk to Edwards and Treen, and even Treen had enjoyed holding mansion parties for House and Senate members. Buddy Roemer would have none of that.

As Tyler Bridges reported,

> Roemer was an unusual elected official. He was a diabetic who needed two shots of insulin a day. He was a loner who didn't like other politicians. He brought books to football games and often

failed to return phone calls, which infuriated many people, especially supporters. When he went to his favorite restaurant in Baton Rouge, a Mexican food place called the Superior Bar & Grill, he would barely talk to any of the other patrons and would sit at a table with his back to the crowd.

Huey Long created an international incident by receiving the captain of a German warship and his consul general in green silk pajamas in his suite at the Roosevelt Hotel. The Germans were offended and left in a huff. Huey was not as upset about the news stories of the incident as the fact that they said he wore silk pajamas. He quickly had himself photographed in a cotton nightshirt to show he was one of the common people. Huey righted his insult by making a show of calling on the captain on his battleship, decked out in a morning coat, with top hat, gloves, and cane. When a new Japanese consul general for New Orleans called on Roemer by appointment at the executive mansion, the governor received him in blue jeans with his feet up on a table. The consul general, deeply offended, publicly rebuked the governor.

Roemer became expert at losing friends and making enemies, and he "faced an increasingly hostile Legislature and public" when he sought to enact his program of fiscal and political reform. The state was suffering through a severe economic depression. Bumper stickers said, "Dear Lord, if you give us another oil boom, we won't screw it up this time." Roemer was determined to improve the secondary education system, reform the state budget, and address an accumulated $600 million deficit. He proposed to reduce the deficit and bring his first budget into line by cutting appropriations for colleges and universities, hospitals, institutions, and the state police.

To finance a pay raise for teachers and other promises, he attained approval of an increase in the state sales tax to 4 percent. It was ostensibly a temporary measure, for one year, but was renewed in succeeding years. A state sales tax exemption on groceries and prescription drugs was repealed. To balance the state budget and avoid bankruptcy, the state had to borrow money by issuing bonds to cover a $1 billion deficit.

These were stopgap measures, and Roemer argued that a reform of state fiscal policies and taxation was needed. He called for "a revolutionary overhaul of the state's fiscal structure."

An October 1988 special session of the legislature was called to enact the fiscal program. Its features were reduced taxes on business, including reduction of the state sales tax on machinery, equipment, and inventories, elimination of the corporate franchise tax, increases in the personal income tax, increases in auto license fees, the gasoline tax, and "sin taxes" on cigarettes, beer, wine, and liquor. Local governments would be allowed to increase their property taxes above a state-mandated ceiling, with the homestead exemption lowered from $7,500 to $2,500 so they could fund services that the state would discontinue paying for.

One observer wrote that "Buddy Roemer's financial package made sound economic sense, but it reflected poor political judgment on his part." It was astonishing that he and his coterie of Roemeristas in the governor's office refused to recognize that the homestead exemption was the "sacred cow" of state politics. The legislature did, and it voted down the entire tax revision package in a stunning defeat for the governor.

Roemer returned to the legislature with a more modest package in 1989. It included an income tax increase, extension of the "temporary" sales tax due to expire, and reductions in some business taxes. The legislature adopted it as a constitutional amendment requiring voter approval. Roemer campaigned for its passage, but the public would have none of it, and in the April 1989 referendum the package was defeated 55 percent to 45 percent.

Roemer did obtain additional state revenues, but through means previously proposed by Edwards in 1986: legalized gambling. The legislature defeated a state lottery and legalization of casino gambling then, and some of Roemer's supporters were surprised to see him embrace gambling now. A constitutional amendment creating the Louisiana Lottery passed by an overwhelming majority, and the lottery began operations in 1991, providing $150 million in new revenue. The legislature also approved, and Roemer signed, legislation approving riverboat casinos. Video poker, passed by the legislature, became law without Roemer's signature when he declined to either sign or veto it. The state constitution required that gambling be "suppressed." Everyone kept a straight face by defining these forms of games of chance as "gaming," which the courts agreed was not "gambling" in contravention to the constitution.

Roemer increased teachers' pay as promised, but he tied the raises to a performance evaluation program, which outraged longtime teachers, who said it was an insult to allow outsiders to pass judgment on their teaching skills. He increased pay raises for college and university professors, but offended their schools and alumni groups by calling for a single board for all institutions.

Midway through his term Roemer suffered a series of personal crises. As Maginnis observed, "the governor was finding that revolutionary fervor is difficult once inside the castle walls." He never learned to return phone calls and was not willing to perform the small things expected of a governor. "The mansion went dark after the Roemers moved in," one politician who had been a frequent guest there under both Edwards and Treen said. The governor spent much of his time brooding in isolation.

In October 1989 Roemer's wife, Patti, left him. She had never liked politics and could no longer deal with her husband's mood swings. She took their young son, Dakota, with her, and Roemer became a lonely figure, Hamlet-like, in the mansion. "I think he liked playing tragic hero," one staff member said.

Roemer reacted by embarking on "a crash journey of personal growth" during his "all-too-public mid-life crisis." He took up ballroom dancing and brought in as his guru a boyhood friend, Danny Walker, a Baptist minister who touted a motivational program called "Adventures in Attitude." Walker exercised enormous influence over Roemer. The governor took his staff on a three-day retreat with Walker to explore their inner selves. Patti Roemer attended, in an effort to repair their relationship, but soon fled. One of Walker's bugaboos was "negative feelings." These were dealt with by wearing a rubber band on the wrist. If a negative feeling intruded, you were supposed to snap the rubber band and say, "cancel, cancel." People thought the governor was nuts, perhaps more so than anyone ever claimed Uncle Earl Long was at the height of his dramatic collapse in the legislature, when they saw Roemer snapping rubber bands and crying, "cancel, cancel."

Roemer, in his newfound self-discovery, decided to share his rebirth in an address to a joint session to open the 1990 legislature. He invited legislators to "hold hands, laugh, and share dreams" with him, and "meet me at the campfire," where they would gather 'round to "build a future for our children." What was dubbed his "touchy-feely" speech left legislators scratching their heads in wonderment.

The legislature finally had enough of Roemer. He had deposed an Edwards ally, Sammy Nunez, as president of the Senate when a reluctant Senate followed a tradition of according an incoming governor his choices for speaker of the House and Senate president. The Roemer men were now voted out, and Nunez returned in triumph to the Senate podium.

On March 11, 1991, seven months before the state election, Roemer held a mansion event to announce that he had changed his registration to Republican. President George H. W. Bush, who Roemer knew while he was in Congress and Bush was vice president, had courted Roemer, and his party switch was negotiated with the president and his chief of staff, John Sununu. Roemer outraged the leaders of the state Republican party by bypassing them. He thought he would be welcomed with open arms, as an incumbent governor and the head of the party in the state, but its leaders had other ideas. They announced a state convention to nominate the party's official candidates. Roemer declined to participate in the caucuses held throughout the state to select delegates to the convention. The state party endorsed Congressman Clyde Holloway, a conservative who actively sought the nomination and won it over David Duke. In making the mistake of believing that his endorsement should have been automatic, Roemer alienated party activists.

While many observers failed to understand the party switch, there was method in what appeared to be Roemer's madness. He believed that, with Edwin Edwards planning a comeback, he had a better chance of defeating Edwards as a Republican. Roemer's eye was already beyond the mansion in Baton Rouge; he was looking at the White House. He thought that President Bush would win an easy reelection but that Vice President Dan Quayle would not have a lock on the Republican nomination in 1996. Roemer knew that he was too conservative for national Democrats and that a run for that party's nomination would be futile. He thought that he could mount an effective campaign in the Republican presidential preference primaries and, with the right breaks, have his candidacy catch fire. Ironically, Louisiana Republicans thought he was too liberal and were not about to let him take over the state party.

Roemer also alienated many Republicans and right-to-life voters when abortion became an issue in the 1991 legislative session. The legislature passed a bill prohibiting abortions in the state, even in cases of rape or when the mother's life was endangered. Roemer had assured legislators that he supported it, but when it came to his desk, he vetoed it. The legislature overrode his veto, the first time that had happened in a century. The U.S. District Court declared the act unconstitutional in light of the U.S. Supreme Court's decision in *Roe v. Wade*. Roemer lost whatever credibility he had remaining with the legislature when he vetoed a legislative reapportionment bill that he had promised to sign. He was described as "a bantamweight at five feet seven inches and 145 pounds." A former supporter said, "He remained a lightweight for the remainder of his political career."

Edwards, announcing his candidacy in the 1991 primary, proclaimed, "I'm the solution to the Revolution." He said that he had learned from his mistakes and pledged to be "a different Edwin Edwards."

David Duke entered the race with an apology for what he termed his "youthful mistakes." Duke had won a special election for a Metairie seat in the state house of representatives, defeating former governor Dave Treen's brother John, a Republican party leader. Duke had paraded in a Nazi uniform while at LSU and made a career out of anti-Semitism and white supremacy. He formed the National Association for the Advancement of White People and was at one time a Wizard of the Ku Klux Klan and the leader of the American Nazi Party. Despite all of his bad baggage, when Duke opposed U.S. senator J. Bennett Johnston's reelection in 1990, he polled 44 percent of the vote.

At the beginning of the gubernatorial race polls gave Roemer 35 percent, Edwards 25 percent, and Duke 15 percent, with 25 percent undecided. Roemer failed to appreciate that an incumbent governor who received only 35 percent in a poll was in trouble. Edwards understood what Roemer did not—that Duke's support was much stronger than his poll numbers because he "flew beneath the radar," with many who intended to vote for him unwilling to disclose their preference. One observer said, "Roemer himself did Duke the favor of campaigning with an air of complacency, acting almost as though the voters owed him another term in office."

Although he had amassed a large war chest early on, Roemer waited until the last several weeks of the election to actively campaign. He was taken by surprise at Duke's strength, and by a $500,000 television advertising campaign mounted against him by businessman Jack Kent. Kent's hazardous waste recycling company, Marine Shale, had been fined $4 million by the state Department of Environmental Quality. Kent said Roemer was trying to put him out of business, so he would return the favor. The clever spots focused on Roemer's broken promises, branding him a hypocrite while a golden halo over his head slowly disappeared.

To the consternation of many, Edwards and Duke went into the general election in what was termed "the race from Hell."

Edwards received 523,195 votes (34 percent), Duke 491,342 (32), Roemer 410,690 (27), and Holloway 82,683 (7). Eight minor candidates polled a total of 40,000 votes. While Roemer partisans claimed that Holloway cost him the runoff spot that went to Duke, even had Roemer received every single vote that went to Holloway he would have barely edged out Duke, and many Holloway voters were Christian conservatives who would not have gone for Roemer regardless, after his veto of the anti-abortion bill.

All of the pundits who had foreseen a runoff between Edwards and Roemer were at a loss to explain events. National attention focused on Louisiana, with Duke the Republican candidate and Edwards the Democrat. The Republican party disavowed Duke; business and church leaders, newspapers, and the leadership of the Republican party all called for an Edwards victory. They were not for Edwards; they were against Duke. One bumper sticker proclaimed: "Vote for the Crook—It's Important." Edwards was bemused by many of those climbing aboard his bandwagon, but was happy to take their checks. President Bush announced that if he could vote in Louisiana, his ballot would go to Edwards. Dave Treen endorsed his former foe, and Roemer said that he would cast his vote for Edwards. The newspapers found virtues in Edwards that they had not seen before. Witty as ever, Edwards said that he would not get the votes of one-armed men because they could not hold their noses and pull the lever for him at the same time. The only thing he and Duke had in common, Edwards joked, was that they were "both wizards under the sheets."

Edwards destroyed Duke in a televised debate, closing with a passionate statement that compared what he had done to build people up, and what Duke had done to tear them down. Edwards recounted how he had served the people of the state for twenty years, while "all he has given us is twenty years of hate and hurt." Many voters, fearful of what a Duke governorship would do to the state's economy, with predictions that new industries would not locate in the state while he was governor, voted for Edwards in a massive turnout. He polled over one million votes, winning by 1,057,031 (61 percent) to Duke's 671,009 (39).

Roemer blamed himself for underestimating Duke, as well as Edwards's continuing popularity, and his own failure to campaign energetically. He nursed his wounds for the next four years, while Edwards went through a difficult administration that won passage of casino gambling but had to continue to deal with economic problems. When Edwards announced to a joint session of the legislature in early 1995 that he would not be a candidate for reelection to a fifth term, a large field materialized.

Roemer announced and ran a "lavishly-financed campaign" in which he promised to abolish the state income tax and put prisoners back on chain gangs. Lieutenant Governor Melinda Schwegmann and State Treasurer Mary Landrieu qualified, as did Congressman Cleo Fields, a black who had represented a Baton Rouge district in the legislature; all were Democrats. State Senator Murphy "Mike" Foster, grandson of a two-term governor, changed his registration to Republican when he filed his qualification papers. Roemer did not think Foster was a threat and anticipated that he would go into a runoff with one of the Democrats, but Foster "pulled a Roemer" on him, imitating the come-from-the-back-of-the-pack campaign that Roemer had waged in 1987. Foster was a small blip in the polls at the outset of the race, but he finished first in the October 21, 1995, primary with 385,267 votes, 26 percent of the total. Fields got 290,921 (19 percent), Landrieu 271,938 (18), and Roemer 263,330 (18). Schwegmann polled a disappointing 71,288 (5), well behind businessman Phil Preis, who got 133,271. Foster's campaign gained ground in the closing days, and Fields edged out Landrieu, making Foster a heavy favorite for the general election, which he won handily.

In finishing fourth Roemer continued his downward spiral, from a plurality win in 1987, to third place in 1991, and fourth position in 1995. He and Foster were both embarrassed by their connections to Duke. Foster was compelled to acknowledge that he purchased a mailing list of supporters from Duke after Duke dropped out of the 1995 race. Critics said that the $152,000 price bought Duke's decision not to make the race. Foster did not use the list, but had to pay a fine for an ethics code violation for failing to properly report the payment to Duke. Roemer was criticized for employing a former Duke campaign staff member.

Roemer mulled over races for the governorship and the U.S. Senate in 2003 and 2004, but stuck to his business involvements. He started the Business Bank of Baton Rouge with a group of investors in 1998 and served as its president and CEO until late 2004, when they sold out to Bancorp South.

One observer said that every time Roemer ran for governor he got fewer votes. "His problem was not to win new supporters; he couldn't hold onto his old ones." He went from 33 percent in 1987 to 27 percent in 1991, to 18 percent in 1995. As one commentator put it, Roemer paid dearly "for his reputation of not being able to work with others and of not delivering on his promises."

—J.B.McG.

"BancorpSouth Buys The Business Bank of Baton Rouge." *Bankers Digest*. 4 October 2004.

Bridges, Tyler. *The Rise of David Duke*. Jackson: University Press of Mississippi, 1994.

Dawson, Joseph G. III, ed. *The Louisiana Governors: From Iberville to Edwards*. Baton Rouge: Louisiana State University Press, 1990.

Kurtz, Michael, ed. *The Louisiana Purchase Bicentennial Series in Louisiana History. Vol. IX: Louisiana Since the Longs: 1960 to Century's End*. Lafayette: Center for Louisiana Studies, University of Southwestern Louisiana, 1998.

Maginnis, John. *Cross to Bear*. Baton Rouge: Darkhorse Press, 1992.

Secretary of State. "The Governors of Louisiana." www.sec.state.la.us.

Wall, Bennett H., ed. *Louisiana: A History*. Wheeling, IL: Harlan Davidson, 1997.

Murphy J. "Mike" Foster Jr.

1996–2004

Baton Rouge was treated to an enormous procession of motorcycles on a clear morning as hundreds of leather-garbed riders gunned their Harley-Davidsons and rode in ranks that filled the streets as they descended on the state capitol to protest legislation that required wearing of helmets. The most unusual aspect of this demonstration was that it was led by Governor Murphy James "Mike" Foster Jr., on his own "Harley Hog." The governor believed that motorcyclists had a constitutional right not to wear helmets, and he had succeeded in amending a law that made them mandatory. Against the advice of his own highway safety director, he pushed through legislation to allow adults eighteen and older to ride helmetless.

Mike Foster's grandfather, Murphy James Foster, served two terms as governor, from 1892 to 1900. His father, Prescott Foster, worked behind the scenes in state politics to encourage reform candidates to seek office.

Foster was born on July 11, 1930, in Shreveport, but the family moved to Centerville, where he went to school. He was active in the Boy Scouts, and one of his proudest achievements was attainment of the rank of Eagle Scout. Foster received a Bachelor of Science degree in chemistry from

Murphy J. "Mike" Foster, Jr., November 3, 1994. Courtesy of the *Times-Picayune*.

Louisiana State University; following service in the air force as a pilot from 1952 to 1955, he returned home to Franklin.

Foster engaged in sugarcane farming on a large scale, becoming president of Sterling Sugars, Inc. He founded Bayou Sale Construction Company and built a personal fortune that made him a multimillionaire.

Elected to the first of two terms in the state Senate in 1987, Foster established a reputation as a conservative, "good government" Democrat. When he declared his candidacy for governor in 1995, few politicians paid much notice. Edwin Edwards announced that he would not be a candidate for reelection, and a field materialized that included former Governor Buddy Roemer, Lieutenant Governor Melinda Schwegmann, State Treasurer Mary Landrieu, Congressman Cleo Fields (who had been redistricted out of his seat), and businessman Phil Preis. All except Roemer were Democrats. The former governor, who had won by a plurality in 1987 when Edwards withdrew from a general election runoff, had failed to make the runoff that Edwards and David Duke went into when he sought reelection as a Republican in 1991. Roemer now expected to have the Republican label to himself.

On the day he filed qualification papers to run for governor, however, Foster changed his party affiliation to Republican. His obscure candidacy gained ground from then on, as he gave Republicans disenchanted with Roemer's inability to work with others, and his broken promises, an alternative candidate. Foster initially financed his campaign himself, pumping hundreds of thousands of dollars into it with personal loans. They were all later repaid as contributions rolled in, particularly when he went into a general election runoff that he was certain to win. He set up headquarters in a trailer at his construction company, and his campaign activities and schedule were handled by secretaries from Bayou Sale, who became famous as "the trailer girls."

Foster's television commercials identified him with working men, hunters, and gun owners. He campaigned as "a gun-toting Christian conservative." He was blunt in stating his opposition to affirmative action programs, and he put his foot in his mouth when he called New Orleans "a jungle." Mayor Marc Morial and many others thought Foster was a racist at worst, insensitive at best. He insisted he was referring to the alarming crime rate in the city, not its majority black population. Foster emphasized the need for improvements in education at all levels and promised that if the pay of schoolteachers was not equal to the Southern average in two years, he would forfeit his salary for the remainder of his term.

In the October 1995 primary, Foster led the field with 385,267 votes, followed by Fields with 280,921. Landrieu and Roemer were close behind Fields, with 271,938 and 263,330, respectively. Phil Preis polled

133,271 and Schwegmann received a disappointing 71,288. In the closing days of the campaign Fields and Landrieu battled, with Fields claiming that Landrieu said that a vote for him would be wasted because he could not win a runoff, while she could, and Landrieu claiming that Fields had "played the race card" on her. In the general election, Foster won by a landslide, 984,499 to 565,861. While Fields increased his vote total from 19 to 36 percent, Foster went from 36 to 64 percent.

At his January 8, 1996, inauguration, Foster assailed the insiders of prior administrations who received state contracts and jobs, calling them "hogs at the trough." One of his first acts was to issue an executive order terminating the state's affirmative action programs for minority and female contractors. There were protests by blacks, and Fields said that Foster's action was "payback," but Foster responded that he had said he would end the programs in the campaign and was keeping his promise. He also kept a promise to allow more people to carry concealed weapons if they filed for permits, rather than requiring that they have a business or other reason for doing so.

Foster made education his priority. Elementary and secondary schoolteachers received salary increases in six of his eight years in office, a total of about $10,000. His administration established the Tuition Opportunity Program for Students, or TOPS, which provides college scholarships for students through opportunity, performance, and honors awards, and for undergraduate students who agree to teach in a Louisiana elementary or secondary school. The higher education system saw pay increases for professors and staff as well as construction of new facilities. When Foster failed to raise teacher pay to the Southern average within two years, he kept his promise to give up his own $96,000 annual salary. He could not legally refuse his salary for the last six years of his terms, so he donated it to a nonprofit fund for teacher awards for developing "innovative character education programs."

Foster's approval rating stayed above 70 percent for most of his eight years in office. In the October 1999 primary his only major opponent was Congressman William Jefferson of New Orleans, a black. Foster was reelected in the primary 805,203 to 392,445, a margin over Jefferson of 62 to 30 percent. Eight other candidates received only 8 percent of the total vote.

Had Foster retired from the governorship at sixty-nine, after one term, he would probably have been regarded by historians as one of the state's greatest reform governors. While his second term had some notable successes, Foster also was widely criticized for lack of leadership in economic development and failure to restrict gambling.

In the 1995 campaign Foster led everyone to believe that he was anti-gambling and would scale it back, if not try to eliminate it altogether. Instead, he expanded it by supporting slot machines at racetracks, renewing agreements with Indian casinos, and trying to get federal approval for an additional tribe for a casino. When Harrah's Casino in New Orleans filed for bankruptcy, Foster renegotiated its agreement with the state, drastically reducing the potential revenue but assuring that hundreds of jobs would be saved. He supported allowing racetracks to have video poker parlors, explaining that the racing season was limited, the tracks were injured by all of the other forms of gambling that had been approved, the thoroughbred industry was important to the state, and the tracks already had gambling.

Some ministers and other anti-gambling advocates said he had broken his promise to curtail gambling. They argued that he could have put his immense popularity on the line for an "up or down" vote on gambling and won it. Instead, he supported local option legislation to allow parishes to keep or ban riverboat casinos or video poker.

Despite the wounds caused by his comment about the "jungle" in New Orleans, Foster not only repaired the damage but lifted his image in the city to become one of its best governors. He worked out arrangements to keep the New Orleans Saints in the city when owner Tom Benson threatened to move the team, although he was later criticized for giving away too much in a deal that guaranteed Benson state incentives and payments. He assisted successful efforts to bring a National Basketball Association team to New Orleans when the Hornets moved from Charlotte and supported state funding for expansion of the Ernest N. Morial Convention Center.

Foster's agreement with the Saints became a source of criticism when the revenues that were supposed to fund it failed to materialize in the amounts expected, and it became a major problem for his successor, Governor Kathleen Blanco. The deal with Benson that Foster negotiated, and the legislature in 2001 approved, called for $186.5 million in incentives and direct state payments to the team over ten years, to keep the Saints in the Superdome until 2010.

The subsidies started at $12.5 million in 2001, with progressive increases to $23.5 million. The guarantees were based on a hotel and motel tax in the New Orleans area, but its take was much less than forecast. In 2004 the state had to borrow $8 million from an economic development fund to make that year's payment of $15 million. In 2005, the shortfall became $10 million.

Governor Blanco sought to renegotiate the arrangement, and meetings with the Saints continued through the first half of 2005. Benson insisted that the state honor the Foster agreement, while Blanco sought to redo it. The issue was further complicated by Benson's insistence that a new stadium be built with minimal financial participation by the team, while Blanco preferred to renovate the Superdome. With legislators from other areas opposed to further direct state funding of the shortfall, in the 2005 session of the legislature Blanco proposed higher taxes on hotel and motel rooms, rental cars, Saints tickets, and Superdome concession sales so that the needed revenue would be raised from the New Orleans area only.

Foster, in a letter to the editor, claimed that the greater part of the inducements was being paid for by out-of-state visitors through the room tax and argued that the economic return to the state from having a professional football team was at least twice what the state was paying to keep it here.

John Maginnis wrote that, in his first term, Foster did a good job of bringing Louisiana politics into the twentieth century as it was closing. Maginnis noted he succeeded where reformers Dave Treen and Buddy Roemer had failed: by getting reelected.

Maginnis contended that "Foster's first term was much better than his second, because the economy was stronger, allowing him to raise salaries for schoolteachers and college professors, establish the TOPS scholarships, and expedite highway construction." When the economy nosedived in 2000, Foster "alienated old allies by trying to raise taxes on businesses."

By the end of his administration, Foster was faulted by most observers for concentrating on education, but failing to give equal priority to economic development, to stem the "brain drain" of young Louisianians who were leaving the state for jobs in Houston, Atlanta, and elsewhere. Ed Anderson, the capital correspondent for the *Times-Picayune*, wrote, "Mike Foster leaves office next month with a strangely contradictory record of sweeping public accomplishments and the personal image of an indolent chief executive." He was credited with "restoring integrity to state government, stabilizing state finances, and creating a solid foundation to begin repairing a badly deteriorated education system." He was faulted for failing to perform on other goals: He promised to reduce the size of state government, but it increased dramatically on his watch. He claimed to oppose gambling, but it expanded. He said he would promote economic development, but he declined to travel to visit corporate executives as his counterparts in other states did.

Foster was skewered for spending too much time at Oaklawn Manor, his showplace plantation home in Franklin, and for indulging his passion for hunting and fishing at exclusive south Louisiana duck clubs and his luxurious camp at Grand Isle. He disdained what he called the "ceremonial b.s." of being governor, and he had no interest in cutting ribbons or greeting convention groups. Even his staunchest supporters in the legislature were disappointed by his failure to be more proactive in economic development. Foster said that people overestimated the effect a governor could have by traveling to corporate headquarters to woo executives. He said that he personally persuaded Northrop Grumman Ship Systems to expand its Avondale Shipyard, and the deal "was made at a duck camp between the CEO of Avondale and myself."

Most observers, however, thought Foster's efforts at economic development were "feeble." John Maginnis wrote that Foster was an old-school politician who thought his job was to oversee government operations in education, highways, and health care, and that economic development should "take care of itself." He was out of touch with the idea that the governor should be in the forefront of economic development initiatives, as the state's number one salesman, personally calling on corporate executives in this country and abroad, "offering tax breaks and infrastructure improvements," and wooing them "as though they were voters or campaign contributors." Maginnis said, "That's not what Mike Foster signed on for," and as a result, "the rank old image of Louisiana festered in the minds of many business leaders, who didn't give a second thought to investing here."

Foster said that he wanted to be remembered for giving the state a "corruption-free administration." When he left office, he said that he was proudest of the integrity of his administration. "The fact is that we stopped the whole idea that government is here to take care of friends and pay off political debts," he said. "This is not something to be taken for granted."

Foster supported the Stelly Plan, named after the legislator who proposed it, which was adopted as a constitutional amendment and ratified by the voters. It reduced sales taxes, eliminating the "temporary" taxes on food and most utilities, which hit the poor hardest, and increased income taxes for those in higher brackets. While it was supposed to be "revenue-neutral," many middle- and higher-income taxpayers thought they had been misled as to its effects when they had to pay their first returns based on it.

Foster also reduced the state debt by $1.6 billion and accumulated surpluses for several years. He practiced good fiscal management, and the state's bond rating was upgraded several times, but budget problems in his final year left a big budget deficit for his successor. He did have the foresight to insist on putting part of the state's tobacco settlement money in trust funds for health care programs. In his second term, he supported efforts to deal with coastal erosion with his "America's Wetlands" program to make the nation aware of the problem. His tort reform was criticized by environmentalists as a "free ride for polluters," but it was the first attempt by the state to address that issue.

Foster's administration was free of corruption, and his own integrity was not questioned—but his judgment on several matters of ethics was. He was the first incumbent governor to be fined for a violation of the state code of ethics, and he was embarrassed by his connection with David Duke. Duke, the former Grand Dragon of the Ku Klux Klan, organizer for the American Nazi party, and founder of the National Association for the Advancement of White People, was defeated for governor by Edwin Edwards in the 1991 general election. He announced for governor again in 1995, but did not run. In 1999, during Foster's reelection campaign, the Ethics Board fined him $20,000 for failing to report a payment of $152,000 to Duke for a mailing list of his supporters and contributors. The payment was laundered through one of Foster's companies. A news article in 2003 reported that "Foster said recently he bought the list as a way to keep Duke out of the race but decided not to use it after he started raising money from other sources." Foster had no apologies for dealing with Duke. "I never thought it was a big deal," he said. "Everybody was trying to buy it."

After Foster broke his anti-gambling promise, it came out that his investments included gambling stock. He also had to deal with his son Murphy Foster's attempt to represent state agencies as an attorney; they sought an Ethics Commission opinion to allow this, but had to be satisfied with obtaining permission for the younger Foster's law firm to represent state agencies so long as he did not share in the fees it received.

Foster was also criticized for the manner in which a donation of thousands of acres of property to the state by oil giant BP was handled by his administration. The property, known as the White Lake Game Preserve, was placed under the control of a private, self-perpetuating board Foster and several friends controlled as trustees. The property contains some of the best duck hunting marshes in the state. The Foster group said that private citizens would be able to draw in a lottery to hunt there, but the exclusivity of the arrangement for management of the preserve generated a firestorm of controversy. The administration of Governor Kathleen Blanco, who succeeded Foster, sponsored legislation that put the property under direct state control.

Foster received a state retirement of $84,000 a year, based on three years' service in the air force, twelve years as an unpaid member of the Board of Commissioners of the Port of St. Mary Parish, eight years as a state senator, and eight years as governor. He took advantage of a lucrative provision in the retirement system for state legislators and officials that lets them "buy time" for service in other governmental positions, with their retirement based on their highest earning period. One critic said that, in the end, the governor himself became one of the "hogs at the trough" he had denounced.

Sensitive to the criticism that he was a "part time governor" who took courses at the Southern University Law School, and often aggravated at the press, Foster had his own radio show, *Live Mike*, in which he made public statements and took questions from listeners. It was a direct line to the governor, and he solved numerous problems in a hands-on manner.

John Maginnis concluded that people "applauded Foster's honesty and progressive policies but were appalled by his roughneck bullying of critics and his self-indulgent preoccupation with law school and fishing trips."

Clancy DuBos, in *Gambit*, made the best assessment of the Foster years when he wrote, "He didn't raise the bar nearly as high as he could have, but at least he raised it."

—J.B.McG.

Anderson, Ed. "Fostering a Legacy." *Times-Picayune*. 28 December 2003.

DuBos, Clancy. "Exit Gov. Foster." *Gambit*. 6 January 2004.

Gill, James. "At last, a Governor Says No to Tom Benson." *Times-Picayune*. 17 October 2004.

Grace, Stephanie. "From Gun-toting Biker to Earnest Reformer." *Times-Picayune*. 30 December 2003.

Hill, John. "Capitol Politics." *New Orleans CityBusiness*. 9 February 2004.

Kurtz, Michael, ed. *The Louisiana Purchase Bicentennial Series in Louisiana History. Vol. IX: Louisiana Since the Longs: 1960 to Century's End*. Lafayette: Center for Louisiana Studies, University of Southwestern Louisiana, 1998.

Maginnis, John. "Gov. Foster Raised the Bar, Then Missed It." *Times-Picayune*. 7 January 2004.

Secretary of State. "Official Election Results" and "The Governors of Louisiana." www.sec.state.la.us.

Wall, Bennett H., ed. *Louisiana: A History*. Wheeling, IL: Harlan Davidson, 1997.

Kathleen Babineaux Blanco

2004–2008

Louisiana's first woman governor, elected in 2003, appeared to be on the way to a successful administration when Hurricanes Katrina and Rita slammed the state's coastal parishes, inundating most of New Orleans and spreading destruction and misery everywhere it touched land. The National Weather Service was quick to label Katrina as the single worst natural disaster ever to befall the United States.

Unfortunately for Governor Kathleen Blanco, it was also the worst natural disaster to hit the Louisiana governor's office as well. Nevertheless, the new governor, a dutiful Democrat who worked her way up the political ladder in a state led by Republican governor Mike Foster for eight years, plunged into the morass left in the hurricanes' wakes, vowed to rebuild the damaged areas, and said the state would seek new industries to replace jobs wiped out by the storms.

With hundreds of thousands of citizens displaced—many evacuated out of state—and tens of thousands of homes destroyed or damaged, the federal government said it would bring in thousands of travel trailers in answer to Blanco's pleas for emergency housing. It was weeks before any

Kathleen Babineaux Blanco, December 13, 2005. Courtesy of the *Times-Picayune*. Photo by Chris Granger.

arrived, however, and other government assistance was slow in coming. In the New Orleans area, the storm was bad enough, but flooding was immeasurably worsened when levees failed or were overtopped. Thousands of people, many of them minorities who had no way to evacuate the city, crowded into the Superdome and the Convention Center, without food or water. The suffering in New Orleans was terrible, as stranded people were lifted from rooftops of flooded homes by helicopter, and thousands gathered on the highway overpasses waiting for buses that took several days to come. It was quickly obvious that the Federal Emergency Management Agency (FEMA) was not prepared for a rapid or effective response.

Blanco found herself in the middle of a media storm, as the finger-pointing began with the dismissal of FEMA director Michael D. Brown. Overworked and exhausted, trying to keep relations with President George W. Bush and New Orleans Mayor C. Ray Nagin on an even keel, Blanco appeared overwhelmed in the immediate aftermath of Hurricane Katrina, which struck on August 29, 2005. The situation was compounded in late September as another hurricane, Rita, slashed through southwestern Louisiana. Hurricane Katrina killed more than 1,100 people, and Hurricane Rita claimed 300 more, according to the National Weather Service.

While this book is about the governors of Louisiana, in the case of Kathleen Babineaux Blanco the political ramifications of the hurricanes are so evident they cannot be overlooked. Blanco's efforts for the state's recovery led to months of political wrangling that stretched through Louisiana and Mississippi to Washington. President Bush made frequent trips to the devastated areas to check on the situation after being roundly criticized for his failure to go there immediately. Distressed public officials and citizens demanded answers and action, but what followed were months of backbiting among the various governmental agencies at local, state, and federal levels. The most immediate needs were to relieve human suffering, provide temporary housing and financial assistance, and address the repair and reconstruction of levees that had failed or were topped.

In an effort to resolve problems created by the hurricanes, the governor called a special session of the legislature and put forward a plan to consolidate eight levee districts in southeast Louisiana. Her proposal included reform of the statute allowing seven assessors for New Orleans, compared with only one in each of the other parishes of the state. New Orleans property owners have loved their assessors because they keep assessments and taxes to a minimum, even though the city always needs greater funds to finance schools and public facilities. Thus, the move to reduce the number of Orleans Parish assessors appeared dead on arrival in the legislature, with Blanco blamed for failing to give it strong support. Later, however, following a grass-roots campaign led by New Orleans women, the legislature proposed a constitutional amendment, which Blanco supported, to provide for one assessor in each parish, and voters ratified it.

Reform of the system of levee boards fared better after Blanco proposed that the eight levee districts in southeast Louisiana be combined into a single authority. Here again the proposal faced a natural barrier—the fact that the Mississippi River splits New Orleans into distinct east and west banks, with each side wanting autonomy. So the legislature provided for two separate authorities to be coordinated under a single state levee board. Some aspects of the new structure were still unclear when the legislature adjourned.

In her push to overhaul the levee system, Blanco joined State Representative Walter Boasso of St. Bernard Parish, a Republican who had campaigned for levee reform in his low-lying parish, where General Andrew Jackson and his forces defeated the British army in 1815.

Perhaps Blanco's biggest struggle in the storms' aftermath was to obtain federal funds to assist in repairing or rebuilding some 217,000 homes destroyed or damaged. After Bush turned down a buyout plan proposed by Congressman Richard Baker, Blanco called for more federal participation, and Bush promised additional billions in aid for the Gulf Coast.

Blanco showed creative style and lots of backbone as she sailed through her first legislative session in early 2004 after a surprising victory at the polls in November of 2003. She lost no time in establishing a firm grip on the governor's office and exerted leadership in dealing with the state's lawmakers.

The first big issue confronting Blanco as she settled into her governorship was an impasse between the shipping industry and the way Mississippi River pilots are commissioned and paid, some $340,000 each per year. In 2001 proposed legislation to revamp the archaic river pilot system got nowhere, and action failed again in 2003. Here was a sacred cow waiting to be reformed, with no leader.

Blanco stepped in and worked out a compromise, the most significant change being that pilot rates will be determined in the future by an eleven-member commission. In theory, rates will be based on the public good and not excessive salary. This will remain a thorny issue because there are three pilot groups.

An unexpected problem developed suddenly with the actions of the Orleans Parish School Board, which had hired a tough new superintendent and given him authority to reform the school system but then tried to fire him when he tried to make significant changes. Governor Blanco stepped into the middle of the fight at the request of some school board members and supported legislation that prohibited the school board from dismissing the superintendent, Anthony Amato. The case landed in federal district court, which upheld Blanco and intervention by the legislature to protect the new superintendent (who, ironically, ended up resigning).

Blanco's accomplishments were spectacular, considering she was a novice in the job. Recent governors had been criticized for not being able to attract new industry. In her first six months, Blanco garnered a $100 million tank-car manufacturing plant to be located in the Alexandria area and employ 850 people. In early 2007 she set her sights on acquiring a colossal German steel plant; a southern state location was sought for this billion-dollar manufacturing operation. She traveled to Germany to promote a site on the Mississippi River in St. James Parish as its location. While Louisiana lost to Alabama's Mobile County, after a spirited competition that involved hundreds of millions of dollars in inducements by both states, Blanco gained respect for her aggressive tactics in seeking the plant.

Blanco drew considerable attention from the sports community with a proposal to build a new stadium for the New Orleans Saints, the city's National Football League team that had been campaigning for a new facility. Blanco's idea was to place it next to the big Morial Convention Center overlooking the Mississippi River, but the plan did not generate much enthusiasm. Rather, support for remodeling the Superdome appeared to be favored by most interests, and Governor Blanco later on endorsed the idea, although she asked Saints owner Tom Benson to pay part of the cost.

At the outset of her administration Blanco faced a shortfall in the budget for state colleges and universities, which she solved with a small increase in fees. She provided financing for preschool programs for four-year-old children from low-income families and pledged to support an ethics package that would set strict guidelines for legislators and state employees. She also resurrected a law that required motorcyclists to wear helmets while riding, even though the former governor, Mike Foster, had been successful in making helmets optional.

Kathleen Babineaux was born near New Iberia in Coteau, a village on Louisiana Highway 88 among the sugarcane fields, on December 15, 1942. She grew up playing with the boys of her family, fishing, climbing trees, and shooting pellet guns at nutria on the pond of her grandfather's farm. She had a strong Catholic upbringing.

In 1964, after obtaining a degree in business education from the University of Louisiana at Lafayette, she taught high school business in Breaux Bridge and was married to Raymond Blanco, a high school football coach and educator. She quit teaching to devote time to the couple's six children but soon got into politics, winning office in 1983 as a member of the House of Representatives and later the Public Service Commission. From that background, in 1996 she was elected lieutenant governor, and used her office to promote tourism and expand it to a billion-dollar industry. She won reelection to a second term based on her record.

Blanco moved out from the pack of candidates seeking the governorship in a forum among the group at the end of the primary. As the forum drew to a close, a reporter asked each candidate if he or she had experienced a "defining moment" in his or her lifetime. The candidates responded mostly in unemotional terms. When Blanco's turn to speak came, her answer was something special.

This was to be a sad moment, not just a defining moment. She straightened up in her chair, took a deep breath, and with a slight tremble in her voice, told of the industrial accident in which her seventeen-year-old son Ben was killed. The painful details of the accident—the tone of her voice and the expression on her face—left television viewers with a picture of a heavy-hearted mother with a determination to overcome. It was indeed a defining moment, the defining moment of her life and possibly of the campaign.

In the October 2003 open primary the Republican candidate, Bobby Jindal, received 443,389 votes, Blanco 250,136, Attorney General Richard Ieyoub 223,513, and former congressman Claude "Buddy" Leach 187,872. Several trailing candidates received a total of 257,614 votes. While Blanco emerged from the Democratic field to enter the runoff with Jindal, his lead of over 193,000 votes put him at 33 percent to her 18 percent.

Although Jindal was heavily favored, and led in several polls until the last week of the general election, Blanco came from behind to win, 731,358 to 676,484, in the November 15, 2003, balloting. When First District Congressman David Vitter was elected to the U.S. Senate for the seat of the retiring John Breaux, Jindal won the election to replace him, and speculation built that while serving in the House of Representatives he would lay the groundwork for a rematch with Blanco when she sought a second term in 2007.

On January 11, 2004, Blanco was inaugurated as governor, taking the oath of office in both French and English. During her term she was one of only eight women among the nation's fifty governors.

Kathleen Blanco made many sacrifices in her personal life and political career, but throughout, she was devoted to her family, to public service, and to her state and people. With low poll numbers, disarray and delay in the Road Home Program to disburse grants of up to $150,000 to assist homeowners in covering their uninsured losses from hurricanes so that they could repair and rebuild, and a determination to concentrate on the state's continuing recovery rather than politics and her own political future, Governor Kathleen Blanco made the greatest sacrifice possible. Despite a campaign fund with over $3 million in the bank, on March 20, 2007, she announced that she would not be a candidate for reelection.

Polls showed that Congressman Bobby Jindal, with over $4 million already raised, would defeat Blanco by a two-to-one margin. With her withdrawal from the race, however, and many leaders in the Democratic party opposed to the candidacy of Public Service Commissioner Foster Campbell of north Louisiana, who they regarded as too liberal, former U.S. Senator John Breaux announced his interest in the race. The Breaux boomlet was short-lived, however, when questions were raised about his ability to meet the legal requirement that the governor be a Louisiana citizen. A Washington lobbyist, Breaux maintained his residence and voter registration in Maryland, and while he could register to vote in Louisiana again prior to the primary, the question of citizenship for the preceding period was open to challenge. Breaux sought an opinion from Attorney General Charles Foti to clarify the issue, but with a Republican court challenge looming, Foti declined to rule. While Breaux mulled his options, the state Republican party ran ads saying that Breaux should not be above the law, characterized him as a Washington wheeler-dealer, and showed aerial views of his multimillion-dollar home on the Maryland shore.

Although state courts had generally ruled against disqualifying candidates who were challenged, preferring to let the voters decide, Breaux was reluctant to run in the face of a suit to remove him from the ballot, which the Republican party was sure to file once the deadline passed for filing qualification papers to run. With that prospect, the need to raise millions of dollars in a short period of time, and polls showing Jindal leading him, Breaux announced he would not run. Breaux had teased that he would run for reelection to the Senate before announcing his retirement from that post, and in 2003 he had teased state Democrats with the possibility that he would run for governor then. After his flirtation with the 2007 race, in which he knew he would be challenged before announcing his intention to run, many state Democrats were tired of the Breaux sideshow that had left them without a strong candidate.

Democrat Lieutenant Governor Mitch Landrieu, who had indicated that he would run if Breaux did not, decided to seek reelection instead. On the Republican side, State Senator Walter Boasso, outraged when the state party's executive committee endorsed Jindal in a move intended to discourage other Republicans from running, changed his registration to Democrat for the race. New Orleans businessman John Georges changed his registration from Republican to Independent and put $10 million of his own money into his campaign.

Jindal participated in only three of the numerous forums, campaigned against what he dubbed the "culture of corruption" in Baton Rouge, and spent over $11 million in achieving a primary victory.

When her term ended on January 14, 2008, Blanco left a $1 billion surplus to Jindal. Despite the crushing unfavorable ratings she had received following the hurricanes, when she left office she had climbed back to a 50 percent favorable job performance rating as the recovery progressed, Road Home checks were distributed, and many people came to believe that she had gotten a "bad rap."

—W.G.C.

Anderson, Ed. "Blanco Asks More of Saints." *Times-Picayune*. 11 January 2005.

Scott, Robert Travis. "Final Face-Off: Many Punches Thrown, But Few Land in Debate." *Times-Picayune*. 13 November 2003.

Times-Picayune. Coverage of special session of the Louisiana legislature, February 7 to February 17, 2006.

Times-Picayune. Daily reports of Blanco's legislative proposals.

Bobby Jindal

2008–

Bobby Jindal's October 20, 2007, primary election as governor was greeted with raucous celebrations on two continents. One was in the ballroom of the Holiday Inn Select in Baton Rouge, Louisiana, where the hierarchy of the state Republican Party gathered for the election returns. The other was in his family's hometown, Maler Kotla, in the Punjab state of India. The celebration in Baton Rouge featured a jazz band, catfish, and Abita Beer. In Maler Kotla, Jinda's relatives and their friends gathered at the ancestral home his parents had left forty years before, to celebrate with traditional folk dances, drums, firecrackers, and large trays of sweets. While family members were disappointed by his failure to visit his ancestral village and see his aunts, uncles, and cousins over the years, they were overjoyed by his victory. His aunt, Vijaylakshmi Jindal, told the press, "We're so proud of our child. He's achieved so much at such a young age. Now we want him to become president next. If he can become a governor, then he can also be president." News of his win came on the Dussehra holiday, described as "a religious festival celebrating the victory of the Hindu god Rama over the demon king Ravana in a triumph of good over evil."

Bobby Jindal, November 2006. Courtesy of the *Times-Picayune*. Photo by Chuck Cook.

Jindal, the "Boy Wonder" of Louisiana politics, was the odds-on favorite to win the election throughout the campaign. Stephanie Grace, a political columnist for the News Orleans *Times-Picayune*, wrote, "The main suspense, other than whether Jindal would clinch it in the primary or be forced into a runoff, was which Jindal voters would be taking home from the store." She contrasted the 2003 model Jindal, who lost the runoff then to Kathleen Babineaux Blanco, with the 2007 model. According to Grace:

> There's 2003 Jindal, a relatively unguarded policy expert who spoke in detail about his plans, who courted educated, urban voters, moderates, and African Americans. Then there's the Jindal who showed up on the campaign trail this season. Jindal fell below expectations in conservative, rural parts of the state that normally opt for Republicans last time out. So this year he focused most of his energy on winning over voters who were more comfortable with Blanco four years ago, whether because of his Indian heritage, his overt braininess, his track record as a budget-shaving government bureaucrat, or simply because he talked fast. This time he appealed to voters' sense of kinship. He talked about guns and God. He wore cowboy boots, slowed his cadence, and while still putting multi-point policy proposals on paper, stuck more to general themes in personal appearances. He pointedly sidestepped talk of his heritage, even during the final debate when he was asked point-blank to address the topic.

Jeremy Alford, in a *Gambit Weekly* piece on Jindal, wrote, "This time around, Team Jindal is managed by a set of tight-fisted handlers; the candidate isn't the easygoing thirty-two-year-old who granted all-access passes to the media in 2003. Today, it's all business. The new Bobby Jindal has been packaged, mass-marketed, and slapped on a bumper sticker—literally."

Jindal spent most of his time talking about the need to improve ethics in government, promising to call the legislature into special session to enact tough new ethics laws as soon as he took office; otherwise, "he limited debates, media interviews, and other situations in which he might lose control of his carefully honed message."

"If I go down as one of the more boring but effective governors, I'll take that as a great compliment," Bobby Jindal told a news conference the morning after his election. "Our people don't want to be amused by our politics anymore. We don't want to be entertained." While the 376,000 who voted for country music singer Sammy Kershaw for lieutenant governor may have disagreed with Jindal, there was no doubt that the majority of voters who gave him a primary victory did not view him as colorful in the tradition of Louisiana politicians. Instead, they saw him as a bright technocrat with lots of good ideas and, hopefully, the ability to implement them in an increasingly partisan legislative process.

There was an immediate temptation to compare Jindal to Buddy Roemer, "the last brainy, glib Ivy League governor, who promised a revolution," but "failed to deliver" according to political writer John Maginnis. Maginnis posed the question, "Has Louisiana elected another Buddy Roemer, and, four years from now, will the newly disheartened wonder what went wrong again? Like Roemer, will Jindal prove incapable of overcoming the forces of the status quo and of putting his lofty words into action?" Answering himself "Possibly so, but probably not," Maginnis said Jindal is no "Roemer redux," because he had won a majority, not the plurality that put Roemer in office after outgoing governor Edwin Edwards withdrew from a general election runoff. Unlike Roemer, Jindal "learned better about how to work with others" and "to win over instead of run over" the opposition.

While Jindal, unlike Roemer, relates well to people, observers comparing the two saw similarities in their approaches to staffing the governor's office with young people rather than old hands in state politics. Like Roemer, Jindal's first appointments, as chief of staff, policy director, press secretary, and communications director all came from his congressional office staff, with his congressional chief of staff tapped for the same position in Baton Rouge. His selection of Rolfe McCollister Jr. as chairman of the transition team came as a surprise to political observers. Publisher of the *Baton Rouge Business Report*, McCollister was treasurer for Jindal's campaign. He had served as state finance chairman and treasurer for Roemer's campaigns for governor and was Roemer's transition chief. Roemer appointed him to the LSU Board of Supervisors. Pollster Bernie Pinsonat of Southern Media and Opinion Research noted that McCollister had finished third with 20 twenty of the vote in a losing race for Mayor of Baton Rouge in 2000, and said he was "a sidekick of Buddy Roemer" and business partner with the former governor in a bank. The Jindal transition set up a website to receive applications for employment, saying that every state job controlled by the governor was open, and the governor-elect solicited resumes from "the best and the brightest," speculating that "Maybe there's a 24-year-old who wants to be head of DHH," the cabinet position Governor Mike Foster appointed him to at that age, as Secretary of the Department of Health and Hospitals.

In a forum two days before the election, candidates were asked which past governor they most admired and would try to follow. Jindal surprised many people by failing to name his mentor, Foster, and instead said his model would be John McKeithen, whose administration promoted economic development and made great progress in race relations. Jindal, who campaigned against the "corrupt crowd at the capitol," must not have been familiar with the corruption and ties to organized crime that plagued McKeithen's second term, despite his other accomplishments. Always calculating whatever he said, Jindal may not have wanted to name Foster because his patron had purchased David Duke's mailing list and was criticized for his failure to travel out of state to seek new industries.

Jindal carried sixty of the sixty-four parishes and racked up a 54 percent vote statewide; in the runoff with Kathleen Babineaux Blanco in 2003, he won just twelve parishes. The only parishes he failed to carry were Orleans, St. Bernard, Red River, and Bienville. Wayne Parent, an LSU political scientist, said, "This is sort of an earth-shattering landslide. I think it was an amazing win." Parent said that voters who had picked Kathleen Blanco over Jindal in 2003 and were disappointed by her performance following Hurricanes Katrina and Rita were a major factor in Jindal's victory. Jindal's campaign theme was that Louisiana had a "second chance" to get it right, by giving him a second chance. "He really played on this buyer's remorse," Parent said. He also attributed Jindal's victory to his success in bringing North Louisiana social conservatives into his camp during what amounted to a four-year campaign. Without any "big name" Democrats in the race, "he began to get this air of invincibility." Robert Goidel, a political science professor at LSU, said "He's got a 31-point plan for anything. He's portrayed himself in terms of competence. And he's built up an aura of inevitability." For many, he was the "governor in waiting," just as Edwin Edwards was during the Dave Treen administration.

During his three years in Congress, Jindal spent every free moment possible touring the state, emphasizing the need to make inroads in its northern half. State Republican Party Chairman Roger Villere said "He changed his strategy, going out to meet conservative Democrats all over north and central Louisiana, where his Indian heritage and dark skin frankly might have been a minus. Now they accept him more for who he is."

Jindal kicked off his campaign on January 1, 2007, in anticipation of a rematch with Governor Kathleen Babineaux Blanco. Although Blanco raised $3 million for her reelection campaign, she was blamed for the slow pace of the hurricane recovery and problems in administration of the Road Home program. With the prospect of having billions of dollars in grants of up to $150,000 to distribute to cover uninsured losses to homeowners, to repair, rebuild, or have their property bought by the state, she proudly named it "Governor Blanco's Road Home Program." Republican legislators cried foul, claiming that she was injecting politics into the recovery, but when the problems in running the program caused a backlash, they were delighted to call it her program. The out-of-state company Blanco selected to administer the program had too few employees, too little information to distribute, and was slow in taking and processing applications.

Blanco's poll numbers dropped to a range of 30–35 percent favorable, and after months of indecision, on March 20, 2007, she announced that she would not seek reelection but put politics aside to devote all of her energy to the recovery. While she agonized over a decision, former U.S. Senator John Breaux, now a high-powered Washington lobbyist, who had toyed with running for governor in 2003, announced that he would consider running if she did not. Breaux's gambit helped push Blanco off the stage while keeping "name" Democrats from mounting it. Once Blanco bowed out, Breaux said that he would run, but he was faced with the prospect of a Republican challenge to his candidacy on the grounds that he did not meet the residency requirement in the state constitution. Breaux had registered to vote in Maryland, and his driver's license and other documents establishing a place of residence were there. Breaux said he was confident that he met the state requirements, as he could change his voter registration prior to the election and was paying property taxes in Louisiana.

A legal challenge to the eligibility of a candidate to seek office must be filed after he qualifies, and the state Republican Party made clear it would do so. Concerned that he would be tied up in court during the primary campaign, Breaux sought an opinion from Attorney General Charles Foti. After further delay while he considered the matter, Foti declined to rule, saying that the issue should be decided by the courts. He noted that state courts generally supported allowing candidates who were challenged to run, although there were some instances where candidates were barred from the ballot for failing to meet residency requirements. Breaux then pulled the plug on his candidacy.

Ironically, Blanco's approval rating rebounded substantially within a few days of the election. As the Road Home program got on solid footing with expedited application approvals and thousands of closings on grants, and as more people saw the federal government rather than the governor as the villain of the recovery problems, a week before the election voters divided evenly on her job performance, with 45.6 percent approving and 43.6 percent disapproving, with the remainder having no opinion or declining to say. It made one wonder whether she regretted her decision to forego the contest, although the improved ratings did not mean that in a head-to-head contest with Jindal, the same numbers would apply. Jindal even had kind words for Blanco during the campaign, saying at one point, "I really think she has gotten a bad rap. Governor Blanco feels like someone I've known my entire life. She's very approachable and likable, like a grandmother."

Throughout the lengthy period while Blanco considered her options, and Breaux played "Hamlet on the Bayou," any decision by other Democrats to enter the race was put on hold. By the time both Blanco and Breaux were out of the picture, it was too late for several others to enter it. Congressman Charles Melancon had been urged to run, but declined. Lieutenant Governor Mitch Landrieu and State Treasurer John Kennedy both decided to seek reelection, and Kennedy changed to Republican after no one filed against him. Reporter Jan Moller said, "The Breaux boomlet had the effect of temporarily freezing the field of potential top-shelf Democratic contenders, leaving Foster Campbell as the only declared Democrat in the race. By the time Breaux was gone, there was little time for another major candidate to raise the money and build the organization necessary to run an effective statewide race."

With Blanco's late exit from the race, and John Breaux's dawdling, Campbell ran a one-issue campaign that never really got off the ground and lacked for funding. Campbell served in the state senate for twenty-six years prior to his election to the Public Service Commission in 2002. His platform called for creation of an oil processing tax that would tax oil coming into the state from overseas and elimination of the state income tax.

John Georges, also a Republican until the state party threw its weight behind Jindal rather than let contenders fight it out, changed to Independent. He put $10 million of his own money into his campaign and said that by financing it himself he would be free of political debts. Georges had built his family-owned Imperial Trading Company into a multistate enterprise distributing tobacco products and liquor and turned a tugboat company he bought into Dolphin Marine, a worldwide operation. He unveiled a detailed plan for economic development, healthcare, education, and ethics in government.

The state Republican Party and the Jindal campaign relentlessly attacked Georges for his involvement with video poker. While he sold his gambling machine distribution company to a business partner, he held a financial interest in it until the transaction was completed. The Republican Party gleefully quoted former governor Edwin Edwards, who talked about the upcoming race in a prison interview with *Times-Picayune* columnist James Gill. Edwards said he liked Georges, "but he's running as a businessman, which could be a good thing, except that his business is selling cigarettes, alcohol, and gambling machines." Edwards predicted that Georges, who had opened his campaign account with $5 million of his own money, would "pull out and put the money back in his personal account when reality strikes." Edwards was wrong in that prediction as well as when he said that Jindal's problem was that he was too black for North Louisiana whites, and not black enough for New Orleans Negroes.

State Senator Walter Boasso of Arabi, owner of a shipping container business, started the race as a Republican but, incensed by the state party executive committee's endorsement of Jindal, changed to Democrat. Boasso said he did not leave his party, it left him, blaming the Bush administration for failing to properly fund the recovery from Hurricanes Katrina and Rita. Boasso said, "George Bush left me in nine feet of water at my home and business."

Boasso, a self-made multimillionaire who said he started his business cleaning shipping containers with a mop, bucket of water, and box of Tide detergent, had taken on one of the sacred cows of state politics, the system of levee boards, following the hurricane, and was successful in consolidating them with passage of a constitutional amendment that received widespread public support. He dismissed Jindal as "big brain, no heart," and said, "Bobby Jindal has attacked every one of his opponents ruthlessly, while skipping almost every debate and refusing to answer questions." Boasso ridiculed Jindal's call for ethics reform, saying:

> He talks as if he were the only honest man in Louisiana yet he's amassed a war chest of almost $11 million. Nearly $2 million came from out of state, and much of it came from people who do business with the state, no doubt seeking favors and contracts. Just last Saturday, the Baton Rouge *Advocate* revealed how Bobby has taken more than $50,000 at one lunch from owners of a toxic waste dump seeking to locate in Baton Rouge, over the opposition of the community, Mayor Kip Holden, and environmental officials.

Jindal acknowledged receiving $50,000 in contributions from the Colorado-based company's executives, owners, and business associates but refused to comment on the story. His spokesperson said their application for an industrial waste landfill permit was not discussed during the luncheon at which checks for $5,000 were given to Jindal.

Boasso branded Jindal a "hypocrite," claiming "he's selling the Governor's Mansion before he's even been elected," and "despite his pious talk about how ethical he is," Jindal had taken money from gambling interests, architects, engineers, contractors, lobbyists, representatives of Harrah's Casino and Indian gaming, and lobbyists for IFC, the Road Home contractor. Boasso asked, "With hands this dirty, how can Bobby Jindal clean up anything?" Boasso also castigated Jindal for voting to send troops into combat in Iraq and Afghanistan, but voting against increases in veterans' healthcare and benefits.

Boasso, Georges, and Campbell found themselves debating each other when Jindal failed to participate in most of the forums sponsored by business, trade association, and civic groups and universities. Georges said he was "just tired of this guy not showing up." Jindal participated in just three of the numerous programs, refusing to leave his bus tour of the state for more forums. He could not plead the need to go back and forth to Washington to vote, as he did not show up there to vote after September 10, 2007, missing 134 consecutive roll calls, including votes on affordable housing, energy, expansion of the S-chip child healthcare program, and, as *Gambit Weekly* pointed out, "improving governmental accountability, one of his campaign's war cries."

The vote total was 110,000 less than four years earlier, with 60,000 fewer ballots cast in New Orleans, which had previously voted heavily democratic. New Orleans consultant Greg Rigamer said that overall turnout was only 46 percent, with 51 percent by white voters and only 35 percent by black voters. His analysis indicated that Jindal received 63 percent of white votes and 10 percent of black votes. John Georges led Jindal by 1,000 votes in Orleans Parish, but that was attributed to his lavish spending on get-out-the-vote efforts by black political organizations. Georges got 56 percent of the black votes in the city compared to 24 percent outside it.

Boasso finished second, with 17 percent of the vote, Georges got 14 percent, and Campbell 12 percent.

At thirty-six, Bobby Jindal was the second-youngest person to be elected governor; Huey Long was thirty-five.

Jindal was born in Baton Rouge on June 10, 1971, son of Amar and Raj Jindal, who had immigrated to this country to attend graduate school. He became the state's first minority governor since Reconstruction, when P. B. S. Pinchback served briefly. Jindal, whose given name was Piyush, took the name Bobby from a character on the *Brady Bunch* television series. He graduated from Baton Rouge Magnet High School at age sixteen and while still a teenager converted to Catholicism.

While opponents said that he has "never held a real job" and that his three years in Congress were his longest stretch in any position, Jindal boasted an impressive resume.

He graduated from Brown University in 1991 with honors in public policy and biology, and from Oxford in 1994, as a Rhodes Scholar with a master's degree in political science from New College. He briefly worked for a consulting firm and served as a staff aid to Congressman

Jim McCrery, who introduced him to Governor Mike Foster. Foster, impressed, appointed him DHH Secretary in 1996. He left that position after two years to serve as executive director of the nonpartisan Breaux-Thomas Commission on the Future of Medicare in 1998. Named President of the University of Louisiana system at Foster's behest in 1999, he resigned that post when President Bush appointed him Assistant Secretary for Planning and Evaluation of the U.S. Department of Health and Human Services in 2001. He left that position in 2003 to run for governor. When First District Congressman David Vitter won election to the U.S. Senate, Jindal moved from Baton Rouge to Kenner, into the district, to seek the open seat. He was elected with 77 percent of the vote in 2004 and reelected with 88 percent in 2006.

As a Congressman, Jindal proclaimed himself "100 percent against abortion, no exceptions," supported a constitutional amendment making flag-burning a federal crime, and received an "A" rating from Gun Owners of America. He was elected president of his freshman class in Congress, voted with the Republican caucus 97 percent of the time in 2006, and in 2007 a nonpartisan group, Congress.org, ranked him "432 out of 439 in terms of overall effectiveness in the U.S. House." Environmental groups gave him low marks for his support for elimination of the moratorium on oil and gas drilling on the U.S. Outer Continental Shelf. He was "an enthusiastic supporter of the war in Iraq" and aligned with the religious right and cultural conservatives in the Republican Party, opposing stem cell research as well as abortion while supporting teaching of Intelligent Design in public schools. When Democrats tacked on an amendment calling for the phased withdrawal of American troops from Iraq, he voted against an appropriations bill that included billions of dollars of additional funds for hurricane recovery in Louisiana.

According to a website that tracks Congress, forty-seven of the fifty-six bills Jindal sponsored failed to make it out of committee; four were successfully enacted.

In the 2003 race, Republicans coalesced around Jindal, while two Democrats holding statewide office, Lieutenant Governor Kathleen Babineaux Blanco and Attorney General Richard Ieyoub ran, as well as former Congressman Buddy Leach. Jindal was endorsed by Governor Mike Foster, the New Orleans *Times-Picayune*, and Mayor C. Ray Nagin, a black Democrat. Jindal went into the runoff with a big lead over Blanco, 33 percent to 18 percent but, in the eyes of many, snatched defeat from the jaws of victory by coasting during the last ten days of their runoff contest and failing to respond to her attacks on him as a cold-hearted technocrat. He lost the runoff 52 percent to 48 percent. One observer said that in 2007

"Jindal spent about $15 million on this year's primary trying to avoid the same fate."

In 2007, opponents sought to revive the 2003 charges that he was insensitive and lacked compassion, pointing to his vote in Congress against expanding the child health insurance program. He aired television spots with his wife and children saying that he would improve healthcare and schools. He and his wife, Supriya, have three children; during his campaign, Jindal received much publicity for performing an emergency delivery of the youngest at home when there was not time to get to the hospital. One critic claimed that the delivery was a publicity stunt and said the Blanco-Jindal faceoff was "a choice between a housewife and a midwife."

"Big brain, small heart" was how Walter Boasso described Jindal, but the frontrunner stuck to his anticorruption, good-government message in a series of clichés and overcame the 2003 campaign impression that he was "an overachieving bureaucrat who has little empathy for the poor in a largely poor state." In 2003, Blanco ran commercials claiming that he was insensitive and as state health secretary had denied care to needy people. As an article in *Time* magazine noted, Jindal "guided the bloated department through a rough period of cutbacks, both in jobs and reimbursements to health care providers." Blanco painted him as "a cold-hearted numbers cruncher," an image Boasso resurrected in 2007. Boasso ran a commercial featuring a middle-aged woman who "in a calm voice, barely concealing her grief and rage, tells of her mentally disabled brother who was evicted from a nursing home during Jindal's tenure." The tag line was "Bobby Jindal threw my brother out on the street, and no one even bothered to call me. Bobby Jindal has no heart." In 2003, Jindal failed to defend himself against Blanco's charges, but in 2007 he struck back, running ads featuring a doctor who claimed that the "corruption crowd" Jindal ran out was back in. Although none of the other candidates had been tainted by the slightest whiff of scandal, and Blanco's administration was clean, Jindal lumped them together with lobbyists and others and said that he was fighting "the corrupt crowd and incompetents in state government."

Jindal's strategy was to concentrate on north Louisiana and Acadiana, rolling from one small town to another in a huge tour bus, to make strong inroads in areas that he had lost to Blanco. Stephanie Grace who wrote that "Jindal strategizes as instinctively as most of us draw breath," said "that's where he spent the bulk of his time, leaving some in his hurricane-stricken home base to wonder where they fit into his grand plan." As soon as he won, however, he focused on hurricane recovery, turning President

Bush's call of congratulations into a request for an early meeting to talk about needs and seconding Governor Blanco's position that the multibillion dollar shortfall in the Road Home program is a federal obligation.

During the campaign, Jindal played down his ethnic background and said little about the recovery of storm-ravaged areas. The *Times-Picayune* hailed his election with an editorial that said, "Many New Orleanians were disappointed that Mr. Jindal did not make the recovery of our region and the rest of South Louisiana a centerpiece of his campaign. Nothing less than the state's future is at stake." In his victory statement election night, however, Jindal recounted how his parents came to this country to follow the American dream, and in a press conference the next day he addressed hurricane recovery. He accepted Senator Mary Landrieu's invitation to meet with Democratic leaders in Congress, and he and Blanco went to Washington together to lobby for more funds. To the dismay of some Republican operatives, who had hoped to gain control of one or both houses of the Legislature, he said that he would not campaign for Republicans in the general election, including the runoff for attorney general. "I want to be governor for everybody," Jindal said. "For me the campaign is over." Unlike his recent predecessors, he also said he would not seek to influence selection of the leaders of the House and Senate, unless there was a deadlock.

On election night, Jindal said that the days of "the corruption crowd" were over. Throughout the campaign, he had crusaded against it without ever naming names, but he now said they knew who they were, and if they tried to hold on to power, he would "call them out," and if they did not leave of their own accord, he would "throw them out" of state government when he took over. The next day, he downplayed these statements while unveiling the five "core provisions" on his 31-point ethics plan. John Maginnis said these were "prohibiting legislators or companies they own from holding contracts with state agencies; barring legislators from working as lobbyists or governmental consultants; disclosing sources of income for legislators and state officials; more detailed information from lobbyists on their clients and expenses; and criminal sanctions for breaking ethics laws."

Following a ninety-minute conference with Blanco several days after the election, Jindal expressed his appreciation for her wholehearted cooperation in the transition. Although he crusaded against what he called Louisiana's "culture of corruption," Jindal praised Blanco for heading "a scandal-free administration."

When Jindal took the oath of office on January 14, 2008, he had a four-year term ahead of him, which was twice the two-year average he stayed in all of his other positions. Blanco left him a $1 billion budget surplus as a cushion to begin the Jindal era in Louisiana politics.

—J.B.McG.

Alford, Jeremy. "Missing Big Votes." *Gambit Weekly*. 23 October 2007.

Anderson, Ed. "Jindal Picks Transition Chief." *Times-Picayune*. 23 October 2007.

Barrow, Bill. "Jindal, Blanco Team up for Recovery." *Times-Picayune*. 27 October 2007.

Blum, Jordan. "Jindal Gets Colorado Help, Landfill Company, Allies Donate $50,000 to Campaign." *Advocate*. 13 October 2007.

"Bobby Jindal." GovTrack. 18 October 2007.

"Bobby Jindal." Wikipedia.

Goldman, Henry. "Louisiana Favors Jindal in First Post-Katrina Governor's Race." Bloomberg.com. 18 October 2007.

Grace, Stephanie. "Jindal Shifts out of Campaign Mode." *Times-Picayune*. 23 October 2007.

Jervis, Rick. "Louisiana's Governor-Elect Pledges to End Corruption." *USA Today*. 22 October 2007.

"Jindal's Era Begins." *Times-Picayune*. 21 October 2007.

Maginnis, John. "Jindal to Lay It on Line with Ethics Package" and "They Said It." *Louisiana Political Fax Weekly*. 26 October 2007.

McCulley, Russell. "The Second Coming of Bobby Jindal." *Time*. 4 October 2007.

Moller, Jan. "Jindal Wins." *Times-Picayune*. 21 October 2007.

———. "With Campaign Over, Jindal Calls for Unity." *Times Picayune*. 22 October 2007.

Naqvi, Muneeza. "Relatives in India Overjoyed by Election." *Times-Picayune*. 22 October 2007.

Ponnuru, Ramesh. "Meet Bobby Jindal." *National Review Online*. 5 September 2003.

Republican Party of Louisiana. "I like Him, But" mail-out. Author's collection.

"Right Signals on Recovery." *Times-Picayune*. 24 October 2007.

Scott, Robert Travis. "India Relishes Jindal's Success." *Times-Picayune*. 28 October 2007.

Sentell, Will. "Jindal Carries 60 Parishes in Landslide Win." *Advocate*. 23 October 2007.

———. "Jindal Win Sign of Gop's La. Strength." *Advocate*. 23 October 2007.

"There's a Word for Bobby Jindal: Hypocrite." Walter Boasso for Governor mail-out. Author's collection.

Index